Market Efficiency Versus Equity

Market Efficiency Versus Equity

Editors

B. Hessel
J.J. Schippers
J.J. Siegers

ISBN 90-5170-437-2
NUGI 695/681

Layout/editing: G.J. Wiarda Institute, Utrecht University Institute for Legal Studies
Cover design: Mirjam Bode
AWSB-logo cover: BRS Premsela Vonk

Table of Contents

Balancing the Welfare State
Bart Hessel, Joop Schippers, Jacques Siegers   1

Market Efficiency, Equity and the Future of the Welfare State: A Contribution
to an Interdisciplinary Discussion
Bart Hessel   9

Reintegration of Partially Disabled Employees:
From Market Efficiency *versus* Social Justice to Market Efficiency
and Social Justice?
Stella den Uijl, Saskia Klosse, Tineke Bahlmann, Joop Schippers   45

Activation Policy and Equity
Jeroen van Gerven, Robert Knegt   69

The Day-Care Efficiency, Quality and Equity Trade-off
Rudi Turksema, Jacques Siegers, Hetty van Emmerik   87

Flexible Labour and Social Security
Yvonne Konijn   105

36-Hours Working Week in Banking: Efficient or Socially Justified?
Tineke Bahlmann, Maaike Lycklama à Nijeholt, Stella den Uijl,
Bart Verkade   125

The Pension Dilemma: A Matter of Efficiency Versus Equity?
Mies Westerveld   153

From Maastricht to Amsterdam: Towards Integration of Social and Economic
Policy in Europe?
Inge van Berkel, Gerrit Faber, Joop Schippers, Jacques Siegers   171

About the Authors   195

About AWSB   199

Balancing the Welfare State

Bart Hessel, Joop Schippers, Jacques Siegers

1 Bipolarity in the Welfare State: Market Efficiency Versus Equity

The growth of the welfare state is characterized by a process in which individual citizens are given more and more rights. The government seemed the most likely party to take care of effectuation and enforcement of these rights. The obligation of individual citizens and companies to give up an important (and growing) part of their income in the form of taxes and social premiums was balanced by the guarantee that the citizen would be cared for from cradle to grave.

Apart from the fact that an increasing number of people experienced this care as suffocating, the high taxes and social premiums proved more and more to put a brake on private initiative. The idea that a high individual financial burden negated any wish to entreprise and that the high collective burden used up such a significant part of community means that insufficient means remained for private initiatives ('crowding out'), gradually gained ground during the eighties. The initially positive effects on welfare of extending government responsibility and interference turned sour. The distribution issue which had until then been fairly easy to resolve because each year there was more wealth to be distributed, now became a problem because the first time in ages it was not growth but rather scarcity that had to be distributed. Thus the market sector, which still gives priority to market efficiency, and the collective sector, which opts for (distributive) justice, became more and more each others opponents.

A change occured when Mrs Thatcher and Ronals Reagan became prime minister and president in the United Kingdom and the United States respectively. Both are inspired by a group of economists who became known as the 'supply-side' economists. Income security in the form of high and longterm benefits negates, according to these economists, the incentive for the unemployed to apply for a job, for the partially handicapped to try and earn some money with their remaining abilities and for lowskilled people who are not in demand to try qualify for a job via retraining. High (marginal) tax rates disencourage entrepreneurs to take new initiatives or to introduce innovations whereas high tax rates fail to entice employees to work harder, strive for promotion of learn new skills and techniques. The 'supply-side' economists plead for strengthening of the price mechanism as a way out of the crisis. On the supply side of the economy this would have to result in extra stimuli to entice employees and employers to one again take initiatives and more risky behaviour. Keywords in this policy context are: market, deregulation and privatization.

The policy recommendations based on the supply economy model resulted among other things in lowering of social benefits, abolition of statutory minimum wages (in the United Kingdom), relaxation of dismissal regulations and privatization of former state companies and government services.

Although by now reduced to no more than a strong wind, this storm did not simply pass by the Netherlands. Especially the no-nonsense governments of the Christian-Democrat Ruud Lubbers preached fervently for the government to step back: the government should relinquish its hold on the national income, benefits were to be granted less easily and the height of benefits too ought to be revised. Economize was the word and citizens would now due to the 'benefit principle' have to pay themsleves for what used to be simply paid out of public means. Thus, university charges went up, rent subsidies down, 'personal contributions' were introduced in the health care sector and public transport companies had to get by with significantly less government subsidies. Employers joined in by pleading for lower taxes as well as less and less complicated legislation, including for example relaxed dismissal laws. Employees would have to be more flexible and be more willing to, e.g., work evenings or during the weekend. Whereas on the one hand the government started an operation titled *'Marktwerking, deregulering en wetgevingskwaliteit' (MDW*; market function, deregulation and legislative quality) employers on the other hand demanded more flexibilization of labour contracts and relations during labour condition talks.

Whenever less means are available, higher contributions are imposed, or certain provisions restrict the rights of people, this has an effect of the welfare of those people. While the growth in welfare during the Sixties was accepted by everybody without much ado and as if it were natural, subsequently giving up a part of that welfare was rather more difficult. Public spending power calculated to two decimal places are a convincing illustration. The ever recurring question was: 'Who can we ask to make more sacrifices?' Civil servants and students proved easy targets. Other groups in society managed to defend themselves more effectively and to avoid the reduction trap to a large extent. It is particularly the accumulation of subsequent cutting, reduction and reorganization operations that give rise to the question whether certain groups in society did not get hit too heavily.

Furthermore, and that is especially important for this book, the question of where to draw the line as regards government withdrawal and therefore also as regards at what point a welfare state stops being a welfare state, became more and more pressing. Whereas at first it was merely a matter of removing excess trimming, the continuation of cuts and reductions subsequently also peeled off the outer and second skins of the welfare state. The debate of the last few years concerns the question what constitutes the core of the welfare state (some people feel that that has already been infected too). Then it must be indicated how a new but also more stable balance can be struck between aggregating sufficient welfare for all people together and constructing a mechanism which will attribute each individual person such a share of that welfare – even if he or she is unable to earn that share independently – that the end result concurs with what the majority of people consider fair and just.

This core issue takes various forms. Sometimes it is translated into a discussion on rights and obligations. At other times it is translated in terms of market and government. However, it always concerns the bipolarity of the welfare state between distribution and production.

Both theoretic and empirical research in the various disciplines show that the way in which the processes of distribution and gathering are structured and the institutional arrangements chosen have an independent – and mutual – effect on the results of those processes. Numerous examples may clarify this. We will limit ourselves here to those that will be discussed in more detail later in the book. A country such as the Netherlands has extremely high labour productivity for working people. At the same time a lot of people are excluded because of disability and large groups of people experiences (too) much stress at work. The obligation for employers to hire a certain percentage of partially disabled workers would (possibly) lower labour productivity but this would in principle be countered by the fact that fewer people would have to rely on social security benefits. This would bring down the level of contributions and lower labour costs which would allow employers to hire more people or reduce working hours per person. A not unlikely (but to be further substantiated by empirical research) assumption would be that the overall level of welfare of the population will be higher as a result of such a quota regulation. The (implicit) choice made over the last few years is to have an ever smaller part of the population work ever harder and to have this shrinking group carry the financial burden of everybody else's unemployability. It will be obvious that both the collective and individual welfare levels are different from what they would be under the indicated alternative situation.

A second example discussed in the book is the tension between flexibility and security (again: a translation of the general bipolarity of the welfare state). The last few years have shown a shift in the labour market where rules that were too strict according to many are substituted by more relaxed legislation (for example concerning dismissal rules). On the one hand such regulations offer the employers the chance to more easily 'get rid' of employees. On the other hand the consequences for the individual employee who gets sacked are so significant and disastrous that one could ask whether this revised legislation does not rather upset the balance. It is true that one could say that such relaxation allows to generate extra welfare. However, the redistribution of that welfare between (in this case) employer and employee is so drastic that there may yet be sufficient reasons to reject such a (new) institutional arrangement.

2 An Interdisciplinary Approach

Each of the following contributions shows the struggle as it occurs in the various policy areas to find an acceptable balance between the two poles of market efficiency and equity. Jurists are struggling just as much as economists. Their different approaches though allow for useful cooperation. Especially two differences are of importance in this context.

The first and well-known difference is that economists work mostly positive analytical and empirical, whereas jurists are mostly normative researchers. As is obvious from the various contributions in this collection, economists primarily aim to obtain a clear insight in the actual relationship between market efficiency and equity. In this their research targets very concrete developments in a specific sector such as the developments in the day-care sector or the 36-hours working week in banking.

Norm-oriented jurists approach the issue from a different angle. They primarily tend to pronounce a clear value judgment on existing relationships between market efficiency and equity. The jurists included in this book appear to be general of the view that these days more attention should be paid to equity.

Secondly, this book shows that major differences exist between economists and jurists in their interpretations of the concepts of market efficiency and equity. Economists conceptualize market efficiency as a combination of technical and economic efficiency. Technical efficiency means that with a given amount of goods a certain goal is realized as well as possible. Economic efficiency exists when, in addition, these goods are used to realize the goals which take highest priority.

4

Jurists sometimes give a different meaning to these notions. Thus, for instance, equity for jurists is primarily tied in with the guarantee function of the law. Such an interpretation of equity often entails that a phenomenon as flexibilization is equalled to market efficiency. Within the normative approach of the law equity usually has a more positive connotation than market efficiency. If the link between equity and guarantee function is not made or to a lesser degree only, this results in a differing view on efficiency and equity which leaves room for a more positive interpretation of efficiency.

Ergo, the issue of the relationship between market efficiency and equity not only requires that economists and jurists study it together but also that the jurists pay attention to both the guarantee and the instrumental functions of the law. The way in which this has been dealt with in the various contributions shows how economists and jurists, who in daily life and research differ somewhat in orientation, may learn a lot from each other in discussions about the structuring of the welfare state. Thus, for example, Den Uijl *et al.,* as well as Van Berkel *et al.* show how efficiency and equity objectives can be (made) complementary. Analogously Konijn indicates that the instrumental function and the guarantee function of the law do not need to be competitive, but may actually be mutually reinforcing.

3 Set-up of this Book

In chapter 2 Bart Hessel approaches market efficiency, equity and the future of the welfare state from a legal point of view. In doing so he first reviews some general economic and juristic interpretations of these concepts. Subsequent to the meaning given to these concepts in economics and market research, where Hessel equals equity to solidarity, he indicates that the tension between market efficiency and equity/solidarity in the welfare state may take three forms:
At the government level of social security policy there is a tension between market efficiency and equity/solidaritity with the economically weak.
At company level there is a tension between market efficiency and solidarity in two varieties:
a. market efficiency versus internal solidarity as concern for the interests of employees;
b. market efficiency and external solidarity as concern for the interests of society.
Hessel considers that in future the emphasis with respect to the welfare state should not only be on strengthening the market but also on strengthening the various forms of solidarity.

In chapter 3 Stella den Uijl, Tineke Bahlmann, Saskia Klosse en Joop Schippers discuss the issue of reintegration of partially disabled employees. This chapter elaborates the first two variations of tension mentioned by Bart Hessel. A particular plea is made for further strengthening of internal solidartiy within the company with the employees.

Jeroen van Gerven and Robert Knecht in chapter 4 discuss the issue of activation policy and equity. Contrary to widespread ideas this issue of the furtherance of labour participation has a long history in Europe. Different means of reaching a higher level of activity have been used in different combinations and under different conditions: institutionalising facilities and rules promoting coping abilities, strengthening financial ties between citizens and the provision of care, stressing responsibilities and duties belonging to the users' right to these provisions and reinstating responsibilities of actors indirectly involved. The authors show these means to return in different appearances throughout the whole period since the 18th century, with the exception of the second and third quarters of the 20th century. However, concepts of labour mobility, flexible labour relations and tripartite administration can be seen as mainly based upon ideas already brought into practice a long time ago. Arguments in favour of and against activation policy also remain much the same: financial independence, individual well-being and a contribution to the national economy have been brought forward in favour of activation policy, while doubts with respect to success, coercion and abuse plea against activation policies.

In chapter 5 Rudi Turksema, Jacques Siegers and Hetty van Emmerik develop an explanatory model to analyze the day care's transition from welfare sector to market sector. They theoretically identifiy what elements play a role in the efficiciency, quality and equity trade-off in the day-care market. The authors also show that imperfections such as asymmetric information obstruct full competition in this market. Government efforts to correct existing market failures or reduce inequalities prove to have been only partly succesful. The answer to the question in which direction the supply of day care will develop may be: downward – the first day-care centres have already gone bankrupt. However, this downward tendency may be stopped if day-care centres are given the opportunity to complete their transition from infant industry to ordinary enterprises.

Chapter 6 comprises Yvonne Konijn's review of social security and flexible workers. She points out that the legal guarantees for flexible employees in case of illness and unemployment show quite a few loopholes and she pleads to further strengthen these guarantees in a way which reconciles efficiency and equity.

Chapter 7 analyzes the introduction of the 36-hours working week in banking. The authors, Tineke Bahlmann, Maaike Lycklama à Nijeholt, Stella den Uijl en Bart Verkade, investigate the arguments that have been put forward in the discussion concerning this reduction in working hours and especially those relating to efficiency and to social justice, respectively. This discussion has a wider implication because the banking sector in the Dutch economy may serve as an example for other branches of industry. The authors conclude that employers and unions have been able to establish a balanced agreement, which offers both parties enough advantages to make the agreement acceptable for their respective 'parties' in the negotiations. By including the introduction of the 36-hours working week in a package deal which includes for instance an extension of business and agreements on automation the package as a whole contributes both to more efficiency in the banking sector and to social justice: the trade unions have been able to prevent as many redundancies (due to automation) as possible. So, in this case efficiency and equity do not oppose each other, but may be considered mutually dependent and reinforcing.

In chapter 8 Mies Westerveld discusses the pension dilemma as a problem for the future. As regards the question whether there is tension between efficiency and equity, in which context she uses daily speech interpretations of the terms, she finds that the key problem with pensions cannot be interpreted in terms of that tension. According to her the main point is that the future of pensions should not be left to the market but needs to be mainly the government's concern. Only the government can guarantee the future quality and security of workers' pensions.

Finally chapter 9 by Inge van Berkel, Gerrit Faber, Joop Schippers and Jacques Siegers discusses the European dimension of the possible tension between market efficiency and equity. After a description of the development of social policy at the EU-level the authors conclude that EU-policy has always given priority to matters concerning efficiency, i.e. the functioning of the internal market and the efficient allocation of resources. Equity issues have always remained the primary responsibility of the individual Member States. Still, there are several arguments in favour of a common social policy at EU-level. Very briefly, these arguments can be summarized in the statement 'economic wealth cannot be built in a social desert'. The Maastricht Treaty set some necessary steps towards such a common social policy. Yet, the coming about of such a policy is a gradual process. Even then, this process will not lead to a coherent and complete unified set of policy measures. It is most likely that the development will give rise to a system of minimum norms and standards in different fields of social policy. Even though efficiency has recieved much more attention during the forty years of European integration, this chapter and the ongoing discussion at European level clearly demonstrate that also at European level market efficiency and equity are two sides of the same coin: even though they represent different angles, they cannot be seen apart from each other.

As pointed out in paragraph 1 there is a lot more to be said about the relationship between market efficiency and equity and all its dimensions than is possible within the context of this book. Still, the book offers some interesting insights in the possibilities and limitations to influence the precious balance between efficiency and equity underlying the late 20th century welfare state. It also shows that a lot of research still needs to be done.

All chapters are revised versions of papers presented at a workshop held in Utrecht in November 1996, which was organized by the Netherlands School for Social and Economic Policy Research (AWSB). The editors would like to thank the Netherlands Institute for Social and Economic Law (NISER) of Utrecht University for their assistance in translating and editing the contributions to this volume.

Market Efficiency, Equity and the Future of the Welfare State: A Contribution to an Interdisciplinary Discussion

Bart Hessel

1 Introduction

Striking the right balance between market efficiency and equity is one of the major problems of the modern welfare state. As is well-known, the crisis in the Dutch welfare state which may be explained by overrating equity in comparison to the disadvantage of market efficiency, has over the past few years resulted in significant emphasis being put on market efficiency. Economists, social scientists and politicians play major parts in this discussion whereas jurists only join in marginally. What is more, and that is confirmed in this book, the latter speak a different language from economists.

In this contribution I wish to review the relationship between market efficiency and equity from a legal point of view. Firstly, both concepts will be elaborated a bit further and delineated on the basis of economic market theory, and equity will be given concrete form by translating it into solidarity (section 2). In doing so I will try to use the same language as economists. Subsequently, the reasons why jurists play only a minor role in the discussion will be reviewed and I will look at how jurists may have come to define the concepts differently (section 3). The possible difference in language between them and economists will thus be explained further. Following an inventory of three points of tension between market efficiency and equity specified as solidarity, which developed as the modern welfare state developed (section 4), I will elaborate from a legal perspective the currently once again very trendy neo-liberal approach where this tension is unambiguously resolved as regards the future in favour of market efficiency (section 5). From a legal and social science point of view this neo-liberal theory seems to fail by presenting a far too one-dimensional view on society in which the essential importance of equity is denied (section 6). As an alternative I should like to argue in favour of a multi-dimensional approach where the three points of tension between market effiency and equity are not merely discarded and where reinforcement of the market is accompanied by reinforcement of solidarity.

2 The Concepts of Market Efficiency and Equity

Whereas the concepts of market efficiency and equity seem fairly obvious to economists they generally present a number of interpretative problems to jurists. Below, I will opt for a definition which to my mind meets two criteria. Firstly, it connects with the interpretation given to these concepts by economists and their market theories. This will prevent the concurrence of different languages. Secondly, this definition gives the best indication of the problem we are faced with in discussing the future of the welfare state.

As regards the definition of the concept of market efficiency I will link up with the definition given by Bahlmann *cum suis*.[1]

a. Market Efficiency as Technical and Economic Efficiency
Market efficiency exists if the criteria of technical and economic efficiency are met. In the words of Hennipman technical efficiency exists 'if in order to achieve a quantitatively and qualitatively determined independent goal the smallest possible quantity of goods is used, or if with a given quantity of goods a certain goal has been achieved as best as possible from a quantitatively and qualitatively point of view'.[2] Furthermore, the requirement of economic efficiency is met 'if the goods are used to meet the correct, that is most urgent, needs'.[3] Within the context of the individualistic market concept these most urgent needs are determined by the individual choices or preferences of the consumers.

Thus, market efficiency is defined in terms of individual exchanges between market parties in which transactions these parties solely look after their own interests.

b. Equity as Solidarity
The concept of equity is, especially for jurists, multi-interpretable. Equity may be taken to mean: (1) the quality of being fair and reasonable in a way that constitutes equal treatment for everyone or (2) the principle used in law which allows a fair judgement to be made in a case where the existing laws fail to provide a reasonable answer to the problem; a technical term in law.[4]

---

[1] See the article in this book by Tineke Bahlmann *et al.*, 36-Hours Working Week in Banking: Efficient or Socially Justified?
[2] Hennipman, 1945, p. 240; also referred to in: Hessel, 1987, p. 15.
[3] Hennipman, 1945, p. 240 and Hessel, 1987, p. 15.
[4] Collins Cobuild English Language Dictionary.

For a sensible demarcation as regards market efficiency the second interpretation of equity, a juridical method for reaching fair judgements, seems irrelevant and we will have to focus on the first interpretation.

Equity then has to be linked to fairness, being reasonable, and equality. These notions, to my opinion, however, do not allow for a sensible demarcation as regards market efficiency. After all, market efficiency too presupposes some form of equality and may also be considered reasonable and fair. This first description also fails to pay sufficient attention to the problem involved in discussing the future of the welfare state, which is what we may describe as the relationship between economic and social dimensions.

In this book the concept of equity will be used as equivalent to what in the Netherlands is literally called 'social justice'. Against this background I will further give concrete form to the concept of equity and equal it to solidarity.

Equity in its meaning of solidarity plays a role when the individualistic exchange relation which is characteristic to the market, no longer suffices in reality (*Sein*) or when it is considered insufficient (*Sollen*), and when subjects heed or should heed to at least some extent the interests of others. Equity or solidarity presupposes some concern for the interests of others (other subjects or the general interest) which transcends individualism. We encounter solidarity in this meaning particularly in the context of the social security system as it developed in the welfare state (see especially the contribution in this book on Re-integration of Partially Disabled Employees).

The difference between market efficiency and equity or solidarity (hereafter I will speak of solidarity) is thus related to the perception of man (*Menschenbild*): market efficiency presupposes individualism or sheer concentration on private interests and solidarity presupposes in addition to or correction of this the further concern for the interests of others.

This concept of man may of course be either descriptive or normative. If we describe reality we may conclude that people only strive for their own interests or sometimes also appear to protect to some extent the interests of others. If we take a normative approach we rule that people may either concentrate on their personal interests or that they should also practice some degree of solidarity. As befits a proper jurist I will in this contribution present not only a description but also a normative judgement, namely that society requires a certain degree of solidarity.

The fact that the concepts of market efficiency and solidarity are related to the perception of mankind is essential for the following reasons.

As far as economics is concerned, in doing this we may relate to the key concepts of that science such as methodological individualism, individualistic welfare theory and Pareto efficiency.

In the normative context we link up with political philosophical or, if one so prefers, legal philosophical writers such as Nozick and Rawls who come into the picture if we consider the future of the welfare state. Whereas Nozick propagates individualism and thus individual freedom and equality, Rawls on the other hand feels that individualism falls short and attributes importance to solidarity as well.[5]

Essential for the future of the welfare state is the question whether the individualistic perception of mankind should be standard or whether there is still a need for solidarity and that importance should be granted to it. Answering that normative question we must of course also keep in mind people's actual behaviour. Normative conclusions that bear no relation to reality will serve no purpose.

For a proper understanding the following remark must be made as regards the perception of man.

Individualism which is at the basis of market efficiency is not limited to the market alone. Whenever the government in reaction to certain market imperfections (such as competition frustrating cartels on the goods and services market or unequal power balances between employers and employees in the labour market) or market failure resorts to socio-economic policies, these policies may also be structured based on individualism.[6]

Juridically speaking it can be said that the substantive legal principles of individual freedom and equality are at the basis of those policies. For example one could mention competition policy, price policy possible due to the *Prijzenwet* (Pricing Act) and wage policy as it is conducted under the *Wet op de loonvorming* (Wages Act). Economically speaking, such policies then fit in with the individualistic welfare concept and methodological individualism. This would still involve efficiency but of

---

[5]   Nozick, 1974, Rawls, 1971, p. 105. Rawls, by the way, tends to interpret solidarity somewhat differently. For him solidarity means that those better off do not wish to improve their situation unless those worst off will also gain. This does not mean that those well off need to lose out in favour of the people less well of.

[6]   We speak of market imperfections when reality fails to meet the conditions for an efficient functioning of the market, such as that of full or workable competition. Market failure occurs when in reality complications occur which fall outside the scope of the market model, such as collective goods and positive or negative external effects. These shortcomings of the market must be clearly distinguished from the possibility that in society the opinion prevails that the market requires corrections from a social justice or solidarity point of view. That aspect will be discussed later.

the Pareto type. Government intervention is Pareto efficient if no single individual may improve its welfare without diminishing that of another individual.

Ergo, the question of how the future balance of efficiency and solidarity in the welfare state should be, should not be equalled to the for the future equally important question of how the relation between market and government should be.

The domain of the individualistic welfare concept and of (Pareto) efficiency is left behind once solidarity enters the scene, that is to say the moment the personal interest is or should be infringed upon in order to reckon more or less with the interest of others.[7] Such balancing of interests which no longer concerns the mutual advantage of the exchange relation but where one person will possibly lose is now outside the scope of economic non-normative science.[8] This is a normative problem of weighing interests.

3 Can Jurists Complement Economists?

It is remarkable that where non-normative economists fail to find an answer, normative jurists come into the picture. After all, one could say, jurists are specially trained to think in terms of weighing conflicting interests of parties, where in a specific situation one party will win and the other lose. Although this entices one to think that jurists could thus nicely complement economists, we have to face the fact that jurists partly inhabit a different world and also speak a different language which hinders a troublefree connection. The fact that they live in different worlds cannot be helped but does require some explanation. The difference in languages may be solved if jurists would take the trouble to (somewhat) familiarize themselves with that of economists.

---

[7] In that case efficiency is no longer the ultimate value in society and we are faced with the problem that the market may need correction from a point of view of solidarity (see note 6).

[8] The limitations to Pareto efficiency are especially bothersome for legal economists. There the scope of economy and efficiency have been extended with the Kaldor-Hicks criterion. Pursuant to this latter criterion changes in legislation are considered allocatively efficient if the profits of those that gain are large enough to possibly compensate those that lose, and still retain sufficient margin. Such possible compensation then helps with the costs-benefits analysis. However, the ultimate legal judgment that one will have to lose in order for the other to gain, is not pronounced.

3.1 Jurists Partly Inhabit a Different World

It is very important to realize that jurists inhabit to some extent a different world. What it boils down to is that for jurists the weighing of interests of both losing and winning parties not only occurs once the Pareto efficiency domain is left behind but even before it is entered. This perhaps cryptic remark deserves some explanation.

Let us assume that economists view reality from a market model point of view. If a number of conditions for optimum functioning have been met and there are no market failures, the market results in efficiency. If in reality the market does not meet the conditions of the model, the economist is faced with problems of inefficiency. His task is then to indicate how efficiency may yet be attained. For him the problem of someone losing out only presents itself when in society the values of equity or solidarity also play a role alongside efficiency and when market results need correction for that reason.

For jurists this problem of losers occurs at a much earlier stage, namely not only in connection with solidarity but as soon as the market fails from an efficiency point of view. After all, they then have to draft legislation, such as competition laws in reaction to market imperfection or environmental laws in reaction to market failure. Such legislation may aim at achieving efficiency as yet, but to that purpose it often interferes with actually existing relationships between (categories of) persons. This generally entails advantages for some and disadvantages for others. An example thereof are social law acts which strengthen the employee's feeble position and limit the employer's powers: the employer will lose. It is up to jurists to reinstate the balance of powers and that involves a limitation of the strongest force. For jurists therefore it is essential that first the weak position of the employee should be improved in order to allow employees and employers to conclude labour agreements on fair terms. With agreements aiming at mutual advantages for both parties we now enter the domain of Pareto efficiency. As we have seen, jurists have faced this problem of weighing interests before then. This difference with economists can be explained from the fact that to economists thinking in terms of efficiency, the unequality in starting position for parties concluding a deal is irrelevant. For jurists who think in terms of justice, on the other hand, this inequality is the very crux of the matter. The criterion of Pareto efficiency bears no relation to differences in starting position and therefore bears no relation to equity.

3.2 Jurists Speak a Different Language

The connection between economists and jurists is further impeded by the fact that the latter speak a different language. Something can be done about that and I think we ought to because jurists are now handicapped in joining other scientists in contemplating the future of the welfare state as regards efficiency versus equity.

We have to conclude that Dutch jurists are in general not very familiar with the concepts of market efficiency and solidarity in their above described interpretations. There are two reasons for this that may be mentioned.

Firstly, there is the strong influence which legal positivism still has on jurists. Somewhat exaggerated one could say that as a result of this influence jurists have for long years learned to start thinking only once an act has been introduced. Combined with their approach which mostly focusses on procedural justice, the result is that jurists are not primarily orientated on the substantive notions of justice which are or could be at the basis of such legislation. This means that substantive legal principles such as freedom, equality and solidarity as well as the related notions of exchange relations, individualistic or non-individualistic perception of mankind and the ideas of authors such as Nozick and Rawls are as yet far removed from many jurists' worlds.[9]

Secondly, fields of law where these substantive principles of law do receive special attention are (public) economic law and, to a lesser extent, social law. However, here the problem is that in the Netherlands economic and social law are traditionally almost completely separated. Generally speaking one could say that in public economic law the emphasis is on market efficiency and government measures aiming to restore the efficient functioning of the market if due to market imperfections this situation does not occur automatically. Public economic law practitioners often feel they do not encounter social justice (or solidarity) within their field of study. Below I will prove that I do not share this point of view (section 7). In social law, however, the emphasis is on social justice and solidarity but here jurists are unfamiliar with the concept of market efficiency. Among social law jurists market efficiency often has a negative ring to it.

Against this background it should not surprise that the legal contributions to this book, except for this one, are all from social law jurists. In as far as economic and social law jurists pay any attention to the concepts of market efficiency and solidarity this attention is rather one-dimensional and the danger exists that the relationship between the two is underexposed.

The above will explain why until now jurists have played such a modest role in the discussion on the future of the welfare state as regards the relationship between

---

[9]   However, this situation is changing. A few years ago the Utrecht law faculty published a study about substantive principles of justice within several fields of law; see Hessel, 1993.

market efficiency and solidarity. This is regrettable because a legal angle may shed a special light on this relationship and particularly on the role of solidarity in society and the social order. However, before discussing this subject in detail (see section 6) I want to point out that the noted differences in language and perceived reality between economists and jurists may result in jurists interpreting the problem of market efficiency versus equity differently from economists. Some examples are the contributions to this book by Yvonne Konijn and Mies Westerveld.

3.3 A Different Interpretation of the Problem

If market efficiency, an individualistic perception of man, individualistic exchange relationships and solidarity, as a supplement or correction, play no role in jurists' language, it is quite feasible that jurists should come to a different interpretation of the concept of equity or social justice. In the world they inhabit (see section 3.1) it then seems sensible to consider social justice or equity as a characteristic for social law in its entirety and not only for certain social security acts which are based on the principle of solidarity which transcends individualism. Then, the line of reasoning followed in social law studies is the following: all social law acts are based on a weighing of interests and many social law acts may be interpreted as reactions to the weak position of the employee as regards the employer. Protecting this weak position is a matter of social justice or equity.

Once such a broad interpretation of equity is chosen it seems logical that market efficiency should then be equalled to flexibilization which involves diminished protection of the employee. (However, it is doubtful, even to me as a jurist, whether flexibilization is actually efficient.)

With this approach we encounter another problem essential to the development of the welfare state. After all, current neo-liberal theory leads to more flexibilization of the labour market which is countered by jurists quite rightly asking after the protection of the employee (see the contribution of Yvonne Konijn about Flexible Labour and Social Security).

It is, however, of the utmost importance to note that here the interpretation of the concepts of market efficiency and equity is clearly different from an economic market perception, which is what I would opt for and which we also come across in the contribution on the Reintegration of Partially Disabled Employees and the article about the 36-Hours Working Week in Banking. I am tempted to say that in the article of Konijn we are faced with the tension between the instrumental and protective functions of the law rather than with the tension between market efficiency and solidarity and that those two areas of tension should not be equalled. If, for example, politicians want a social security act that aims at solidarity in the sense that the economically weak deserve protection, the instrumental function of that act aims at the same solidarity. The protective function expressed for instance by the complex procedure of legislation and the allowance for appeal, could then hinder that solidarity or at least impede its (timely) realization.

In contrast to the above described interpretation I should like to consider the matter of market efficiency versus solidarity specifically as regards the question that is essential for the future of the welfare state, i.e. whether besides market efficiency, individual freedom and the pure protection of one's own interests, reality still leaves room and should leave room for solidarity in the form of some concern for the interests of others.

As far as social security legislation is concerned this means that we must review whether the principle of solidarity should be retained or whether in future new legislation should be introduced based on the principles of individual freedom and equality which are related to an individualistic perception of man. This would result in seeking security by means of individual insurances in the market. The tension between market efficiency and solidarity in the welfare state, however, is not restricted to social security but occurs elsewhere as well. So before we make any normative statements we should trace where exactly solidarity and the tension with market efficiency evolved in the welfare state.

4 The Welfare State: Three Areas of Tension Between Market Efficiency and Solidarity

a. The Actual Development of Solidarity

Market imperfections and market failures as they occur in the reality of the modern welfare state have resulted in extensive government activities and legislation which are aimed at as yet achieving market efficiency or economic efficiency. This not only includes economic legislation but also important parts of social legislation. This aspect would elude the social law jurist if he interprets all social legislation as a reaction to the weak position of the employee. However, from a market theory point of view in social law, as in economic law, one should distinguish between legislation which is a reaction to market imperfections and which aims at re-establishing the optimum functioning of the market, and legislation which aims to correct the market in view of solidarity with the economically weak.[10] Only this latter category of legislation, therefore, involves solidarity in the sense of solidarity with the economically weak.[11] Furthermore, the development of the welfare state has brought the acknowledgement that the model of market efficiency and individual exchange relations proves insufficient in reality as regards equity. For in reality aspects of solidarity have developed in the meaning of concern for the interests of others. Thus, some areas of tension developed between market efficiency and solidarity.

We may distinguish the following three aspects of solidarity with three subsequent areas of tension:

At government level we encounter solidarity as solidarity with the economically weak in relation to the goal of a just income distribution. Here the tension occurs mostly as regards social security, as was pointed out above.

At company level we encounter solidarity in two varieties.

1. internal solidarity, i.e. concern for the interests of employees. It is nowadays understood that the relationship between employees and the company they work for is not limited to an anonymous exchange relation to which the employees' only contribution is, according to economic market theory, the production factor labour. The social component of labour as a means to development and self-fulfilment for man has become ever more important. Within the organization elements of internal solidarity and mutual concern play their roles. This has created tension between the aim of profit maximization and internal solidarity in the sense of concern for the

---

[10] Examples of social legislation in reaction to market imperfection are the *Wet op het algemeen verbindend en onverbindend verklaren van CAO's* (Act on declaring collective employment agreements generally binding or non-binding) and the *Wet op de loonvorming* (Wages Act) – the twin sisters of the *Wet Economische Mededinging* (Competition Act) and the *Prijzenwet* (Pricing Act), respectively, of economic public law – which aim at re-establishing the optimum functioning of the market. Examples of legislation aiming to correct the market from a point of view of solidarity with the economically weak would be certain acts concerning social security. (See the contribution on Reintegration of Partially Disabled Employees.) These have no equivalent in economic public law. (See Hessel *et al.*, 1997, p. 323-330.)

[11] I do not feel that this is very obvious in the contributions by Yvonne Konijn and Mies Westerveld. This does not mean, by the way, that social and economic legislation not aimed at solidarity with the economically weak is entirely devoid of solidarity. Below I will distinguish – as opposed to market theory – internal and external solidarity at company level alongside solidarity with the economically weak at government level. If one agrees with me on the existence of internal and external solidarity and that this solidarity needs reinforcement, then solidarity plays a role in all legislation.

employees' interests. This development has in law resulted in the introduction of the principles of proper entrepreneurship.[12]

2. External solidarity or social responsibility of the company. In contrast to pure market theory the conviction has grown that companies should supplementary to certain statutory norms exercise some social responsibility, for example as regards the environment or investments in countries with deplorable regimes. During the heydays of the welfare state South Africa was a good example thereof. Such ideas create a tension between profit maximization and external solidarity or social responsibility.

This condition of social responsibility primarily developed as it became clear that the legislator by nature fails in adequately settling the conflicts of interest that occur in a rapidly changing society. Particularly in the United States there was a flood of publications at the time on 'social responsibility' and subsequently on 'business ethics'. An example is the book by Christopher D. Stone which is also well-known in the Netherlands, Where the Law Ends, The Social Control of Corporate Behaviour (1975). In the Netherlands we can mention the publications of Kuin (1977) and Van Luijk (1985).

b. The Crisis in the Welfare State

The tension between market efficiency and solidarity usually receives most attention at government level, but we must not disregard the aspects of solidarity at company level. The fact that the latter receive less attention may perhaps be explained by the fact that the crisis in the welfare state mostly developed at government level. Vast unemployment, the rigidity of the labour market and the prohibitive costs of the extended social security system − not least because of improper use and insufficient control − has resulted in a radical change during the second half of the Eighties when deregulation and reinforcement of the market became primary goals. This change of policy in itself may be considered necessary and wise because attention for the market had largely disappeared and the expectations of government policies were far too high. It is, however, regrettable that in general the one-dimensional approach which is characteristic for neo-liberal market theory was thus chosen. Disappointment in government policies was replaced by great expectations of the free market economy. Market efficiency now threatens to become the key issue and solidarity a practically and normatively outdated principle. The areas of tension between market efficiency and solidarity are then 'resolved' and the individualistic perception of man becomes the rule.

---

[12] See Van Leeuwen, 1989; Van der Heijden, 1988.

5 The One-Dimensional Approach of Neo-Liberal Market Theory

Even though over the last few years, also because of concrete experience with deregulation and privatization, there is increasing criticism of neo-liberal theory and the present government of liberals and socialists, the Kok administration, also distances itself further from the pure neo-liberal approach, yet a number of aspects of neo-liberal theory even now dominate the discussion on the future of the welfare state. (Neo-liberals here have the advantage that they can rely on traditional, unambiguous and therefore politically attractive ideas while critics lack such common milestones.) As regards the subject of this article two aspects of neo-liberalism are of particular importance as they pertain to the relationship market efficiency–solidarity and two further aspects which pertain to the role that the law plays in neo-liberalism.

As regards the relationship between market efficiency and solidarity the following applies according to neo-liberal theory.

a. Price Mechanism and Market Efficiency Has Been Made Absolute
The price mechanism being the only coordinating mechanism, sufficiently coordinates the actions of economic actors. Market efficiency is the highest principle and should therefore absolutely prevail over solidarity with the economically weak. This solidarity is incompatible with the efficient functioning of the market and is at most a sort of left-over category: solidarity as the safety net of the market.
Unmodified application of this theory will in the end result in cutting out all elements of solidarity from our system of social security, a drastic cut in social benefits and the introduction of a so-called mini-system which is claimed to serve the efficiency, flexibility and dynamics of the market. The unconditional plea to abolish minimum wages fits this line of thought. Such a return to the market does not allow for any kind of government interference. We should let the market have its way.
Nor is there any room in neo-liberal theory for internal or external solidarity of the company. The role of the employee within the company should be played as much as possible in accordance with the market: flexible supply of the production factor labour to be determined by the aim of profit maximization. External solidarity in the sense of social responsibility of companies is a residue of the soft approach of the Seventies. According to proven neo-liberal recipe the social responsibility of companies exists in making profits. To the extent that reality still contains elements of the three aspects of solidarity these may easily be eliminated for the future.

b. Solidarity Neither Present nor Wanted

The neo-liberal market model involves a strictly individualistic perception of man, at least as regards market actors. The relationship between market parties is characterized by an anonymous exchange relationship based only on personal interests. This relationship is governed by individual freedom of choice and equality in the meaning of equal competition conditions. Furthermore, there is no actual or normative room for solidarity in the sense of being alert to the interests of others. This sort of solidarity does not exist and need not exist in order for the economic process of production and distribution to function properly. The free price mechanism and the thesis of natural harmony of interests will, after all, see to it that the market functions both efficiently and justly.[13]

As to the role of law in neo-liberal theory I should like to point out the following two issues.

c. The Law Creates Order

The market model is not legally neutral and presupposes the existence of a certain band of legislation around the market. In the ideal liberal market economy this band may be limited to classic private and criminal law;[14] in the welfare state this band of legislation has been extended considerably with social and economic regulations due to occurring market imperfections, market failures and market corrections necessary from a solidarity point of view. According to neo-liberal theory it is the law's task to impose order among rational individuals who are only concerned with their own interests. It is assumed that law is capable of *creating* by itself actual order among individuals. The law is one-dimensionally able to solve possible conflicts of interest beforehand by providing unambiguous abstract rules which suffice to solve concrete conflicts. Thus, within the band of legislation individuals are allowed to strive for their own interests. In this, jurists recognize the rather optimistic traditional view of legal positivism. In this approach to law the emphasis is on providing legislation. Whether these laws are indeed observed is of no or less importance. In as far as the problem of observance of legislation is acknowledged, the solution too is one-dimensional and simple: deterrence by means of criminal law is the motto. If

---

[13] It will be clear that a non-normative economy does not pass the normative judgment that man, at least the market actor man, may or should act individualistic. In as far as neo-liberals give the idea that with some actual insight in the economy one must come to such a conclusion, their conclusion is based on a hidden value judgment.

[14] The parties on the liberal market are supposed to have private property and freedom of agreement and are supposed to buy their goods and not to steal.

21

rules nevertheless get broken one will have to opt for heavier sentences and increased chances of arrest, which will convince the rational calculating citizen to behave in accordance with the law. The role of the subject is limited to sufficient recognition of his obligations stemming from the unambiguous rule and to calculating and passive observance of his obligations. The subject's only question is: 'What are my chances of getting caught and what will it cost me?' This model leaves no room for legal principles alongside and supplementary to legal rules such as the principles of proper entrepreneurship. After all, legal principles require that a person is actively involved with the law in that he must in some way weigh his interests against those of others. Legal principles involve ethics and neo-liberalism leaves practically and normatively no room for ethics in addition to legislation.[15]

d. A Businessman Is Supposed to Act Amorally

Market theory presents a strict division between the role someone plays as a citizen and member of the community on the one hand and the role the same person may play as a market party on the other hand. The two roles may not be mixed. This means, for instance, that an entrepreneur as an entrepreneur may only and should only be led by market signals, although within the clearly visible boundaries set by legal rules. Privately he may hold certain ethical or legal opinions and he may share a legal conscience with others. This legal conscience relates to the question of how the interests of various (groups of) people must be weighed against each other. Thus, for example, an entrepreneur may privately feel that the environment must be protected and that special activities should be organized to help handicapped people or foreign workers to a job, but in his role of entrepreneur in the market this sort of political consideration is out of bounds. Political or legal consciences and the market are strictly separate areas and should remain so. The entrepreneur is supposed to act amorally.

---

[15] The difference between rules and principles has aptly been phrased by Dworkin: 'Only rules dictate results, come what may. When a contrary result has been reached, the rule has been abandoned or changed. Principles do not work that way; they incline a decision one way, though not conclusively, and they survive intact when they do not prevail' (Dworkin 1977, p. 35).

6 Points of Criticism

Neo-liberal theory is open to a lot of criticism not least from an economy point of view because economy is not merely limited to the market.[16] Here I should like to discuss the criticism which one may have on the role attributed to the law.

6.1 Legislation Cannot Impose Order Among Individuals

As shown, market theory may be based on a positivistic view on law. This assumes that conflicts in society can easily be solved by legislation, by simply imposing statutory rules which are subsequently enforced in court. Via the traditional legal order of law and judiciary an actual social order could be created within society. In other words: the law determines the rules of the social game and this allows the game to proceed in an orderly fashion. This model is therefore characterized by the primacy of the legal order; the actual social order follows from there. *Ergo*, a one-dimensional approach.

Jurists no longer have such an optimistic belief in the powers of statutory rules. The law is indeed indispensable in society but that does not mean that it can simply mould society. Particularly the development of legal sociology and the attention for the actual influence of law on society have taught jurists that the simple determination of a statutory rule is something entirely different from concluding that the social game is indeed played according to those statutory rules. Even the simple traffic rule which forbids us to ignore a red traffic light illustrates this all too clearly.

Legal sociology teaches us that law and statutory rules cannot by themselves impose order on a society which consists only of individuals. Legal order cannot create social order. For the law to have effect, for an appeal to statutory rules to have effect, social reality must comprise at least a minimal social order in which statutory rules may take root. This minimal social order is characterized by solidarity or loyalty between people to the extent that they mind other people's interests at least to some extent.[17]

---

[16]   Even if one only thinks in terms of efficiency and the individualistic welfare concept, the neo-liberal pleas to abolish minimum wages and relinquish the declaration of general binding of collective labour agreements, may be questioned. See Den Hertog, 1977, p. 262.

[17]   See Schuyt, 1973, p. 170-171.

6.2 Adam Smith Already Mentioned 'Fellow Feeling'

This is, by the way, not so much a new perception presented by sociology of law but rather a confirmation of the topicality of an old notion. Thus, for instance, Paul Scholten, who is legendary among Dutch jurists, in combating simple legal positivism, stated already in the Forties that the law does not take effect as regards mere individuals but that the law assumes a solidarity which transcends individualism.[18] Within economics we can perceive in this context a clear connection with several authors who over the last few years have reminded us that The Wealth of Nations by Adam Smith must be seen in connection with the latter's earlier publication, Theory of Moral Sentiments. Alongside the market order a certain spontaneous social order (once more) may be discerned in the form of 'fellow feeling', 'social passions of generosity, humanity, kindness, mutual friendship and esteem' which lessen the effect of pure personal interest even to the perception of the founding father of market economy.[19]

In this concept of law, therefore, man is not merely *homo economicus* but also a social being. This solidarity entails that citizens not only look after their own interests but are also to some extent concerned with those of other people and of the community in general. As a social being a person takes into account other people's norms and expectations of him.

As regards the law this solidarity (or fellow feeling) forms the reason why people should observe the rules.

Whoever assumes in accordance with the market model that a person in his approach to legislation is led solely by an individualistic cost-benefit analysis, 'What are my chances of getting caught and what would that cost me?', completely ignores such questions as 'What is expected of me?' and 'Surely you can't do that?'

The example of the red traffic light may clarify this. The fact that the majority of cyclists nowadays ignores red lights shows that legal order cannot impose social order. For years the majority of cyclists stopped before red lights. The legal norm was supplemented by social solidarity: 'People want and expect me to stop' and 'One does not ignore red traffic lights'. The fact that these days cyclists behave differently is not due to the fact that calculating citizens now reach a different conclusion on the

---

[18] Scholten 1949 (reprint 1980), p. 47.
[19] See Canterbery 1980, p. 51. See also Kastelein 1976, p. 53: 'It will be obvious that Smith rejected this Robinson perception of man. That is to say that he rejected the position that society existed of a collection of unrelated individuals which could only achieve an orderly society by means of some sort of contract or obligatory behaviour imposed from outside.'

basis of a cost-benefit analysis. The problem is rather that for cyclists the spontaneous solidarity that one does not ignore traffic lights, has largely disappeared. In contrast to the traditional positivistic recipe the law has even been adapted and now generally allows cyclists to ignore the red light when turning right. This does not as yet apply to car drivers. A driver who ignores a red light is still considered a 'scoundrel'.

6.3 Spontaneous Solidarity and Legal Standards

In order to indicate that social solidarity cannot be created by law but has to be present in society to some extent from the start, I speak of spontaneous solidarity. Spontaneous therefore in contrast to imposed by law. However, this concept of spontaneous solidarity must be considered in its right proportions. The fact that the legal order does not take primacy does not mean that we should turn 180 degrees and say that society can do without any form of legal order. The assumed existence of spontaneous solidarity does not mean that citizens will of their own accord take sufficient notice of other people's interests so that legislation is no longer necessary to solve conflicts of interest. That of course would be nonsense and another typical one-dimensional approach. Spontaneous solidarity presupposes a certain involvement in the interests of others which provides fertile ground for the legal rule where those interests of others gain some importance. The point is that legislation in itself is insufficient and that it needs spontaneous solidarity to supplement it. Legislation must relate to the minimal social involvement of people and enhance it by further specifying it into legal rights and legal duties. Thus we have a multi-dimensional approach to law.

What we should think of when talking about spontaneous solidarity may be illustrated by means of the developments around the *Wet Arbeid Gehandicapte Werknemers* (WAGW, Handicapped Workers Employment Act). This act shows that legislation alone is not enough but that we should not rely on mere spontaneous solidarity either. Reality is far more intricate.

According to legal positivism, the legislator who feels that employers should employ a certain percentage of handicapped workers may without problem authoritatively impose such a percentage. Law then creates order. This is a far too simple perception of reality as experience with the WAGW learns. As soon as the legislator announced his intention to impose a statutory quota on employers, the latter protested against such a duty in vast numbers. Quite rightly the legislator then did not follow the legal positivistic recipe but opted for an alternative to imposing authoritatively. However, the chosen alternative proved no solution but rather taught us not to assume that employers will of their own free will employ handicapped workers. In reaction to the protests, namely, the legislator opted for an introductory period of three years during which the realization of set goals was left to the social partners. This too resulted in failure. In reaction authoritative imposition was once again chosen albeit that the duty may now be activated by means of an Order in Council. This has as yet never happened, so that we have now reached a stalemate. As early as in 1991 Hessel and Klosse have argued that instead of imposing a quota duty authoritatively, legislation should be made which appeals to the already to some extent existing social involvement or solidarity of businessmen. Instead of the detached instrument of a quota duty the legislator could, as in Canada, oblige (larger) companies to draft an affirmative action plan, the goals and terms of which may be adjusted on a yearly basis. 'The advantage of this method over quota duty is that employers have some discretion in interpreting their duty to employ handicapped workers. Compliance with this statutory duty may be reinforced by means of "contract compliance" which entails in short that government contracts are preferably granted to companies that execute a positive plan of action.'[20] However, at the time there was no interest in this approach. (See further section 7.3.1 sub c.)

To conclude this section I would like to point out one very important social complication which comes to light with the multi-dimensional approach to law. The spontaneous solidarity in social order necessary for the law to take effect, may be absent or diminished and the rules of legal order may actually contribute to that. That is the case when legislation applies traditional, unambiguous standards which reduce people to mechanical docility. If spontaneous solidarity disappears then the law is left empty-handed. After all, how to persuade cyclists to once more stop before a red light? How to persuade society to again accept certain statutory rules concerning solidarity with the economically weak if that spontaneous solidarity gets eroded?

7 A Multi-Dimensional Approach to Market Efficiency and Solidarity

The fact that the law needs a certain amount of spontaneous solidarity within the social order in order to achieve results, has very important consequences for the perception of social reality and the process of production and distribution which takes place within that reality. What it amounts to is that the handling of the welfare state crisis cannot be limited to promoting market efficiency according to neo-liberal

---

[20]   Hessel and Klosse, 1991, p. 7.

recipe. The three aspects of social solidarity should also receive special attention. In this context I perceive an active role for the government as well. Below, I shall elaborate on this further. Remarkable is that during the last two or three years obvious developments have taken place in the Netherlands that seem to fit the approach argued by me. Apparantly there is a slowly growing understanding that the neo-liberal approach is in the end too simple. Unfortunately, I must conclude that within my own field of experience, public economic law, the one-dimensional approach still reigns. It seems that here we pay the price for the traditional one-sided attention for market efficiency (see section 3.2). Besides, the government policy as executed by the Ministry of Economic Affairs does not exactly stimulate to acknowledge the shortcomings of neo-liberalism.

7.1 Solidarity with the Economically Weak Must not be Considered a Left-Over Category

The understanding that some degree of spontaneous solidarity is necessary in society in order for legislation to function properly is, of course, a major setback for the traditional formally oriented jurists who adopted the one-dimensional belief that society functions well if proper procedures are agreed upon and the acts concerned are published in the National Official Journal. However, social reality is far more complicated than this traditional picture. In view of the necessity of some spontaneous solidarity, namely, we have to acknowledge with legal sociologists such as Schuyt that in reality there is a multi-dimensional tension between material distribution of chances (in life) in the social game and the degree to which that social game is played in an orderly fashion.[21] If the results of this social game differ too much among the various players and if for instance a group of permanent losers is formed, spontaneous solidarity is under pressure. This has its effect on the willingness to accept the rules of the game. And if that willingness disappears the law is left, as we saw, empty-handed.

This understanding of how the law works makes it obvious that for the economic process of production and distribution, yes even for the rule of law (*Rechtsstaat*) itself, to function well it is dangerous to regard social solidarity with the economically weak as unimportant for the market economy. Should we create a dichotomy within society this will not be a problem which only affects a small group of socially involved people who wish to stick to the by now outdated ideals of the welfare state

---

[21]   Schuyt 1973, p. 172.

in its heydays. From a legal perspective we must conclude that that would amount to jeopardizing the rule of law which is the jurist's *raison d'être*.

In social reality the relationship between market efficiency and solidarity with the economically weak is far more complicated than the supporters of the market model want us to believe. They emphasize that the crisis in the welfare state has taught us that too many social regulations and too much protection results in economic rigidity and prohibitive costs. Too much solidarity therefore, undermines the market and calls for a boost in market efficiency. This is in itself correct except that it shows only one aspect of the problem. On the other hand we must bear in mind that efficiency measures which lessen the protection of employees and social security beneficiaries may at first sight boost the market but reduce at the same time the existing element of solidarity and will thus in time undermine acceptance of the rules of the efficient market game. If we acknowledge that side to the market efficiency–solidarity balance the question forces itself upon us whether the government policies executed until now have not been determined disproportionately by considerations of finance and efficiency. Does not this approach pose a major threat to the constitutional state? For instance, the *Wet op de Arbeidsongeschiktheidsverzekering* (WAO, Disability Insurance Act) was revised extensively some years ago. Induced by excessive reliance on disability allowances the government has reduced both height and duration of the allowance. Furthermore, the criteria for qualification have been made stricter. So in the end fewer people receive less allowance for a shorter period. Those who now no longer qualify for disability allowances, however, are not immediately able to rejoin the labour process. They will have to apply for unemployment benefits pursuant to the *Werkloosheidswet* (WW, Unemployment Act). Such a legislative operation is not based on a clear vision of how market efficiency and solidarity should be balanced in future. The basis here is a so-called volume policy which seems successful when the number of disability benefit claimants drops. The fact that we encounter the very same people on the unemployment lists shortly afterwards and, after subsequent tightening of the admission criteria for that act, on the dole, does not seem to spoil the fun for now. The fact that thus strengthening of the market as coordination instrument results in a disturbance of spontaneous solidarity, which is also a coordination instrument, fails to be understood because the latter instrument is not considered.

7.1.1 Recent Developments in the Right Direction

Now, how may we achieve increased attention for solidarity with the economically weak as well as achieving the necessary financial and market economic reorganization?

First, let me emphasize that I do not consider restoring the much discussed automatic linking of benefits, minimum wages and civil service salaries to salaries in the market sector the right solution.[22] Such an interpretation of solidarity is too much against the grain of the market. This instrument which was wielded in the heydays of the welfare state in the Netherlands around 1980 and which was for a short while reinstated in 1990, has a number of fundamental flaws.[23] It is in fact a one-dimensional instrument as it leaves no room for the complexity of society and the necessity of balancing efficiency and solidarity.

Automatic linking may at face value seem very sympathetic but the toll it takes on the market and the financial position of the government soon becomes too much for the government to bear and it is obliged to let go of this link very soon. That is why it lasted only very shortly in 1990. Within a socio-economic context where (quite rightly) more than in the past importance is attributed to a proper functioning of the market, a government should do no more than consider on a yearly basis whether its financial situation allows for some form of linking. I therefore strongly support the idea of the *Wet koppeling met afwijkingsmogelijkheden* (WKA, Act on Linking with Possible Deviations) which was introduced in 1991, as well as the fact that after considering the actual situation the link has been restored by the socialist-liberal Kok administration for 1996 and 1997.

Besides linking in situations where this is economically and financially possible, I think that solidarity with the economically weak should be realized in a way which is not contrary to strengthening the market but rather supplementary. This means that the economic measures to strengthen the market must be supplemented by active government policies aimed at the economically weak. Instead of the neo-liberal idea of simply back to the market which must then play its part, the government should resort especially to significantly intensifying its reintegration policy. Pleas to that effect, such as that by Klosse, found little or no support in the early Nineties.[24] However, the socialist-liberal Kok administration has taken some important steps as

---

[22] See also Hessel and Klosse, 1991.

[23] As a result of automatic linking the decisions taken by the social partners in the market sector to increase wages, take direct and uncensured effect within the civil service sector. Irrespective of the financial-economic problems this system could once again create, this structure is most unfortunate also from a procedural and distribution of responsibilities and competences point of view. The government was in 1980 forced to combine the automatic linking with planned wages policies. The Wages Act (*Wet op de loonvorming*) was used to curb budget deficits. Such policy was not only juridically unacceptable because the act was now used for something entirely different, but it also disturbed the functioning of the market.

[24] See Klosse, 1989; Klosse, 1993; Klosse, 1995.

regards reintegration. Consider for instance the introduction of the so-called Melkert jobs for the long-term unemployed and the *Wet uitbreiding loondoorbetalingsverplichting bij ziekte* (WULBZ, Act on Extended Duty to Pay Wages in Case of Illness). These measures indicate that in striving for more employment the government no longer solely relies on the market (flexibilization, possible reduction of minimum wages and reducing if not abolishing the possibility to declare collective labour agreement clauses generally binding), but also resorts to aspects of solidarity. (See further the contribution on Reintegration of Partially Disabled Employees.)

7.1.2 We Are Not Out of the Woods Yet

The fact that there are some developments in the right direction, where one-dimensional neo-liberal theory is left behind, does not mean we are there yet. To my opinion a more balanced relationship between market efficiency and solidarity deserves consideration in general and not only as regards social security. At the moment the situation is still too much that of two camps not understanding each other's language. On the one side we encounter the economic-financial camp where reducing the budget deficit takes priority, also limited by the requirements for entering the future EMU. In my own field of expertise all eyes are focussed on that. On the other side there is the camp which, supported by predictions of the Social and Cultural Planning Bureau and research into poverty in the Netherlands, is focussed on ghetto formation in the larger cities and the dichotomy of society. If both camps are maintained the results of relevant discussions on the future of rent subsidies, the volume of council housing *et cetera* will be influenced too much by the political power balance of the moment.

Whatever it will be, the following three notions will have to be included in these discussions:
1) not only the market but spontaneous solidarity too is an important coordination instrument in society;
2) when looking for a balanced relationship between market efficiency and solidarity one must bear in mind that economic reality does not confront us with the *fait accompli* that solidarity is subordinate to market efficiency. There is some room for discretion as regards the advantages of solidarity compared with the disadvantages of any disturbance of the market. This discretionary leeway is more extensive than neo-liberal theorists want us to believe on the basis of their hidden value judgements. However, it is also smaller than we thought during the heydays of the welfare state;
3) the rate at which the budget deficit of the government is reduced is not dictated by economic reality but is subject to political choice. However, it must be understood

that social policies have their price and that the various options are of necessity limited by the financial elbow room of the government.

As the government has these days far less financial elbow room than (private) companies, one could imagine realizing the necessary solidarity (also) by means of these companies. This leads me to the following.

The understanding that some degree of spontaneous solidarity is necessary for the law to function also influences the way in which one perceives the role of companies within the economic process of production and distribution. Thus, primarily influenced by the legal sociological perception of the actual role of legislation as regards industry, over the last twenty years an extensive attack has been launched in Anglo-saxon literature on the simple perception of company behaviour as promoted by traditional market theory. The one-dimensional view that industry is led only and solely by market signals and the wish to maximize profits, is rejected in literature because it does not concur with reality. An alternative developed which I have referred to in earlier publications as the school of social responsibility.[25] Supporters of this school such as the earlier mentioned authors Kuin and Stone (see section 4), describe the consequences of the actual restrictions of law to create order both as regards the internal functioning of the company and as regards its approach to the outside world. Essential is that companies in reality focuss both internally and externally on profits and market efficiency as well as on aspects of social solidarity. The role of the internal social climate and of social responsibility are emphasized.

In contrast to what the name of said school might indicate it does not replace one-dimensional market theory with an equally one-dimensional absolute acceptance of solidarity. *Au contrair*, the authors involved entertain a typical multi-dimensional view of reality which comprises both market efficiency and solidarity and which assumes a complicated and strained relationship between the two. I have already admitted to adhering to this theory in earlier publications.[26] Within my own field of expertise, however, where market theory prevails since deregulation, there is as yet little support for this approach. In general, though, I get the impression that the multi-dimensional approach has been gaining recognition over the last few years in the Netherlands as well. Remarkable is that this recognition comes from those who are involved with the daily practice of company behaviour such as social scientists and organizational advisors.

---

[25] See Hessel, 1987; Hessel, 1995, p. 350.
[26] See Hessel, 1987; Hessel, 1995.

Applying the multi-dimensional approach of the school of social responsibility I will now discuss the meaning of both internal and external solidarity in relation to a strenghtening of the market.

7.2 Internal Solidarity (Social Climate) Also Needs Improvement

What was said above (section 6.1) as regards legal rules being the rules of the game of society as an organization, also holds true for the rules of the game that apply to the company as an organization. In order for the internal organization of the company to function properly it does not suffice if proper juridical procedural rules and competences are being introduced, but it also requires some sort of spontaneous social solidarity or internal social solidarity. The understanding that the ordening possibilities of legislation are limited, entails the understanding that the proper functioning of the company in the production and distribution process requires not only a strong competition position in the market but also that the internal social climate is good. In neo-liberal theory this internal social climate has no place. Quite the opposite, supporters of 'back to the market' emphasize that the crisis of the welfare state has learned us that too much internal solidarity leads to keeping workers employed who cannot (or no longer) keep up sufficiently with the demands of the market which in turn results in excessive labour costs, weakening of the competition position in international markets and technical innovations grinding to a halt. Here too their conclusion from the past is that too much internal solidarity undermines the market and requires a boost of market efficiency. This in itself is correct but represents only one side of the coin.

At first sight a strictly efficient internal company climate may perhaps contribute to a strong market position of the company. By means of a hiring and firing policy in reaction to the market's demands and by demanding quick adaptation of employees to changes in that market, the company may cut back on all kinds of social aspects. However, having to work in such efficient and dynamic surroundings does not suit many people and it is far from stimulating. The workers' understanding that their meaning and value for the company are determined solely by the market will result in diminished internal solidarity. This is irrelevant to neo-liberals. They ignore the fact that that diminishing will have its effect on society by diminishing the willingness to loyally apply the company's rules of the game. Such a standstill in the internal organization will in the end affect the company's market position.

If we include these complications of reality in our considerations it appears that the company's behaviour is not only coordinated by market signals but rather by a complex multi-dimensional combination of market and solidarity. On the one hand there are the relations underscored by the supporters of the market: strengthening of solidarity by too soft personnel policies for the sake of employment will harm the market position of the company which reflects negatively on solidarity. For if you want to execute social policies you need financial strength.

On the other hand, the following relations should also be acknowledged: reinforcing the market position by, for instance, innovations may lead to internal social tensions which in turn reflect negatively on the market position. Reversed: strengthening internal solidarity may contribute to a better market position.

Particularly these latter relationships should be used and this is where I see the government's task.

Let me confirm first, that the increased attention for internal solidarity does not mean that we must return to the policies executed during the heydays of the welfare state. By the end of the Seventies, early Eighties it was usual for the government, especially the Ministry of Economic Affairs, to temporarily financially support economically weak companies and sectors in order to improve their positions. Although that was not the intention, this policy did result in a standstill. The number of weak companies burdening the Dutch economy grew. Since the mid-Eighties on the other hand, it has, in the context of maximizing the market, become customary for the financial means of the government to be used rather to stimulate relatively strong companies or sectors. These may give an extra impulse to the economy. In this context one may consider all sorts of stimulating regulations as regards innovation, technological renewal and such. Deviating from neo-liberal theory such stimulating regulations should, to my opinion, be used to reinforce the market as well as restore the welfare state. This the more so as the Netherlands, compared to other countries of the European Community, spend rather few resources on technological renewal.

However, the innovation and technology policies followed until now have been directed rather too one-sidedly at reinforcing the industries' market positions. In this the importance of internal solidarity gets lost. Both from a point of view of good market positions in future – preventing social unrest in case of innovation – and from that of internal solidarity itself, the government should not consider strengthening the market position as the ultimate aim but rather as a step towards strengthening internal solidarity. This may be achieved if the innovative measures mentioned above are subject not only to economic conditions, such as the company having to predict permanent profits, but also to social policy conditions.[27] An example would be internal education programmes, adequate support for elderly workers who cannot keep up (sufficiently) with technological developments, sufficient openness of the management towards its employees and loyalty towards the works council.

In my view companies who have no or a bad social programme should not qualify for innovative or technological stimulation premiums. Bad social policies are unwanted both for economic and social reasons.

7.2.1 Recent Developments in the Right Direction

As regards internal solidarity too the last few years have shown some developments in the right direction which acknowledge the limitations of one-dimensional market theory.

a. Organization Consultancy

In organization consultancy we see clear reactions to the reorganizations characteristic of the early Nineties which aimed only at flexibilization and market reinforcement. Consider for instance the criticism uttered by organization expert Colijn concerning human resource management where the value of people within the organization is determined entirely by short-term market theory, where personal and organizational principles of integrity are sacrificed.[28] Colijn emphasizes that within modern industry where the performance competences of people determine the degree of success, it is disfunctional to disregard the emotional bond within the organization.[29] According to him it is desirable, and not only from a humane perspective, to take into account the stamina of workers in times of crisis. The reverse may in practice result in significant, mostly invisible costs due to loss of involvement. Contrary to the perhaps too soft approach of the Seventies Colijn pleads to take distance from emotional considerations which may weaken the harshness necessary during the phases of analysis and strategic planning. Following a strict analysis, however, solidarity must then be taken into account during the executional phase in order to gain sufficient acceptance and commitment.[30] This means that superfluous or disfunctioning workers no longer remain where they are but that following a clear strict review of their position the management will look for other work for them within the company, perhaps after retraining, or elsewhere via outplacement.

---

[27] It goes without saying that making economic policy subject to such social conditions must be based on explicit statutory authorization.

[28] Colijn, 1996, p. 19.

[29] Colijn, 1996, p. 24.

[30] Colijn, 1996, p. 24.

b. Another View on Flexibilization and Protection

If we include internal solidarity as an aspect of reality into our considerations, we may also take a different view on the tension between economic flexibility and job protection. Thus, for instance, research is currently undertaken within the framework of the Netherlands School for Social and Economic Policy Research AWSB and upon request of the Ministry of Social Affairs and Employment, into the possibility to protect workers via internal procedures within the company as an alternative to the preventive dismissal check which is criticized by the market. This is an appeal to internal solidarity and not merely the traditional legal dominance of legislation and court. This development, by the way, seems to indicate that the Ministry of Social Affairs and Employment has developed an interest in internal solidarity as well as the market. That is a good thing provided this happens along the lines Colijn has set out with a proper understanding of the necessary harsh analysis of the market and not the traditional soft approach of social policy with a negative ring to market efficiency.

7.3 External Solidarity (Social Responsibility) also Needs Reinforcement

The understanding that some degree of spontaneous solidarity is necessary in society in order for the law to function properly also has its influence on the view one takes as regards the industry's approach to the legal rules which apply to them. Here too it appears that market theory has a far too simple perception of the coordination of market subjects.

a. There are Three Coordination Instruments

The economic process of production and distribution in the market not only comprises coordination via the market within ready-to-use statutory regulations that will satisfactorily solve conflicts of interest between the company and its surroundings. There is rather the necessary combination of three coordination instruments namely the market, legislation and solidarity or loyalty in the sense of concern for other people's interests.

In law one can even come to this point of view without the legal sociological understanding that some spontaneous solidarity is necessary for rules to be effective. After all, as the welfare state developed it became clear that statutory rules can never sufficiently solve the conflicts of interest between companies and the outside world. An abstract legal rule always leaves the subject some discretion depending on the phrasing of and concepts used by that rule. The person may never resort to passively recognizing the 'preconditions' that apply to him, but when interpreting the law will always to some extent have to weigh his interests against those of others. Furthermore, legislation always lags behind in solving the problems that may occur, especially in a society as changeable as ours.[31]

This sort of notion, familiar to the jurist, has in Dutch literature hardly ever been connected to the behaviour of entrepreneurs in the market. This is different in the United States. Stone has even managed to summarize the crux of the matter in the title of his book: Where the Law Ends. The Social Control of Corporate Behaviour.[32]

The perceptions gleaned from legal sociology and law bring us to conclude that some measure of external social solidarity or social responsibility is necessary for the proper functioning of rules which apply to companies as market parties. In other words: entrepreneurs in reality cannot act amorally in contrast to what market theory assumes. Because of the limitations of law and legislation they have to behave morally to at least some extent for legislation to be effective.

What is remarkable is that in the Netherlands the economist and entrepreneur Kuin already acknowledged this necessity in the Seventies. In het earlier mentioned book 'Management is meer.... de sociale verantwoordelijkheid van de onderneming' (Management is more...social responsibility of the corporation) he criticizes for instance the market theory assumption that competition imperfections in the market can only be solved by means of clear anti-cartel laws imposed on corporations. Kuin quite rightly points out that such legislation only applies to flagrant cases. 'The only guarantee for the proper functioning of the system is the responsibility of the strongest. If this is absent the market economy will perish due to its own perver-

---

[31] That is what Stone has called 'the time-lag problem'. Stone says: '[T]he law is primarily a reactive institution (...) until they [laws] are passed a great deal of damage – some perhaps irreversible – can be done. Thus, there is something grotesque – and socially dangerous – in encouraging corporate managers to believe that, until the law tells them otherwise, they have no responsibilities beyond the law and their impulses (whether their impulses spring from the id or from the balance sheet).' (Stone, 1975, p. 94.)

[32] Stone gives the following general conclusion: 'Thus, the overall picture is that our strategies aimed to control corporations by threatening their profits are a very limited way of bringing about the internal changes that are necessary if the policies behind the law are to be effectuated. Indeed, I would go so far as to suggest that those who deplore 'the fact' that corporations are motivated solely by profit are not only wrong, but missing an important point.' (Stone, 1975, p. 57.) With reference to Stone in the same period Steiner and Steiner conclude concisely: '[T]hat in the past social responsibility doctrine did not work and we therefore needed the law. Today the law does not work and we need to throw social responsibility back on the corporation.' (Steiner and Steiner, 1980, p. 200.)

sion – the law of the jungle.'[33] Here too the notion is that legislation in itself is insufficient and requires the accompaniment of some degree of social solidarity. In Kuin's example this consists of the willingness of the economically strong to somewhat limit the possibilities in the market to protect their own interests in favour of the general interest. In economic terms: a certain spontaneous limitation of actual economic power for the sake of workable competition.

Somewhere else in his book Kuin cites a passage from the English Watkinson Report (1973) on the subject of The Responsibilities of the British Public Company, which describes the relationship between the insufficient statutory rule and the required moral attitude of the company as follows: 'A company should behave like a good citizen in business. The law does not (and cannot) contain or prescribe the whole duty of a citizen. A good citizen takes account of the interest of others besides himself and tries to exercise an informed and imaginative ethical judgement in deciding what he should and should not do. This, it is suggested, is how companies should seek to behave.'[34] This is a despicable point of view to a neo-liberal.

According to neo-liberalism after all, companies always act amorally because they should act amorally (see section 5 sub d.). They think it absolutely ludicrous that reinforcing competition legislation as now happens in the Netherlands requires supplementary external solidarity and reinforcement of business ethics.

Remarkable is that the market economy assumption that companies must act amorally is discarded as unrealistic by supporters of the school of social responsibility. Thus, for instance, Kuin emphasizes in his criticism of market theory the patterned and unreal nature of this division of roles. Reality is not like that. Kuin therefore says: 'Organizations are run by people. Although these people will defend their organization whenever it is attacked, they are also citizens of the same country and they partake of the same culture as their fellow human beings outside the organization. They share the same changes in awareness though perhaps somewhat slower and slightly altered by loyalty. That is why they may be appealed to also on the basis of values and insights they have only recently become aware of. However, due to their more extensive knowledge of their own field they will understand better than others what may be involved in applying those values and insights.'[35] I will return to this issue later (see section 7.3.1).

If on the basis of the legal sociological insights in law and legislation we reach the conclusion that companies must have some degree of external solidarity or social

---

[33] Kuin, 1977, p. 149.
[34] Kuin, 1977, p. 95.
[35] Kuin, 1977, p. 25.

responsibility we must not of course forget the aspect of market coordination. This involves a multi-dimensional approach and tension may grow between the demands of the market and those of external solidarity.

What was said about company internal solidarity of course also applies to external solidarity. Social policies have their price. This means that a company which has trouble in keeping afloat cannot be expected to show a lot of social responsibility. Here too it is true that a strong position in the market is a precondition for external solidarity. It should be noted that an increasing number of companies have already realized that taking social responsibility by for example offering environmentally sound products, may actually improve the company's economic position. The sales of unbleached (coffee) filters, free range eggs, ecologically grown potatoes, candies without colouring agents and the like are really very profitable for food producers. Here too improvement of solidarity will enhance the market position.

b. Deregulation Requires More Business Ethics

If we acknowledge that there is a multi-dimensional combination of market and external social solidarity we also look from a different angle at the reorganization of the welfare state and the aim of more market and deregulation. According to market theory it would suffice to reduce legislation as well as government interference. According to the school of social responsibility, however, deregulation and strengthening of the market entails that 'the level of ethics and morality in business must continue to rise'. That is obvious. If we do not work according to ideology and if we do not succumb to the enticings of the free market model, we acknowledge that the actual functioning of the market, in contrast to what economists say, does not yield a natural harmony of interests but rather results in numerous conflicts of interest that call for solutions. Should the government retreat together with its public rules, these conflicts will once again become manifest unless companies solve the problems by means of selfregulation. To do that they will have to be sufficiently concerned about the interests of others or in other words show sufficient external solidarity. It is, after all, completely senseless to believe in selfregulation by people who only consider their own interests.

Linked to the ideas of the school of social responsibility I stated in the late Eighties that the aim of optimum market and deregulation should be combined with enhancing social responsibility and promoting business ethics.[36] The initiative taken in the Seventies must be further elaborated. This may lead within company law to a further development of the principles of proper entrepreneurship towards external solidarity.

---

[36] Hessel, 1989, p. 134.

However, we must conclude that this link between market and more social responsibility or business ethics is hard to trace in the Dutch approach to deregulation as it developed in the early Nineties. That approach seems to be based on market theory *sec* and the theory of business ethics, separated from no-nonsense company law, thus ended up in the 'soft' corner. An appeal to business ethics then draws the following reaction. 'Someone who thinks he can still appeal to social responsibility, the morality and solidarity of companies is no longer of this day and age, sticks to certain ideals of the heydays of the welfare state and has no inkling of social reality. Companies in reality only pay attention to market signals and it is correct they should do so. You may want them to feel socially responsible but they will not and cannot.' Whoever knows his neo-liberal 'classics' may then support this judgement with the well-known neo-liberal opinion that social responsibility of companies exists in aiming for profit maximization.

Whereas this neo-liberalism still rules public economic law, important developments towards a multi-dimensional approach can be perceived in other fields.

7.3.1 Recent Developments

a. Growing Interest for Business Ethics

Whereas in the early Nineties hardly anyone in the Netherlands spoke of business ethics, this situation has changed drastically over the last two years, not only within university circles but also in organization consultancy. Large commercial organization consultancy agencies such as Coopers & Lybrand and Moret, Ernst & Young, for instance, show a marked interest and KPMG in 1996 actually set up a separate consultancy branch for Integrity Consulting.

One problem, however, is that this in itself correct interest for business ethics as yet fails to adequately pervade legal fields such as business law and economic law and the legal question of how the government/legislator should approach companies. In general, business ethics supporters and jurists talk at cross-purposes. Yet some recent developments seem to indicate that the importance of social responsibility is beginning to penetrate law.

b. Empirical Confirmation of the Multi-dimensional Approach

Persistent supporters of neo-liberalism might be tempted to belittle Kuin's point of view which I supported earlier by saying that he, though apparently bitten by the 'soft' bug of the Seventies, would now have come to a more realistic stance.

However, in recent social research in the Netherlands too the correctness of Kuin's point of view has been confirmed.

Thus, for instance we encounter the same criticism of market theory with the empirical criminologist Van de Bunt, independent of Kuin's ideas.

Van de Bunt rejects the idea that organizations act rationally and amorally and that they may be controlled by the government via criminal law by means of deterrence, an idea that can be linked to neo-liberalism (see para. 5).[37] When an organization is set up, according to Van de Bunt, a certain division is created between the outside world and the organization, and between what is profitable for the organization and what is not, but the amorality of industry is a myth.

'So although each organization is to some extent inherently "a-moral", this "a-morality" is as much a myth as is the rationality of organizations. Organizations consist of people with a conscience and feelings and even organizations function within a society where values and norms regulate interactions. A by now classic study of legal sociology by Macaulay shows that in commercial transactions the organizational contacts are not governed by specific contracts with concretely described sanctions in case of non-performance, but rather by values such as honesty ('one does not shirk one's promises') and reliance ('one is obliged to deliver a good product'). From the many publications and symposia on business ethics one may furthermore deduce that companies are increasingly aware of their social responsibilities. One can be cynical about that, but I regard it as an interesting and hopeful sign.'[38]

Van de Bunt subsequently refers to the results of empirical research conducted in 1991 into the social responsibility (civic responsibility) of 51 managers of average to large multi-national companies in Rotterdam. It appears that this responsibility most certainly exists but is interpreted rather 'strictly'.

'In most cases there is no sense of responsibility for the solution of social problems (unemployment, foreign workers policy), but besides (of course) feeling responsible for the guaranteed continuity of the company there is also a sense of responsibility for observance of legislation and restricting as much as possible the nuisance created by the own company for the environment.'[39]

In this paragraph we find empirical confirmation for a number of essential aspects of the multi-dimensional approach. Here too a sound economic position in the market appears a precondition for accepting social responsibility. Furthermore, social responsibility or external solidarity does not go as far as entrepreneurs of their own accord attributing so much importance to external interests as to spontaneously

---

[37] Van de Bunt, 1992, p. 18.
[38] Van de Bunt, 1992, p. 18-19 (incl. references).
[39] Van de Bunt, 1992, p. 19 (incl. reference).

employ foreign or handicapped workers. Social responsibility also refers to the willingness to comply with the expectations of outsiders, responsibility for observing legislation and the willingness to reduce as much as possible the nuisance for others. Their attitude towards the law therefore is not only determined by an individualistic cost-benefit analysis and the question 'what will it cost me to break the law?', but also the social consideration of 'what does society expect of me?'

Van de Bunt then reaches the conclusion that the deterrence notion of criminal law is based on an incomplete perception of what makes organizations tick. In applying deterrence, the government and legislator run the risk of diminishing existing spontaneous solidarity – Van de Bunt prefers social responsivity – whereas in contrast they should appeal to it. Van de Bunt thus offers a current confirmation of the notion that the government must appeal to what Kuin called 'the sense of civic duty of entrepreneurs'. This sense of civic duty does exist to some extent as is confirmed by Engbersen's research and it is therefore not unrealistic to appeal to it.

c. Need for Alternatives to Traditional Legislation
A third development to be mentioned is that most people by now understand that legislation traditionally imposed from above does not work in cases where the government for instance wants businesses to employ more handicapped or foreign workers.
The problems related to the WAGW as mentioned earlier (para. 6.3) recently also occurred in relation to the *Wet ter bevordering van de instroom van allochtone werknemers* (WBEAA, Act on the Improvement of Labour Market Access for Immigrant Ethnic Minority Workers). Here too it is obvious that on the one hand the imposed standards do not work whereas on the other hand the social responsibility of companies is not such that entrepreneurs will of their own accord hire more immigrant ethnic minority workers. While in 1992 there was as yet little attention for contract compliance as an instrument for the government with which to draw on the spontaneous solidarity of companies, the research school AWSB is currently conducting some research into contract compliance commissioned by the Ministry of Social Affairs and Employment. Recent publications, furthermore, mention other possibilities for the government with which to appeal to spontaneous solidarity. Thus, for instance, Van Heertum-Lemmen and Wilthagen propose covenants between central and branch organizations as well as the possibility of national collective labour agreements in order to get more immigrant ethnic minority workers a job. These national collective labour agreements would then have to be detailed per sector but it would mean an end to noncommitment without putting on pressure from

above.[40] Interesting is that within AWSB research is done, once again commissioned by the Ministry of Social Affairs and Employment, into labour condition agreements as alternatives to government regulation. No unconditional selfregulation where the government refuses to interfere but rather stimulating social responsibility or business ethics via government influence.

These examples help to illustrate that within a multi-dimensional approach much importance is attributed to consultations between government and industry. One-dimensional neo-liberal theory on the other hand leads to abolishing all sorts of consultation elements in the economic order which hamper – short term – market efficiency. Finally I would like to point out the approach taken in the contribution on Reintegration of Partially Disabled Employees. The authors draw attention to the fact that to achieve reintegration, solidarity at company level needs to be reinforced. This presupposes a different frame of mind on the part of the entrepreneurs which may be enhanced by changing the image of the partially disabled worker. According to the authors the emphasis should be on the strong motivation such workers display. The government must actively contribute to this change of image by setting the right example.

8 Concluding Remarks

The crisis in the welfare state which developed by the end of the Seventies has resulted in increased attention for market efficiency. This in itself is correct and necessary. However, it speaks of a far too simple perception of society and law to take the neo-liberal point of view and make market efficiency the highest standard and consider solidarity unimportant. The understanding that legislation needs a certain amount of spontaneous solidarity in order to be successful entails that the future of the welfare state requires reinforcement of both market efficiency and solidarity. This means that solidarity with the economically weak is far from unimportant, that internal solidarity within the company must be enhanced and that the social responsibility of the company, business ethics, deserves increased attention alongside striving for deregulation.

---

[40] Van Heertum-Lemmen and Wilthagen, 1996, p. 234-238.

References

Bunt, H.G. van de, Organisatiecriminaliteit, Gouda Quint, Arnhem 1992.

Bunt, H.G. van de, Het besef komt van binnenuit, NJB 1994, afl.45/46, p. 1576/1677.

Canterberry, E.R., The Making of Economics, Belmont, California, second edition 1980.

Colijn, A.C., HRM in crisissituaties; weg met HRM? Een profielschets voor P&O managers, In-, door- en uitstroom, nummer 1, 1996, p. 19-29.

Dworkin, R., Taking Rights Seriously, London 1977.

Heertum, A.H. van, A.C.J.M. Wilthagen, De doorwerking van aanbevelingen van de stichting van de arbeid, sinzheimer cahiers 12, HSI, Sdu, 's-Gravenhage 1996.

Heijden, P.F. van der, Algemene beginselen van behoorlijk ondernemerschap, OR Informatie 13 september 1988, p. 12-14.

Hennipman, P., Economisch motief en economisch principe, NV Noord-Hollandse Uitgevers-maatschappij, Amsterdam 1945.

Hertog, J.A. den, Economie, recht en economische politiek, in: B. Hessel, et al., Sociaal en economisch recht, grensvlak van markt en overheid, Wolters Noordhoff, Groningen, second edition 1997, p. 235-309.

Hessel, B., Rechtsstaat en economische politiek, W.E.J. Tjeenk Willink, Zwolle 1987.

Hessel, B., Het Nederland economisch publiekrecht in de jaren negentig: een pleidooi voor interdisciplinaire samenwerking, in: Op zoek naar juridisch onderzoek in de jaren negentig, NISER, Utrecht 1989, p. 125-139.

Hessel, B., S. Klosse, Sociaal beleid na de no-nonsense tijd, Juncto February 1991, p. 5-8.

Hessel, B. (ed.), De knikkers van het spel, facultaire gedachten over materiële rechtvaar-digheid, Lemma, Utrecht 1993.

Hessel, B., et al., Sociaal en economisch recht, grensvlak van markt en overheid, Wolters Noordhoff, Groningen 1995; second edition 1997.

Kastelein, T.J., Sympathie, eigen belang, rijkdom en geluk bij Adam Smith, in: Adam Smith, 1776-1976, 200 jaar sedert de 'Wealth of Nations', Leiden 1976.

Kimman, E.J.J.M., De maatschappelijke betrokkenheid van de ondernemer, Bedrijfskunde, special bedrijfsethiek, jrg. 61, 1989/4, p. 349-354.

Kimman, E.J.J.M., Marktethiek, Van Gorkum, Assen/Maastricht 1990.

Kimman, E.J.J.M., Organisatie-ethiek, Van Gorkum, Assen/Maastricht 1991.

Klosse, S., Menselijke schade: vergoeden of herstellen?, Maklu, Antwerpen/Apeldoorn 1989.

Klosse, S., Vrijheid, gelijkheid en solidariteit in ons stelsel van sociale zekerheid, in: B. Hessel (ed.), De knikkers van het spel, facultaire gedachten over materiële rechtvaardigheid, Lemma, Utrecht 1993, p. 243-268.

Klosse, S., Bevordering van arbeidsparticipatie ofwel: werk boven 'wig' of 'wig' boven werk?, Samsom H.D. Tjeenk Willink, Alphen aan den Rijn 1995.

Kuin, P., Management is meer.... De sociale verantwoordelijkheid van de onderneming, Elsevier, Amsterdam/Brussel 1977.

Leeuwen, B. van, Beginselen van behoorlijk ondernemingsbestuur, Tjeenk Willink, Zwolle 1989.

Luijk, H.J.L. van, In het belang van de onderneming, aantekeningen voor een bedrijfsethiek (Delft 1985).

Luijk, H.J.L. van, Bedrijfsethiek in drievoud, Bedrijfskunde special bedrijfsethiek, jrg. 61, 1989/4, p. 330-337.

Luijk, H.J.L. van, Om redelijk gewin, Boom, Amsterdam 1993.

Nozick, R., Anarchy, State and Utopia, Basic Books, New York 1974.

Rawls, John, A Theory of Justice, Oxford University Press 1971.

Scholten, P, Kenmerken van recht, Verzamelde Geschriften, Deel 1, Tjeenk Willink, Zwolle 1949 (reprint 1980), p. 1-120.

Schuyt, C.J.M., Recht, orde en burgerlijke ongehoorzaamheid, Universitaire Pers Rotterdam, 2nd. ed., 1973.

Steiner, George A., John F. Steiner, Business, Government and Society: A Managerial Perspective Random House Business, Division New York, third edition 1980; recent edition John Wiley & Sons, New York 1991.

Stone, Where the Law Ends. The Social Control of Corporate Behaviour, 1975.

Reintegration of Partially Disabled Employees: From Market Efficiency *versus* Social Justice to Market Efficiency *and* Social Justice?

Stella den Uijl, Saskia Klosse, Tineke Bahlmann, Joop Schippers

1 Introduction

1.1 Increasing Number of Non-Employed People

On the threshold of the 21st century, the Netherlands are wrestling with a practically uncontrollable increase in the number of people who, for want of suitable paid work, have to rely on benefits instead of on wages.[1]
Radical changes in the nature and substance of (paid) work are to a considerable extent accountable for this situation. Automation, mechanisation and rationalisation have, besides creating new forms of work, also lead to an increase in the productivity of labour. Moreover, with a view to competitiveness, labour saving investments have proved necessary. Advanced technological production processes have, furthermore, brought about a change in the nature of the demand for workers: more and more unskilled workers have had to make way for higher skilled, well trained personnel. Increasing numbers of people with too low, unsuitable or inadequate training, or who were simply not productive enough, have been excluded from employment as a result of this complex of factors.[2]

In turn, this development has brought about a rise in the number of people who have to live on income substituting benefits. These benefits serve to soften the blow for those who, because they lack the required qualifications for the labour market, are written off like obsolete machines. It is characteristic for the Netherlands that disability benefits have served this purpose for many years already.
Because of the rise in numbers of beneficiaries at the same time, a negative spiral has come into effect. The continuous charge on society for those who are unemployed drives the rates of taxes and insurance contributions ever upwards and thereby the

---

[1] Ctsv, 1995a.
[2] Seyfried, 1992; Commission of the European Communities, 1993; OECD, 1994.

costs of labour. This induces more labour saving investments and increases in productivity, which in turn result in yet larger numbers of people entitled to benefits.

It will not come as a surprise that the combination of these factors have placed the financing of the benefit scheme under severe pressure. There are, after all, limits to the insurance contributions the continually shrinking group of working people can be asked to pay. Furthermore, the financial problem is intensified by the prospect that, as a result of the ageing of the population, the ratio between the number of employed and non-employed will only decrease in the decades to come.[3]

1.2 Reconsideration of the Concept of Social Security

Driven by the need to find an effective solution for these problems, the Netherlands are engaged in reconsidering the concept of social security. In this process, two general tendencies can be identified.

1.2.1 Reduction of Government Intervention

First of all, there is a strong tendency to consider reducing the expenditures on benefits a solution to the problem. Cost containing measures, such as lowering the level of benefits, restricting the duration of benefits, and/or tightening the conditions for awarding benefits, are popular.[4]

An example of such measures can be found in the changes the Dutch legislature introduced in disability regulations in August 1993 and March 1996. The 1993 changes brought about an extension of the possibility of awarding someone either no long term disability benefit, or at least less money than before. The changes made in 1996 may be regarded a first step towards a social security system that only provides a minimum 'safety net' level of protection, leaving it primarily to the employer to ensure an adequate level of income maintenance during the first year of absence due to illness. These changes will be elaborated further in section 4.

In the final analysis, this type of measure amounts to a curtailment of the State's responsibility to guarantee social security. This collective responsibility is, to some extent, shifted onto the private sector, or as the case may be, onto individual people, who in principle have to provide their own supplementary social security. This is

---

[3]   International Social Security Association, 1993.
[4]   Berkowitz, 1990; Aarts *et al.*, 1995; De Jong *et al.*, 1992.

based on the assumption that the notion of individual responsibility has been gradually stifled by too much government intervention. From this point of view, it seems necessary to encourage private initiative by reducing government intervention, and more specifically, by making the social security scheme more 'market-orientated' and more selective.

Some regard this evolution as an evolution from the so-called collective solidarity market model to a selective market model. This is related to the fact that privatisation (indeed, even commercialisation) of social security at the same time substantially limits the degree of solidarity which people living in a civilised society will tend to have for each other. In so far as social risks are, once again, insured collectively in the private sector a certain degree of solidarity continues to exist within this new collectivity; it is rather a matter of shifting. However, this does not alter the fact that it remains uncertain whether appropriate arrangements will be made; whether or not this will happen depends on circumstantial factors. If the arrangements fail to be made, then those who need most protection will be found to foot the bill. Solidarity with the socially weak then loses its meaning. This will be discussed further in sections 2 and 5.

1.2.2 Promoting Reintegration

A second important trend is the high value which is presently attributed to measures aiming to promote the return to employment of those entitled to benefits. Evidence for this can be found in recent changes in the law and in the introduction of new measures to bring about reintegration.[5]

In view of the budgetary problems with which the Netherlands are struggling, the decision to enourage reintegration should not come as a surprise. After all, an effective policy, which brings those claiming benefits to participate in productive work again, limits the duration of the benefits and consequently represents a reduction of social security expenditure. Moreover, it is also significant that such a policy increases the number of people paying insurance contributions, thereby strengthening the financial basis for the social security system.

Another motivation lies in the awareness that there could well be a shortage of labour in the near future as a result of demographic developments.[6] Sprouting from this awareness, the idea is gaining ground that failing to try and make beneficiaries return

---

[5] Berkowitz, 1990; International Social Security Association, 1993; WRR, 1990.
[6] Van der Veen, 1994.

to employment may result in an enormous and unnecessary loss of potential labour. Furthermore, the furtherance of reintegration also seems to be consistent with the previously described tendency to encourage private initiative by strengthening the sense of individual responsibility regarding social security. The combination of these factors fosters the conviction that more energy and resources ought to be invested in the promotion of reintegration. In sections 3 and 4 we will come back to this point.

1.3 Object of Research

At first the tendency to encourage reintegration seems to be in line with the first mentioned evolution from a collective solidarity social security system to a more market-oriented and more selective social security system. And yet, upon closer examination the question arises whether these two developments do not oppose rather than support each other.

A lead for calling this into question springs from the fact that the realization of the reintegration goal depends to a large extent on the degree of (internal) solidarity or, in other words, the willingness of employers to employ disabled persons. This willingness in its turn is to a considerable extent determined by considerations of efficiency. Under the present circumstances, employing someone has to be cost effective. In case of reintegration of partially disabled workers it is precisely this notion which may undermine the willingness to employ them.
Besides real or imagined notions concerning the productivity of partially disabled workers, the possible side effects of necessary changes to the social security system also play a role in this. The intended shift in responsibilities to company level is namely accompanied by a shift in the financial burden for social security from the collective to the private sector. As a result, it is not imaginary that financial arguments will play a (more) significant role in relation to the decision to employ or keep employed partially disabled workers. The necessary (internal) solidarity or willingness of employers to reintegrate partially disabled workers thus threatens to be undermined by considerations of efficiency.

In this contribution the relationship between social justice and market efficiency will be reviewed against that background. To this purpose the above-mentioned two tendencies will first be discussed in further detail. Subsequently, both tendencies will be considered in their mutual relationship in order to finally answer the question whether and if so, to what extent arguments of social justice and market efficiency support or rather oppose each other as regards the furtherance of reintegration of partially disabled workers in the labour process.

2 Evolution From the Solidarity-Collective Model Towards the Selective-Market Model

2.1 The Solidarity-Collective Model

The Dutch social security system is the result of processes of increasing solidarity and collectivity which have taken place in the field of social risks insurance since the last century.

Solidarity may in the widest possible sense be defined as a condition of social relationships determined by the stronger helping the weaker, or the promotion of shared interests. Solidarity manifests itself primarily in a redistribution of the costs and benefits involved between higher and lower income groups (vertical solidarity) or among groups of individuals with a shared, but varying risk (horizontal solidarity).

Collectivity comprises the part of the population where this solidarity occurs and the social level at which the rules of solidarity are determined.[7] Making social security a collective affair means that social insurance is organized at a high social level, covering several social risks and large groups of insured or a major part of the national population.[8] In reality, these processes find expression in the existence of the whole system of obligatory social insurances.

The introduction of the system of obligatory social insurances may be considered the reaction of the government to undesired effects of the free market mechanism. Aspects of social justice are at the basis of this reaction, but efficiency considerations too play their role: without government intervention, widespread and sustained poverty and exclusion will threaten social cohesion, and therefore society as a whole, in the end. From this point of view, the introduction of obligatory social insurances may be seen as a governmental correction of the free market's inadequacies as regards social justice.

In itself this constitutes a recognition of the fact that a labour relationship is more than a mere individualistic exchange relationship, and also of the fact that market actors in this field have to bear in mind the interests of others. The latter fact reflects the solidarity notion in that the economically strong must take the economically weak's interests seriously and must be willing to make sacrifices.

---

[7]   Van Oorschot et al., 1991.
[8]   Van Oorschot et al., 1996.

Within the system of social security this notion is represented on the one hand by the obligatory nature of social insurances and on the other hand by the fact that these are financed by means of contributions. The contributions are not linked to the individual risk but are a percentage of a person's income. Thus, each insured contributes a proportional share in the costs of social insurances, irrespective of that individual's need to actually claim benefits. The situation may occur, for instance, where a thoroughly healthy person pays his contributions year after year without ever having to claim income substitution. In this way he helps in financing the benefits for people in bad health. People in good health (the economically strong) thus share the burden with people in bad health (the economically weak).

The extent to which the solidarity notion is observed was originally limited to specific situations because government involvement in this field only covered those hardest hit by market failure, namely labourers, and was furthermore aimed only at the circumstances which used to threaten labourers' social security most, i.e. loss of income due to industrial accidents, illness, invalidity and old age. Only in these circumstances could workers apply for benefits under the statutorily obligatory social insurance system.[9]

During the crisis in the Thirties, which caused massive unemployment, and the following war years, these limitations exacted their pay. The result was that new forms of poverty and social insecurity developed to which the existing system of social insurances had no adequate answer. Thus, the conviction that an adequate system of social security requires a broader basis took root.

Following the Second World War this conviction of a need for a broader basis took more definite shape. It was expressed in a substantial expansion of social security. The initially limited target group of workers was extended to include all inhabitants and new risks were to be covered by the social insurances, such as the risk of unemployment and the financial risk involved in having children. Social security was furthermore complemented with social assistence which could be claimed in case and to the extent that social benefits proved insufficient.[10]

With this extension of the social security system both the notions of collectivity and of solidarity in the sense of protecting the economically weak, took shape. It was

---

[9]   De Gier *et al.*, 1994.
[10]   Klosse *et al.*, 1996.

against this background that the social security system was realized after the Second World War. This system is also called a solidarity-collective model.

2.2 The Selective-Market Model

In the selective-market model social security is more selectively organized in the sense that the distribution of benefits and costs of insurance are adapted rather more to the individual chance the risk will materialize and the expected extent of the damage. Thus, a distinction is made between 'bad' and 'good' risks. The notion of solidarity loses significance in this way.
A second characteristic of the selective-market model is that the organization of social security is left to the market, that is to say to the interaction of supply and demand between individual citizens, employees and employers on the one hand and insurance companies on the other. Individual responsibility is the key to this model.

Prensently, the transfer to a more selective-market model is promoted by more and more people. The tendency to stress individual responsibility plays an important role here. The shift towards the selective-market model, however, is also directly due to dissatisfaction with the solidarity-collective model. This is no longer considered the best way to offer social protection. The mainspring for this seems to be the growing number of beneficiaries stemming from the collective and solidarity aspects of this model. The most important objection seems to be the anonymity of the system which these aspects entail. In turn, this is supposed to encourage irresponsible behaviour resulting in burdening society with the costs. More in general, this boils down to the notion that the collective-solidarity model allows too much incorrect use, if not abuse. The introduction of more market-selective elements in the social security system intends to counter this problem. By using financial incentives based on personal interest and competition such a system allows a direct confrontation of those involved with their responsibility to reduce the financial costs of the benefits system as much as possible.

Furthermore, the solidarity-collective model is considered to be contrary to the current tendency towards individualization and freedom of choice. Social security thus becomes a subject of general reconsideration of the administration's core tasks. The opinion that the government should limit itself to guaranteeing a minimum subsistence level and that obligatory social insurance for huge collectivities should be abolished where possible, is gaining ground. Furthermore, the idea prevails that the link between rights and obligations should be more explicit. Recent adaptations of the short-term disability scheme illustrate this tendency.

3 Encouraging Reintegration

The development of the social security system from a solidarity-collective model to a selective-market model also entails that reintegration is seen in a different light. Under the solidarity-collective system income protection is the prime issue. Solidarity is apparent in the distribution of benefits and costs between higher and lower income groups or among citizens with shared but individually varying risks. In this way the income compensation function of the social security system is emphasized.

Accentuating this compensatory function of the system, however, does have several drawbacks. First of all, it dissipates almost every incentive to realise the aim of reintegration. Especially in periods of economic decline, any stimulus to promote reintegration, in fact, tends to vanish into thin air. In turn, this brings about that those who find themselves in the benefit system cannot easily get out again. Consequently, a steadily growing group of people with long term disability benefits has come into existence. Given the small chance of their resuming work, one could say that, once on the dole, they are often condemned to a life without paid work.

In the process of reconsidering the existing concept of social security, policy-makers now think it of the utmost importance that beneficiaries should again take their place in the labour market. As already mentioned, this desire to restore the reintegration concept is not very hard to understand when the budgetary problems with which the Netherlands are struggling, are taken into account. After all, an effective policy which brings those drawing benefits back to work, will bring about a reduction in benefits costs as well as in the costs of labour, due to the possible subsequent lowering of insurance contributions rates.
At the same time, giving fresh impetus to the reintegration concept seems to correspond well with the transfer towards a more market-oriented and more selective social security system. An important argument for this is the assumed necessity to strengthen the sense of individual responsibility to co-operate in ensuring (the financial feasibility of) social security. Stimulating an active reintegration policy at company level seems an effective way to meet this responsibility.

From this point of view these two developments seem to be mutually supportive. Whether and, if so, to what extent this is the case, depends on the actual measures taken to substantiate these developments. In order to do so successfully, the two developments will have to be considered in their mutual dependency.

4 Coherence Between the Evolution from the Solidarity-Collective Model to the Selective-Market Model

4.1 Redistribution of Responsibilities

4.1.1 WULBZ

One very concrete and tell-tale example of an actual attempt to strengthen the individual responsibility which fits within the framework of both developments is that of the *Wet uitbreiding loondoorbetalingsverplichting bij ziekte* (WULBZ; Act on the Extension of the Obligation to Continue Paying Wages in Case of Sickness). Introduction of this Act in 1996 namely materializes the need to place at least part of the financial burden as regards social security at company level. The WULBZ intends to concretize this by obliging the employer to pay at least 70% of the employees wages during the first year of disability due to sickness (cf. Art. 7:629 CC). During this period therefore there is in principle no right to benefits out of social insurance funds. The financial burden for sick-leave is thus largely placed on the shoulders of the employer. In this way, the responsibility is put with those who are in a position to do something about the problem of absence due to illness. This change is expected to induce employers to find effective ways of combating sick-leave.

In principle this measure seems very well suited to serve several purposes, such as enhancing reintegration but also making the social security system more selective. It is assumed that if employers are financially responsible for sick-leave within their company they will be more strict with their employees than if the government is primarily responsible. Employers will tend to pursue a preventive sick-leave policy so that employees will less easily end up claiming (longterm) social security benefits. Effective sick-leave policies and reintegration policies, therefore, can contribute to reducing the claims on the social security system, as it will now be reserved for those who 'really' need it. At least, that is the general idea.

The goal of making the social security scheme more 'market-oriented' is achieved as employers may opt to shift the risk of sick-leave costs onto private insurance companies. As these insurers tend to relate the premiums they charge to the individual health of the employees of the company, these premiums may help to further reintegration as well. Thus, the knife is expected to cut various ways.

4.1.2 Stricter Sanctioning

Another example of a measure that may contribute to the enhancement of reintegration on the one hand and a more selective benefit system on the other is the stricter sanctioning policy that was introduced in August 1996. Due to this strict policy insufficient efforts to return to the labour process are in principle punished by loss of benefits. Only if the failure to return to the labour market is not primarily due to the beneficiary's behaviour the situation is relieved in that benefits are continued for 6 months at 50%. That way, the strict system addresses beneficiaries directly as regards their responsibility to really try and return to the labour process. Thus, it aims to achieve that everyone who can work will actually avail himself of his chances. This not only suits the reintegration goal but may also contribute to making the system more selective and (at the same time) more true to its original aim, namely guaranteeing merely a temporary compensation for loss of income. The system furthermore meets the notion of strengthening the sense of individual responsibility by making the incapacitated employee personally responsible for finding or keeping a job.

4.1.3 Stricter Admission Criteria

A final example of measures resulting from the developments described in sections 2 and 3 is the range of measures intended to make the system less easily accessible and so less attractive. In practice this resulted in stricter admission criteria for unemployment and disability benefits. As far as the unemployment benefit scheme is concerned, unemployed employees with relatively little work experience now run the risk that after six months they will receive only social assistence or even no benefits at all. The presumed necessity of making the benefits system less accessible and less attractive has furthermore resulted in drastic changes in the *Wet op de arbeidsongeschiktheid* (WAO; Disability Insurance Act). Now, people are not as easily declared disabled and the benefit itself is of restricted amount and duration. The younger one becomes disabled, the harder the consequences, because one receives either immediately or after a short while benefits only at or around subsistence level.

This measure too is supposed to cut several ways. On the one hand the stricter cirteria are intended to prevent people from getting caught in the social security system. This increases the selectiveness of the system. In case this does not work, the less attractive conditions are supposed to enhance reintegration. Here too, personal responsibility plays its part. The (partially) disabled or unemployed employee is personally responsible for a fast return to the labour market. In his attempts he is stimulated by the unattractive benefit conditions.

4.2 Increasing Employment

In addition to the above measures, there is currently also a strong emphasis on increasing the number of jobs available to beneficiaries. This seems to indicate that their return to work has for years been inhibited by a lack of suitable and affordable job opportunities. Taking into account that many of them are unskilled or limitedly skilled, priority is given to the creation of low productive, labour intensive and low paid work. Increasing the demand for workers at the low end of the labour market seems to be the most obvious way to achieve this goal.

Besides futhering flexible working hours the demand for labour will have to be increased by means of deregulation and by making labour cheaper. As far as deregulation is concerned the proposals to relax dismissal regulations are an example. Proponents of this relaxation consider it necessary because the existing dismissal protection would discourage employers to hire certain groups of workers such as those receiving disability benefits. Relaxing the dismissal regulations is to remove this discouragement. In turn it is supposed to have a positive influence on employers' hiring policies. So, again, the knife will cut both ways.

The demand for labour will furthermore have to be enlarged by enabling employers to avail themselves of cheaper labour.[11] This is achieved by means of various measures that relieve labour costs. These offer, among other things, the employer the possibility of temporary tax and premium reductions or the right to temporarily pay employees less than the statutory minimum wages. Some people propose even further-reaching measures in this context. Thus, for example, one sometimes hears the plea to abolish statutory minimum wages altogether. However, as yet such ideas have not been translated into concrete policy proposals.

In order to give extra impetus to the reintegration process of partially disabled workers, some specific measures, espcially targeting this group, have been introduced. These are positive stimuli to induce employers to improve the labour market position of partially disabled employees. They aim to support the partially disabled worker with his or her reintegration. There is for instance the possibility to be temporarily relieved of the obligation of paying 70% of the salary in case of illness if an employer hires a person receiving a disability benefit. Costs incurred in providing an adapted work space can also be recovered (Articles 6 WAGW and

---

[11] Van Wezel 1995.

57/57a AAW). An attempt has been made to remove obstacles for the employer to employing a partially disabled worker in providing wage dispensation (article 8 WAGW), labour cost subsidies (article 62 WAO) and the possibility to employ partially disabled people on a trial basis for a fixed period of time (article 63 WAO).

Behind these measures hides unmistakeably the belief in the beneficial effect of the market mechanism. At the same time, however, it is acknowledged that this market oriented approach is not enough. This is apparent for instance from the fact that at the same time new additional labour possibilities are created in the fields of, among others, care for the elderly and home care, day care and security jobs. These new, additional jobs are unofficially called 'Melkert' jobs. They are for the most part paid out of collective means. 'Melkert' jobs are, therefore, state subsidized jobs.

The existence and development of these jobs indicates that striving for more employment is not dictated solely by the market. Social justice aspects apparently also play their role. Below this will be considered in relation to the theme of this book: the tension between market efficiency and social justice.

5 The Other Side of the Picture

In section 4 a picture has been painted of the measures with which the government intends to introduce more selectiveness and market efficiency into the social security system. Expectations are that these measures will in turn have a positive effect on the intended enhancement of reintegration. And yet the question arises to what extent these goals will actually be achieved if the possible side effects are also taken into consideration.

The question then is whether these two developments are not mutually frustrating rather than mutually supportive. Will not the intended increase in selectiveness in the social security system result in such a shift of financial responsibility to company level that the willingness to achieve the reintegration goal is undermined? Or, in other words, will not the transfer from solidarity-collective model to selective-market model create a situation where arguments of social justice in the end threaten to be surpassed by arguments of market efficiency which will result in a breakdown of internal solidarity?

In this section the measures discussed in sectoin 4 will be reviewed against this background.

5.1 WULBZ

As we have seen above, the WULBZ intends to use financial stimuli in order to make employers effectively counter sick-leave within their companies. Thus, apparently, both the enhancement of reintegration and a more effective functioning of the benefit system are contributed to. However, one can also imagine other effects.

By burdening the company with the financial responsibility for sick-leave, the WULBZ increases the costs of the organization. This may result in deterioration of the internal company solidarity. Yet, it is precisely this internal solidarity that is needed to achieve the reintegration goal. If reintegration is to happen, then employers will have to benefit by it one way or the other. The benefit may either be financial or social. By introducing measures like the WULBZ, however, it is quite possible that employers will be encouraged to assume that there are no benefits at all involved in employing partially disabled employees. If this assumption is not counterbalanced, it cannot be discounted that this development will induce employers to deal more strictly with giving employment to partially disabled people.

Even if employers choose to shift the risk to private insurance companies this possibility is not imaginary. As these insurance companies tend to base their premiums on the individual physical condition of each employee employed by the company, this may lead to people with (potential) health problems being either excluded from insurance altogether or accepted only at high costs. This in turn may lead to an earlier discharge of high(er) risk employees. Thus, the notion of solidarity with the economically weak, which is so deeply embedded in the social security system, is at the same time undermined.
This will be the stronger if another feared side-effect of this regulation occurs. If financial arguments will have greater impact on the decision whether or not to employ a partially disabled worker, this may increase the tendency to select job applicants on the basis of the risks they represent, as research has proved.[12] This will make it even more difficult for partially disabled workers to obtain and keep a job.

Given this context, it seems justified to conclude that the introduction of the WULBZ may result in a reduction of society's solidarity with the economically weak. At the same time, this measure can be a serious threat to internal solidarity at company

---

[12] Ctsv, 1995b.

level, which will affect the extent to which the reintegration goal will be achieved. After all, one should reckon with the possibility that the measure will encourage employers to keep partially disabled workers out of their company rather than in. It is quite possible too, that they will try to remove partially disabled employees which are 'inside' their organization because of financial reasons. These people then have to rely on the social security system. Thus, the intended goal of making the social security system more selective and market-oriented will not be achieved either. If reintegration fails, the position of the economically weak in our society will only be weaker rather than supported in a positive way.

5.2 Stricter Sanction Policies

The stricter sanctioning policies may also involve a deterioration of the position of the economically weak. As mentioned earlier, the key notion of this measure is that people receiving benefits must take every opportunity of a job, even if the beneficiary is too well educated for the job or has no affinity with it whatsoever. As refusing such a job opportunity is punished by withdrawing the benefit, one could say that this measure actually comes down to the introduction of an indirect form of forced labour.

The fact that this situation could have some reverse effects as well seems of no concern to the government. Seen in itself, this is remarkable. After all, one cannot disregard the fact that being forced to accept a (unattractive) job can easily reduce someone's motivation to perform the job and also increase the chances of sick-leave. In turn, this may negatively influence the employer's decision to fill possible vacancies with people on the dole.

A factor which can yet worsen this situation is that to accept a job is not very desirable for beneficiaries for another reason. Even if employers are willing to engage beneficiaries this will usually be on the basis of flexible contracts without any prospect of a steady job. Such employment does not guarantee lasting reintegration in the labour process. Re-entering the labour market on this basis thus enlarges the risk of having to fall back on the social security system sooner or later, that is to say, if one is lucky enough to meet the (tightened) eligibility conditions. It is not very hard to understand that the awareness of these consequences will not exactly have a stimulating effect on the willingness of beneficiaries to return to the labour market. As they are actually left with the choice to either cooperate in their reintegration or lose their benefits, it is quite possible that the side effects touched on above will occur with all inherent consequences. If that is the case, the intended goals, again, will not be reached.

5.3 Stricter Admission Criteria

As already indicated briefly in section 4.1.2, making the admission criteria for social security benefits more strict may have just the wrong effect as well. This becomes clear when this measure is not seen in itself, but considered in conjunction with other measures. The tendency to tighten admission criteria will, for instance, take on a different aspect if it is considered in combination with the tendency to employ beneficiaries on the basis of flexible contracts. Thus, it becomes visible that stricter eligibility criteria easily can lead to dampening any enthusiasm to re-enter the labour market, which in turn does not help to convince employers to employ partially disabled workers.

All in all, this does not effectively contribute to furthering reintegration. Nor will the social security system function more effectively because of these side-effects. Viewed from this perspective, it seems justified to conclude that the knife does not cut both ways, as was intended. This does not mean that the knife does not cut at all; it rather cuts in another way. What may be the result of this kind of measure is namely that the socially weak become even weaker. The notion of solidarity in the sense of protecting the economically weak thus loses its meaning, whether or not intentionally.

5.4 Positive Stimuli

From Section 4 it follows that the above-mentioned measures are supplemented by another type of measure which are intended to influence employers' employment policies in a more positive way. Proposals to relax dismissal regulations for instance rank in this category. Relaxing dismissal regulations is considered necessary because protection against dismissal could discourage employers to hire new personnel, especially employees who might represent a certain financial risk, such as people with (potential) health problems.

At first sight, this type of measure may seem like a sensible way to strengthen internal solidarity. It looks like market efficiency and social justice go together very well here. However, this only will be the case if the positive effect of this type of measure will, at the same time, prevent employers from trying to keep people with (potential) health problems as much as possible out of their company because of the financial risks involved. If that does not happen, the expected positive effects of more lenient dismissal legislation simply will not occur. The intended strengthening of internal solidarity will than be overshadowed by the aforementioned financial reasons which in the end will tip the balance.

Experience with other positive stimuli for employers, such as labour cost subsidies, seems to go a long way in this direction. Recent research has shown that this type of measure in general fails its purpose.[13] So it was found that, for example, employers hardly ever apply for contributions towards the costs of work place adaptation or schooling, whereas most partially disabled workers need these means in order to function well.

Unfamiliarity with these means on the part of the partially disabled employees themselves and on that of the employers may explain this limited use. In view of the fact that employers will have to apply for the subsidies themselves, this unfamiliarity with the possibilities hampers reintegration. Besides unfamiliarity, the fact that employers have little need for these subsidies may also be a cause for such insufficient use.[14] Furthermore, employers seem to be reluctant because of the 'red tape' involved, and the ever changing and fragmented legislation complicates matters even further.[15]

However, the most structural reason for insufficient use turns out to be the process of risk selection which in turn is induced by enlarging the financial burden for social security at company level. Employers tend to be mostly concerned with finding the right candidate for the job. Candidates with a history of disability then easily disqualify. Apparently, positive stimuli hardly can change employers' behaviour in these matters.[16] What may happen, though, is that employers who are already considering employing a partially disabled worker may be convinced by these positive stimuli. Yet, in general, the process of risk selection proves stronger than the positive stimuli to encourage reintegration. One rather opts for the healthy worker than for the suspected high-risk worker.

The result is that reintegration fails to occur. Consequently, partially disabled workers still have to rely on benefits, even if these are now lower, which means no reduced claim on the social security system and, therefore, no enhanced selectivity.

---

[13]   Ctsv, 1995b; NCCZ, 1995.

[14]   Mul *et al.*, 1995.

[15]   Baar, 1996.

[16]   Ctsv, 1996.

6 Market Efficiency and Social Justice

The present crisis in the welfare state is often attributed to the fact that too many social measures and too much protection leads to economic standstill and financial insupportableness. Too much solidarity may weaken market efficiency and that calls for supportive action.
On the other hand one could say that efficiency measures which lessen the protection of employees and social security beneficiaries, may seem at first to increase market efficiency but will in the end undermine the acceptance of the efficient market game rules by breaking down existing elements of solidarity.

Looking at this side of the relationship between market efficiency and social solidarity the question arises whether the government policies pursued until now as regards the socially weak have not been determined disproportionately by financial and market efficiency considerations.[17] Solidarity with the economically weak should primarily be shaped in a way which does not counter but rather uses a reinforced market. This means that the economic measures taken to strengthen the market must be accompanied by an active government policy aimed at protecting the economically weak. In stead of merely relying on the market to do its job, the government should adopt a policy of substantially improving reintegration. What is certain in any case is that market economic measures alone will not employ any extra partially disabled workers.

It should be noted, that solidarity in this way cannot be imposed as the legislator can only impose or prohibit what is most necessary. However, within the framework of the law there is ample room for the management of a company to take its responsibilities. One should not treat employers as managers of whom nothing may be expected. On the contrary, one should appeal to them to consult their employees and see whether and how the social stance of their companies may be improved.[18] As for the government, this means that it should not limit itself to the traditional onesided imposition of statutory conditions but that it should actively stimulate consultation of employers and government, or, in other words, the internal solidarity at company level.

---

[17] Hessel *et al.*, 1995.
[18] Kuin, 1977.

Anticipating and using the internal solidarity of a company requires a different attitude from the government than merely imposing rules. It requires an attitude where the government does not simply expect managers to passively implement legal rules but rather acknowledges their active involvement. So, if the government wishes companies to reintegrate partially disabled workers, it must not impose binding regulations on the companies. It should appeal to the companies' solidarity by means of consultation and persuasion.

Yet, Hessel *et al.* (1995) point out that consultation and persuasion in themselves are not enough. The government must enter consultations with certain clear standards laid out and must know precisely what it wishes to achieve with these standards. That means that the results of the consultations are not free. Consulation and persuasion according to Van de Bunt (1992) may be the most effective ways to influence behaviour, in view of the interests and powers of the organization they can only be effective if backed up by statutory sanctions. In short, consultation and persuasion with the law as the big stick.

German research[19] shows that this combination of consultation and persuasion with the law as ultimate option is very important. Germany has a quota system which means that in principle 6% of all personnel must be partially disabled workers. However, companies may shirk this obligation by paying a so-called levy. This occurs widespread. The reason given is that the quota is imposed, there is no internal solidarity and there is no adequate statutory sanction.

If there is no solidarity at company level employers will, because of the competative market structure in which we now live, always try to bar from their organization those whom they consider to represent the worst risks. Solidarity at company level requires a change in thinking on the part of the employer and the partially disabled worker himself but presumably also of society as a whole.

7 Conclusions and Recommendations

In this paper the development of the modern welfare state has been typified as a movement of increased collectivity and solidarity. The circle within which people take responsibility for each other's welfare has expanded slowly to now encompass

---

[19] Sadowski, 1992.

the national state. In the course of this development the nature of solidarity has changed as well: from responsibility for those close of kin to solidarity with strangers. This latter solidarity is organized and realized by the State. That involves a number of unavoidable consequences which, however, threaten mutual solidarity. The anonimity of collective solidarity invites shirking or neglecting statutory obligations ('free rider' behaviour). As there is a vast gap between the individual action and the collective result one may say that collectively organized solidarity undermines the sense of individual responsibility of people.

The traditional alternative for collectively organized solidarity is the free market. If people are free to pursue their own interests they will make rational choices weighing the pros and cons of the various options open to them, which – given a few conditions – is supposed to result in maximum welfare and optimum distribution of goods for society as a whole.

If the emphasis of social policies remains mainly on the individual responsibility of people this will negatively influence mutual solidarity. A wider choice as regards social insurances and more competition between insurance companies will certainly result in a more restrained use of social security and will increase the efficiency of the system, but at the same time the market forces the insurers to risk selection and the companies to select healthy, low-risk employees. What is gained in efficiency and cost reduction is lost again in the loss of (collective) solidarity and social security.

That strengthening individual responsibility may result in decreased solidarity is also obvious from the measures to stimulate the employer's individual responsibility as regards reintegration, such as the WULBZ, stricter sanctioning and stricter admission criteria. But it is not only that. The effect of these measures as they are now shows that the individual responsibility of employers as regards their own personnel does not improve either. On the contrary, employers try to shirk that responsibility.
This teaches us that financial stimuli aimed at changing the behaviour of employers or beneficiaries in a negative way, as is the case with all these measures, are risky implements. Measures like the WULBZ show, for instance, that if the financial responsibility of the individual employer is stressed too heavily, this forms a stimulus to avoid that responsibility rather than to take it. From this it follows that too heavy a financial responsibility easily undermines internal solidarity at company level. This is a serious threat to the positive stimuli which are supposed to enhance internal solidarity. Research has shown that these stimuli then become inefficient. Aspects of social justice are thus undermined by arguments of efficiency. This is in contrast to what the government intended i.e. to have the forces of social justice by means of

positive stimuli (such as labour costs subsidies) and efficiency enhancement (measures such as the WULBZ) mutually reinforce each other.

Given this context, the question arises how the government can stimulate individual employer responsibility and internal solidarity at the same time. It is clear that financial stimuli which all in all lead to breaking down the internal solidarity at company level, are ineffective. It is also clear that imposed measures do not have the positive effects that were intended. Taking everything into consideration, it seems preferable to induce companies to take their responsibility by consulting them, persuading them to reintegrate partially disabled workers, using the law as a final threat. Employers must be convinced by means of social stimuli of the necessity to take their responsibility.

This is no easy task in view of the economic climate which demands ever improved productivity. The idea to reintegrate partially disabled employees is hard to match with the competitive structure of modern society. This must be kept in mind when implementing instruments with which to stimulate reintegration. The example of one of the 'solutions', all sorts of subsidies, may illustrate this. Under the present circumstances the decision whether or not to hire someone is determined by his productivity: employment must be cost effective. It is not very likely that subsidies will change this as these do not help to meet any productivity demands. Subsidies are temporary cost reductions. It is doubtful whether they will motivate employers sufficiently to giving long-lasting employment to partially disabled workers. The fact is that most employers fear that especially partially disabled employees will fail to meet today's productivity demands. Subsidies really are not the way in which to change this situation. Without changes in the social and economic climate employers will continue to try and shirk their responsibility to hire partially disabled workers by simply saying they have no suitable work available for them.

So the question remains how to convince employers that partially disabled workers can indeed be sufficiently productive. What can the government do about the prejudices of employers as regards the productivity of the partially disabled worker?

The government in furnishing reintegration implements should aim rather more at employers in placing less emphasis on (negative) financial stimuli and more on attacking the notion that partially disabled workers are less productive. This shift in emphasis could be very important for partially disabled employees. An important option here is to stress the motivation of partially disabled people. For employers highly motivated personnel forms an important precondition for the success of their business.

Government policies should support rather than oppose this, for instance, by taking measures such as stricter sanction policies and tightening eligibility conditions which, whether or not intentionally, tend to reduce the motivation of the target group. Employers on the other hand, must be made to understand that reintegrating partially disabled employees are not per definition demotivated and often ill. The most important aspect in this is putting emphasis on the positive experience employers may have with partially disabled workers. Here lies a task for the government. Firstly, the government should set the right example. At the moment the government has as yet the lowest percentage of partially disabled employees in its various branches. In order to convincingly present an active labour market policy, to increase these numbers could be a first step. Work experience places, apprenticeships *et cetera* for partially disabled workers with employers could also be a step in the right direction. Thus, employers could gain experience with partially disabled employees and a more positive impression of this group would ensue. The process of barring partially disabled workers because of assumed lesser productivity can then be stopped. At the same time this will lead to a situation in which market efficiency and social justice support rather than oppose each other. From this point of view taking serious steps into this direction seems to be worth the effort!

Bibliography

Aarts, L., Ph. de Jong, R. van der Veen, H. Wagenaar, Naar een houdbare verzorgingsstaat: een beschouwing over de dillema's van sociaal beleid, in: L. Aarts, Ph. de Jong, R. van der Veen, H. Wagenaar (red.), Het bedrijf van de verzorgingsstaat: naar nieuwe verhoudingen tussen staat, markt en burger, Boom, Amsterdam/Meppel 1995.

Baar, E., De arbeidsmarktpositie van werknemers met een arbeidshandicap: knelpunten en mogelijke oplossingen, Afstudeerscriptie RGL, Universiteit Utrecht 1996.

Berkowitz, M., Forging linkages: modefying disability benefit programs to encourage employment, Rehabilitation International, New York 1990.

Bunt, H.G. van de, Organisatiecriminaliteit, inaugurele rede Vrije Universiteit Amsterdam, Gouda Quint, Arnhem 1992.

College van Toezicht Sociale Verzekeringen, 1995a, Ontwikkeling ziekteverzuim en arbeidsongeschiktheid: ziekteverzuim vangnetgroepen, Zoetermeer 1995.

College van Toezicht Sociale Verzekeringen, 1995b, Risicoselectie op de Nederlandse arbeidsmarkt: selectieve aanstelling en afvloeiing van personeel op grond van (vermeende) risico's binnen de Ziektewet en de WAO, Zoetermeer 1995.

College van Toezicht Sociale verzekeringen, Toepassing van reïntegratie-instrumenten voor gedeeltelijk arbeidsgeschikten, Zoetermeer 1996.

Commission of the European Communities, Growth, competitiveness, employment; the challenges and ways forward into the 21st century, White paper, Part C, Luxembourg 1993.

Gier, H.G. de, P.J. van Wijngaarden, A.M.E. Roelofs, Sociale zekerheid in Europa: trends en perspectieven, Lemma, Utrecht 1994.

Hessel, B., J.A. den Hertog, C.E.M. Schutte, F.P. Sprik, J.B. Wezeman, Sociaal en economisch recht: grensvlak van markt en overheid, Wolters-Noordhoff, Groningen 1995.

International Social Security Association, Responding to changing needs, Report I, Geneva 1993.

Jong, M.J. de, R. van Schoonhoven, Afscheid van de zorgeloze verzorgingsstaat, Het Spectrum, Utrecht 1992.

Klosse, S., H.J. van Dijk, Met zekerheid naar de toekomst? van reagerende naar activerende sociale zekerheid, in: S. Klosse, J.J. Schippers (red.), Met zekerheid naar de toekomst: sociale zekerheid in Nederland op de drempel van de 21ste eeuw, Maklu, Antwerpen/Apeldoorn 1996.

Klosse, S., (a), Reintegration of beneficiaries, Guest lecture, Oslo 1995.

Klosse, S., (b), Bevordering van arbeidsparticipatie ofwel: werk boven 'wig' of 'wig' boven werk?, Samsom H.D. Tjeenk Willink, Alphen aan den Rijn 1995.

Kuin, P., Management is meer... de sociale verantwoordelijkheid van de ondernemer, Elsevier, Amsterdam/Brussel 1977.

Mul, C.A.M., C.R. Winter, I.D. de Nijboer, H.F. de Haan, Methoden voor de (re-)integratie van gedeeltelijk arbeidsgeschikten, Vuga, Den Haag 1995.

Nationale Commissie Chronisch Zieken, Advies privatisering Ziektewet, opting-out/premiedifferentiatie WAO en de consequenties voor mensen met een arbeidshandicap, Zoetermeer 1995.

OECD, 1994, Economic Outlook (55), Paris 1994.

Oorschot, W. van, Solidariteit in verzekering en sociale zekerheid: analyse van een begrip, Sociaal Maandblad Arbeid, 1991, jrg 46 vol. 7/8, p. 358-374.

Oorschot, W. van, C. Boos, L. Geleijnse, Solidair of selectief, Kluwer/SOVAC, Deventer/Utrecht 1996.

Oudshoorn, C., J.A. Vijlbrief, Nieuwe wegen naar sociale en economische vooruitgang, Economisch-Statische Berichten, 1995, jrg 80 nr. 4024.

Sadowski, D., Die wirkungsweise des schwerbehindertengesetzes, Vollzugsdefizite und Verbesserungsvorschläge, Trier 1992.

Seyfried, E., Requirements for the succesful integration of disabled people into working life, CEDEFOP-report, Berlin 1992.

Tweede Kamer der Staten Generaal, Werken aan zekerheid: bouwstenen voor een modern en houdbaar sociaal stelsel, vergaderjaar 1996-1997, 25 010, nrs. 1-2.

Veen, R.J. van der, Is de verzorgingsstaat overbodig geworden?, in: J. Bussemaker (red.), De verzorgingsstaat tussen individualisme en solidariteit, Amsterdam 1994.

Wetenschappelijke Raad voor het Regeringsbeleid, Een werkend perspectief: arbeidsparticipatie in de jaren '90, SDU, Den Haag 1990.

Wezel, J. van, M. Havekes, Economie en samenleving: een internationale vergelijking van het arbeidsbestel, Lemma, Utrecht 1995.

Activation Policy and Equity[1]

Jeroen van Gerven, Robert Knegt

1 Introduction

1.1 A Recent Turn?

In various publications since the early Eighties a lance has been broken for activating labour market policies. Anyone taking cognizance of these is readily left with the impression that the phenomenon they are dealing with must be a relatively recent one. If in some of them attention is paid to the long-term history of these policies, a fairly 'classical' picture arises: after nineteenth century liberalism was left behind, in the Netherlands new arrangements and insurances have developed since the beginning of the twentieth century, directed at compensation of various social risks. These arrangements were only incidentally (around the First World War and in the Thirties) complemented by relief work projects. Generally, it is said, policies were passive, merely directed at compensation of loss of income. After their culmination in the Seventies it was not before the Eighties that a turn towards mainly activation-oriented policies was realized.

In contrast to this picture, however, the active furtherance of labour participation of unemployed citizens has a long history, in the Netherlands as well as in other European countries. In the sixteenth century already the duties of the 'valid' poor to provide for their own living were stressed, duties which were not only verbalised in humanistic texts but also applied in poor relief practice in many European cities: a strict prohibition of begging combined with the imposition of a duty to work.[2] Arrangements developed which partly had a function of regulating labour and were, except for periods of economic crises, indeed functioning as such.[3] In the second half of the eighteenth century several local initiatives were taken in the cities intending to bring in unemployed poor into industrial institutions, mostly specifically created for this purpose. We will discuss this period, which in a number of respects shows interesting similarities with the last quarter of the twentieth century, in more detail.

---

[1] The authors thank Dr. Saskia Klosse for comments on an earlier version of this paper.
[2] Roebroek, 1995, p. 156.
[3] Van Damme, 1990, p. 266-274.

1.2 Activation in Relation to the Welfare State and the Labour Market

Talking about activation we generally mean the lasting (re)integration of unemployed people on the labour market. Lasting reintegration means that the ultimate aim is to make the activated unemployed find a job in the market sector. Activation policy can be shaped in two different ways. The first way is related to the way social benefits in case of unemployment and incapacity for work are distributed. In this case one may refer to an activating welfare state. Besides, in 1987 the Dutch Scientific Council for Government Policy (WRR) introduced the concept of activating labour market policy. This concept refers to a labour market policy which succeeds in optimally (re)employing the labour force.

Dercksen (1993) in the first case refers to 'a system of state regulations, or regulations assured by the state, which offers citizens not only guarantees against poverty and want, but also urges them to provide *themselves* for others taking care of them'. Supposedly this would in particular mean providing oneself with an independent income by finding a paid job. In this system of reciprocity on the one hand one receives a benefit, but on the other hand this creates a commitment of efforts. In an activating welfare state the arrangements of care provoke this kind of reciprocity. Dercksen (1993) distinguishes four means of reaching a higher level of activation.

1. Institutionalising facilities and rules which promote coping abilities. Examples are schooling, temporary jobs to promote work experience and rules promoting the flexibility of the labour market. The best way to provide for others taking care of you is to participate in the labour process.
2. Strengthening the financial ties between citizens and provision of care. This tie is made more visible by attributing personal contributions and own risks than by charging taxes or social security contributions.
3. Tackling users of provisions on their responsibility by making clear that the welfare state does not only entail rights, but duties as well.
4. Reinstating responsibilities of actors indirectly involved; as a result of decentralization the business community or local residents get involved again. The quality of service can then be raised.

Activating labour market policy is closely linked to the activating welfare state, but it does not mean exactly the same. In a sense an activating labour market policy supports the activating welfare state. It offers facilities to the unemployed to acquire the place in the labour process which is so important in an activating welfare state. Activating labour market policy also has four characteristics, described by the WRR (1987) as follows.

1. Promoting labour mobility. This is necessary to meet the consequences of the shifts in the sectoral pattern of employment. Besides, the need for less traditional labour patterns is growing. Labour market policy can anticipate this by means of schooling, by offering opportunities to get work experience, by more flexible labour relations and an adjustment of dismissal law.
2. An active (re)orientation of unemployed on their labour market perspectives. The criterion of 'suitable employment' could, for instance, be supplemented with 'suitable schooling' or 'suitable work experience'.
3. A tripartite responsibility for the organization and financing of the public employment service. This would especially be relevant for tuning labour market policies to the negotiations on employment conditions, between employers and unions. Due to the (negative) evaluation, however, of the Employment Service Act 1991 by the Commission Van Dijk tripartisation is now under discussion again.
4. Simple and effective instruments which do justice to the diversity of the labour system. Instruments like schooling, promoting work experience, information, help for starting entrepreneurs and employment-finding should be connected with each other as much as possible. Reliable and specified unemployment figures are indispensable.

1.3 The Role of Equity

In this chapter we will argue that, despite the fact that the definitions and characteristics above are quite recent, activation policy already has a long but somewhat forgotten history. Our central perspective will be the relationship between activation policy and equity. We think it is interesting to see in what way arguments, in favour of or against activation, have been, or are playing a part based on social equity. Equity might be considered to be a contradiction of activation policy. One may, for example, prefer protection and legal security to incentives to re-employment. But one may also conceive of certain kinds of social equity, like equal chances of self-fulfilment, as reasons for pursuing an activating policy. To what extent are these reasons only presented to cover up other, financial and economic, arguments?

In the discussion about the question whether activation should be considered equitable an important notion is that of 'suitable employment'. This criterion was introduced at the beginning of this century and offers guidelines on the kinds of jobs that unemployed persons of a certain training and experience ought to accept. The way this criterion was applied and sanctioned in the course of this century is indicative of the importance attached to equity. We will pay attention to the change of this notion.

2 Activating Policies in the Eighteenth and Nineteenth Century

2.1 Activating Unemployed in the Second Half of the Eighteenth Century

Before going into similarities, what should be noted first is that there are no less fundamental differences between the societies of the second half of the eighteenth and of the last quarter of the twentieth. These differences include at least the preindustrial economy of the eighteenth century, its lasting guild system and the dominance in that time of what was called a '*policiële*' conception of the role of the state, in which the state was primarily a guardian of public order but should otherwise not be involved in matters of production and labour. We should not forget about these differences, but it is nevertheless worthwhile to focus now on the remarkable similarities.

These similarities apply to 'activating policies', as will be shown below, but also to some extent to the economic situation.[4] Unlike what is suggested by the way the term 'globalisation' is recently used, in the eighteenth century too the effects of internationalization of economic activities asserted themselves clearly, be it in combination with demographic developments.

In the second half of the eighteenth century the Netherlands faced a decline in employment. The active trade of goods which had brought economic prosperity to the nation shifted abroad; commercial capital was increasingly invested into foreign funds. While employment was thus reduced, the population grew rapidly. As a result of a combination of traditional ways of production and relatively high wages Dutch companies lost market shares in national and foreign commodities markets. As new sources of subsistence were lacking, a structural lack of employment was leading to a 'poverty problem'. Other sources point to the peculiar simultaneity of mass unemployment and a shortage of manpower. The supply of a mass of unskilled and poorly motivated proletarians was facing a limited demand for skilled and hard working labourers. The demand was partly met by hiring foreign, in particular German labourers who, according to contemporaries, worked harder and were satisfied with less wages.

The lack of training and of motivation was then increasingly seen in relation to the quality of the services that poor citizens were able to appeal to. These services were supplied by locally organized administrations (the '*armbestuur*'), usually consisting of local notables. For a long time relief of the poor was conceived of as religious well-doing. Poverty was seen as an evil which was at best related to insufficient

---

[4]   The similarity has been also pointed out by Wilterdink, 1995, p. 181f.

moral development of the people struck by it. Only gradually the ample support supplied to the poor is being criticized for its perpetuating effects. Thus the widespread and religiously inspired charity was criticized for distributing support without considering whether those presenting themselves as needy were actually 'deserving poor'. Thus charity would contribute to making groups of citizens dependent upon support, and to breaking the habit of earning one's own living by working.

At this point already a similarity may be noted between late eighteenth century and recent views and considerations put forward in relation to activating unemployed citizens. For these early criticisms clearly remind of those recently brought forward against the welfare state which would be making groups of people dependent upon benefits and support indefinitly. Legal programmes as well as the ways in which such programmes are implemented, would stimulate 'calculating behaviour' of citizens and in that way eventually undermine the legitimacy of the welfare state.

In the second half of the eighteenth century there is an important change in the way unemployed poor are treated. As from the Seventies of that century, in particular, one looks for possibilities at local level to get the poor to work. For the rise of activating initiatives in this period there may be a dual explanation. The increasing number of poor put an increasing burden upon poor relief administrations which in some places were threatened by financial breakdown. At the same time the rise of Enlightenment brought new conceptions of citizenship and education that influenced the attitude of the bourgeoisie towards the poor compatriots. Every citizen should, as such, contribute to the common interest of the progress of society. It is argued that all people should be citizens, contributing usefully to the wealth of the nation. This enlightenment concept declares labour to be not only a citizen's duty, but also a *wholesome* duty. By working regularly and disciplined man fulfils his destiny. Not only does he contribute productively to society and is he able to provide for his own living – working even will make him happy, it is argued.

It would not be adequate to consider these ideas as only directed at the poor, unemployed layers of society. In the public discussion well-to-do merchants and bourgeois rich are also criticized for their indolence and, from the same background of ideas, are required to dedicate themselves more actively to the promotion of the general interest. As an eighteenth century author declared:

'We ought to be ashamed that in a Nation of such Affluence so many people unnecessarily fall into poverty, for no other reason than our own neglect.'[5]

The notion of poverty as a problem which regards all, the solution of which represents a common interest, inspired industrial and pedagogical initiatives of individual citizens, mostly ministers or entrepreneurs or men combining these qualifications. These initiatives generated what would now be called 'additional supply' of work, and lead to improved education and vocational training.

> Thus in 1777 in Hoorn, a small city in the northern part of Holland, the Baptist minister Cornelis Ris took the initiative to do something about what he called the 'deplorable idleness' ('*veragtenswaardige lediggang*'). First he published a blueprint for a shipping and trading company, the '*Ontwerp ter proeve ter opregtinge eener Vaderlandsche Maatschappij van Reederij en Koophandel ter liefde van 't Gemeenebest*'. Goal of this new company would be to diminish and prevent poverty, to further diligence and to provide for vocational and moral training for children. He then founded amongst others a factory of wall clothing, stair carpets and rugs, and an educational and vocational school. In 1778 already some hundreds of spinsters were working for the company, while the school counted a hundred of pupils learning to read, write and do arithmetic, received instruction in spinning and weaving and in 'all which belongs to Civil Manners and Morals, in order to civilize them in a reasonable fashion' (translation by the authors).

At least in those days additional work was created without adequate understanding of the necessary prerequisites of lasting integration into the regular labour market. Due to that inadequacy many initiatives did not last very long and were abandoned. They usually were geared to market conditions in so far that wages which could be earned in these additional jobs, ought to be higher than public assistance but lower than wages in the market sector. Only then could the goal of getting formerly unemployed poor to flow from there into ordinary jobs, be realized. Moreover, thanks to these additional jobs the poor relief administration was in a better position to sanction a presumed unwillingness of poor to take up labour: people unjustly refusing to take a job consequently lost part of their assistance.

The change in poor relief systems in the eighteenth century was not of an ephemeral nature but contained important new elements that were there to stay. It was not only a conjunctural low causing problems of liquidity. The socio-economic context in which poor relief systems were functioning, was changing radically and structurally.

---

[5]   Ris, Tweede Vervolg tot berigt van den Tegenwoordigen Staat en van de Naaste Oogmerken der Vaderlandsche Maaschappij, ter liefde van 't Gemenebest, Hoorn 1778, p. 182, cited by Van den Eerenbeemt, 1977, p. 7 (translation by the authors).

The gradual rise of industrial capitalism was putting views on, and conceptions of poverty and poor relief into an explicitly economic context: poverty was judged by its usefulness or harmfulness as regards national interests. Poverty was then considered to be an economic burden and to pose a political problem, and the ensuing task was to shape the poor into a productive element of society.

At the same time it should be noted that this new conception distances itself from seventeenth century policies which were directed at isolating or punishing the poor, and which at best tried to elevate them morally by way of religious instruction. The new measures 'at least presuppose a recognition of their fundamental humanity, of their capacity to become humans like all other people'.[6]

Arguments for activating policies in the eighteenth century refered to three different frames. First, they are argued for because of the common interest of mobilising sufficient productive forces, including a sufficient mass of cheap labour. Activating policies should actually contribute to the development of a labour *market* as such. The second framework is *pedagogical*: the poor should be taught to behave decently and civilized, in order to be able to contribute as citizens to the common interests. And, finally, arguments are of a *humanistic* nature: integration of poor into the working population induces 'respectability'. Labour has become a means to educate and (re)integrate.

The first argument may be read as the pursuit of furthering the functioning of the market. At a time Adam Smith was publishing but was not yet read in the Netherlands, improving the market was mainly seen in the light of national interests; these interests were implying obligations to citizens, not only the duty of the poor to work, but also the moral duty of wealthy citizens to invest their capital for the benefit of the growth of the national economy. Justice as a motive is recognizable only in so far as all well-disposed inhabitants should have the opportunity to contribute as citizens to the common interests.

2.2 The Nineteenth Century

In the nineteenth century massive economic transformations and the consequent rise of unemployment and poverty were causing a dip in activating policies. The optimism of the late eighteenth century evanesced and measures directed at the poor again had a more coercive character. The idea that poor relief and creation of jobs were closely related, disappeared behind the scenes. In the middle of the nineteenth century the discussion about how to shape poor relief policies revived: proposals to

---

[6]   De Swaan, 1988, p. 53.

create jobs, among others by way of large investments in infrastructural projects, were opposed by liberal pleas for state abstinence. This discussion lasted until the end of the century, but changed its character under the influence of expanding industrialization.

3 Activating Policies in the Twentieth Century

3.1 Before the Second World War

During the first two decades of the current century, which only around the First World War faced a period of serious crisis, unemployment relief work was considered artificial. The 'State Committee on Unemployment'[7] in 1914 reported that relief work was only considered useful to meet the consequences of seasonal unemployment, by staggering public works over the seasons. Public works for the only purpose of combating unemployment, however, were very rare in this period. They were not seen as a serious solution for the economic crisis. More faith was put into other means of combating unemployment, like employment-finding.[8]

Early in the twentieth century it was suggested to provide for insurance against the risk of unemployment. In that discussion a very strict division was kept between those willing to work and workshy or incapacitated unemployed. Only the first category would be eligible for insurance. The others should remain under the 'educational discipline' of poor relief. The Poor Law was very strict for fear of bringing about more unemployment among the workshy. So social benefit should be very low to prevent voluntary idleness.

Although at the beginning of the twentieth century it was still common sense that people in the strength of their lives should not get money from the state without anything done in return, at the turn of the century the approach of the working class was changing. The aim of improving the position of poor workers and the unemployed was gaining prevalence.

After the First World War, in an initially expanding economy, government aimed at bringing more workers under the unemployment insurance scheme, to raise benefits and to extend the duration of their provision so that these benefits would be sufficient for subsistence. Another reason, however, for this development was severe criticism of welfare regulations which by lack of sufficient inspection and

---

[7]   Staatscommissie over de werkloosheid, 1914.
[8]   De Rooy, 1979.

individualization would allow for a lot of fraud.[9] From 1925 unemployment steadily rose and the arguments of right wing-liberal politicians that the care for the unemployed was becoming a too heavy financial burden for the state and was taking away the 'incentive to work' were increasingly well received. Despite this criticism the idea that the state cannot resign in the face of grinding poverty remained dominant.

Although economic problems were relatively modest, and in spite of the objections to relief work as formulated by the State Committee in 1914, this kind of measures came back into fashion again after 1925. Financially they were of little use: usually at the moment a project of relief work starts the welfare regulation is abolished, and the welfare money used as a subsidy. De Rooy (1979) mentions annoyance about the increasing number of unemployed people strolling around in the streets as the most important motive to start relief work projects. In the big cities it proved to be difficult to set up relief work projects; the number of unemployed as well as the extent of welfare given were growing. Concern about this increased because of the manifest development of a group of unemployed that will only get to work again in case of a serious conjunctural revival. If such a recovery would be delayed, one feared that the moral and physical condition of the unemployed could decrease so much that they would hardly ever again be able to do any work at all.

In the Thirties, characterised by a sharp economic crisis and very high unemployment figures, relief work projects take place too. More than in the Twenties government considers them as a way of combating unemployment. Plans are developed which are based upon privately raised funds, state contributions and upon a level of wages below normal.[10] The works performed were state commissioned or private; private initiatives were stimulated by subsidies. The latter in particular were criticized; enterprises were suspected to cash in subsidies for work they would have commissioned anyhow. Apart from that the unions objected to the low wages. As a consequence successful examples of relief work at national level were hardly seen, but locally several large-scale projects were set up. The best-known example is the construction of the 'Amsterdamse Bos', a large wooded area near the city. In the Netherlands, around 1935, 12% of the unemployed worked in relief jobs.[11] A refusal to participate was punished by a cut in benefits.

During this decade an improvement of the position of people unemployed or living off welfare was not possible. Although many people felt ashamed about the fact that

---

[9] De Rooy, 1979.
[10] De Rooy, 1979.
[11] De Rooy, 1979.

several abuses still were not coming to an end, it was still considered hardly possible to combat unemployment; the level of social benefits even had to be lowered.

3.2 The Years after the Second World War

After, and in fact already during the war, a period began that was to be characterised by a strong expansion of social security. At the occasion of the installment in 1943 of the Van Rhijn Committee, commissioned to develop principles for a new system of social security, the Minister of Social Affairs declared:

> 'The goal of social insurance will be widened. The *desideratum* is: creating freedom from want, thus assuring a reasonable livelihood to all members of the community, under all circumstances this might be lacking' (translation by the authors).

Given this strong emphasis on protection of everyone it is obvious that the idea of activation to some extent faded into the background. In its report the Van Rhijn Committee (1945) resisted the idea that social security would affect the willingness and the initiative to work. The problem that a-social behaviour cannot be completely excluded, is typically implied by the whole idea of insurance. As the Committee puts forward, this is equally true for a fire insurance, which is nevertheless generally considered as necessary. It is admitted that man generally needs an incentive to be active, but Van Rhijn assumes that social insecurity certainly will not provide such an incentive. Continued indigence will not contribute to the mental and physical health of the population. Furthermore, the Committee points out that there still is an incentive to reach an income above minimum level (at which most benefits are positioned at that time) and that interested parties contribute to the costs of the system of social security.

Shortly after the Second World War guarantees of social equity gradually came to dominate the discussion. Sometimes these ideas were put in marked contrast to slogans of Hitler and Mussolini, who were propagating and idealising a life of danger. Nevertheless, the presumption is that everybody may be expected to give his best for rebuilding the economy.

3.3 The Sixties and Seventies

In the General Welfare Act (*Algemene Bijstandswet*) of 1965 welfare is considered a supplement to what income can be realized, either by the person himself or under collective responsibility. Social equity is explicitly mentioned as the main reason for the introduction of this law.[12] Welfare benefits should be sufficient, without taking away a person's responsibility for his own subsistence. Pursuant to article 1, welfare even should be *directed* at enabling the person involved to be self-supporting. Concretely this means that costs of schooling, revalidation, curing, *et cetera* are also compensated for. All this can be interpreted as making demands on persons on welfare which tend to involve them in the labour process. The law thus reflects a compromise between the primary goal of social equity and the state duty of guaranteeing this on the one hand and prevention of lack of responsibility which might be induced by the existence of a state duty to pay welfare on the other hand. Although the Welfare Act was under societal and political debate at a time of tight labour market conditions, there was no direct insistence upon reintegration of those on welfare into the labour market. Almost everyone considers welfare an absolute necessity. Some, out of fundamental Christian motives, wondered whether government regulation of welfare was really necessary. Only in liberal circles the objection might be heard that society also consists of 'workshy, lazy and mal-adjusted' people. For this group too few conditions tending to involvement in labour were said to be connected to the provision of welfare. It is not quite clear whether the term 'own responsibility', as mentioned in the law, refers to being self-supporting by a labour income. It is sometimes pointed out that granting welfare might induce people to insure themselves insufficiently.

In the implementation of the Welfare Act in the Sixties and Seventies hardly any element of activation can be observed. The implementing agencies were soon nicknamed '*uitkeringsfabriek*' (benefit factory). Making sure that rightful applicants received their benefit in time was considered to be their primary task by the civil servants. Usually educated at social work schools or academies, they considered themselves to be social workers. Promoting self-support initially is no prevalent goal of implementing the Welfare Act.

Thus as from 1970 a gap develops between what is socially desirable (more rights and immaterial claims) and what is economically possible (diminished economic growth). The relative embarrassment of living on welfare decreases as the number of those entitled to benefits grows. This results in an emphasis on the *right* to work rather than on the *duty* to work.

In 1965 the Unemployment Facilities Act (WWV) is also introduced, intended as an extension of the Unemployment Act (WW) for long-term unemployment. The introduction of this law has to be seen mainly in the light of an extension of the social security system. The WWV, however, contains some elements of activation of

---

[12] Bijlage Handelingen II 1961-1962, 6796.

the target group. The law provides for some possibilities to get hindrances to involvement in the labour process out of the way.[13] These 'personal hindrances' primarily refer to illness, but also to character. Means provided for by the WWV are medicines, means of transport, technical adaptation of the workplace, courses, *et cetera*.

In 1967 the Disability Insurance Act (WAO) was introduced which discards the concept of *risque professionel* in favour of that of *risque social*, and takes account of the possibility of partial (in)capacity to work.[14] The partially incapacitated constitute a special category of unemployed. Their limited availability and health apparently make reintegration extremely difficult. 'Suitable employment' is a problematic concept for this particular category, the more so when its boundaries are widened, and partially incapacitated persons are presumed to be able to take all kinds of low-skilled, unfamiliar jobs. Between 1973 and 1983 the implementation of the WAO was relatively generous; the additional problems of finding jobs which this category of unemployed was facing, was translated into a high level of disability benefits.

3.4 From the Eighties till the Present

Although the economic crisis had announced itself already at the beginning of the Seventies, a decision to revise the system of social security is only taken in the mid-Eighties. This brings activating policies back on the agenda. During a debate in Parliament State Secretary De Graaf makes clear that regulations ought not to discourage willingness to participate in the labour process.[15] The most important revision was the new Unemployment Act (WW), which took effect in 1987. The WW contains facilities for, among other things, schooling and doing unpaid work while remaining entitled to unemployment benefits.[16] This forms the basis of an active policy directed at preservation, recovery and promotion of opportunities on the labour market and at improving the social circumstances of unemployed people. This kind of social security facilities must be considered as supplementary to more general facilities (like education and health care) and more directly pointed at persons entitled to a benefit. These facilities are also meant to prevent claims to social security to grow in number or to last longer than necessary. So they should promote reintegration at the labour market directly or indirectly. Continuation of payment of

---

[13] Bijlage Handelingen II 1964-1965, 7736.
[14] Bijlage Handelingen II 1964-1965, 7171.
[15] Handelingen II 1985-1986, pag. 4560.
[16] Kamerstukken II 1985-1986, 19261.

benefit during schooling – which in fact means a prolongation of the benefit – has been considered but was not yet incorporated into law.

In the Eighties the implementing agencies tended to pay more attention to guidance of clients. Guidance was thought to prevent unemployed or incapacitated people from remaining dependent on a benefit too long. At the same time there is a growing awareness that there are 'calculating citizens' and especially also 'calculating companies', cleverly making use of social legislation. At the occasion of the parliamentary inquiry into the implementation of social insurances in 1993 Wim Kok stated that, at the time when he was chaiman of the union FNV, 'dumping' redundant workers by way of the WAO was common practice, as this route was much more favourable for the workers involved.[17] Before the same committee a former civil servant of the Ministry of Social Affairs and Employment, Mr Den Broeder, said that the steering committee which was especially established in 1978 to develop policies towards 'non-active citizens' concerned itself mostly with the problem of giving unemployed people at least something sensible to do.[18]

Societal trends that presented themselves in the Eighties and continue in the Nineties are among others the tendency to use welfare money to create employment, and the peculiar phenomenon of a growing shortage of paid jobs, but not of work. This leads to a need for voluntary work, as a result of which working without loosing benefit is more and more allowed. That supplementary income may be kept, even though one lives on a means-tested benefit, is more readily accepted, for reason of stimulating the acceptance of low paid work.

Recently, activation policy has been put on the agenda again very explicitly. The new General Welfare Act (ABW), effective since 1st January 1996, clearly sheds a new light on the principles of the former law. The central principles are still there, but now the principle of promotion of self-support as an integral part of welfare is put to the foreground and is made concrete. In the Explanatory Memorandum[19] the Minister argues for the prevention of a dependency on welfare as a continuous situation for a growing number of people. As an important addition to the existing material goals of the ABW, an obligation was introduced to enable clients to become self-supporting. Instruments are the Youth Work Guarantee Act (JWG), the job-pool regulation and opportunities for nurseries. Furthermore, cooperation between implementing agencies and the public employment service is enhanced. The ABW imposes on Municipalities the obligation to cooperate with the employment service to promote reintegration in the labour process. Municipalities are also charged with

---

[17]   Parlementaire enquêtecommissie, 1993.
[18]   Parlementaire enquêtecommissie, 1993.
[19]   Kamerstukken II 1991-1992, 22545.

informational and mediatory tasks, which should stimulate clients to make use of facilities contributing to their self-support. Government wants to prevent that the existence of a right to welfare will work as an obstacle for efforts necessary to become self-supporting. For this reason the coherence between rights and duties is defined more strictly. Obligations to do unpaid work, using welfare money to create additional labour and widening the possibilities for a supplementary income are issues which are more readily discussed. The provision that the obligation to apply for and to accept 'suitable employment' does not apply during schooling, has been realized in the framework of activation policy too. People backed by a training program are expected to be eventually more succesful in entering the labour market. In short the reorganized ABW should, besides providing guarantees, fulfil an activating function as well. This approach reaches further than welfare; it is an encompassing policy directed at promoting outflow by eliciting the right behavioural effects from people entitled to benefits. The rules concerning 'suitable employment' and the imposition of the obligation to work are sharpened. In the Employment Service Bill, which is discussed now in Parliament, financial incentives will be incorporated so that target groups will also be mediated and targets will be reached by the Regional Employment Exchange Bureaus (RBAs).

Since 1994 a very strong impulse to activation policy has been given by the so-called 'Melkert' banen,[20] jobs created not only in the collective sector but also in the care and market sectors. They have an activating effect because these jobs are supposed not to replace existing regular jobs. The idea is to seduce employers by subsidies to supply jobs that would not have been profitable without this subsidy. The costs of the subsidies are compensated for by using benefit funds. Jobs are always 32-hours-a-week jobs at the minimum wage. Financially most unemployed persons will not be much better off; it is getting work experience which makes the jobs valuable. Meanwhile these 'Melkert' banen are highly criticized. It is hard to know whether these additional jobs really are not created at the expense of regular non-subsidized jobs. Many critics prefer using the money for general labour costs subsidies, making it more profitable for employers to supply jobs in the lower wage scales. More generally the criticism is that employers are primarily interested in good, and only secondarily in cheap personnel.

---

[20] Additional jobs, named after the Minister of Social Affairs and Employment, who introduced them in 1994.

4 'Suitable Employment' as a Mediator between Efficiency and Equity

In the nineteenth century the implicit presupposition underlying all poor relief was that if an unemployed worker were able to get an income, he ought to accept any job. To this rule there were only three exceptions:

1 jobs which entail illegal activities;
2 jobs that cannot be done due to physical deficiencies of the worker;
3 differently 'gendered' jobs (polder labourer, scullery maid).

The expansion of the labour market, of public employment service and of unemployment benefit schemes in the first decades of the twentieth century raised an awareness that it was both unfair and inefficient to expect every worker who is hit by unemployment to accept any job. The claims which in the context of benefit schemes were made to workers' efforts to find a job should be counterbalanced by rules that indicate which efforts may be considered appropriate. Questions as to 'suitable employment' arise particularly in two settings: at the registration desk of the Labour Office, as unemployed comply with a duty of registration imposed by an implementing agency, and at the agency itself when it has to decide whether to sanction a client for reason of insufficient efforts to get a job.[21]

In the context of shifting notions of what may reasonably be demanded from unemployed, the development of a legal notion of 'suitable employment' may thus primarily be regarded as that of a protective device for workers, secondly as a guidance for implementing civil servants and finally to some extent, as far as training and experience are concerned, as an efficiency-promoting instrument of labour market policy. Although the concept is mentioned in the Unemployment Act (WW), in force since 1952, and in later social legislation (e.g. the WAO), development of the legal content of the notion is left to jurisprudence. In particular after WW II the scope of the protection is gradually extended to account for training, work experience, distance between home and location of work and former wage level of workers.

This trend is reversed in the Eighties, when activation policies dominate the agenda. Since 1987 Article 24 of the WW contains an explicitly more restricted wording of the notion of 'suitable employment', which is now negatively defined as work 'acceptance of which cannot be demanded for reasons of a physical, mental or social nature'. In the Explanatory Memorandum training, previous work experience, former wage level and distance from home are explicitly exluded as reasons to refuse an

---

[21] Van het Kaar, 1995.

offer of a job.[22] In the revised WAO (1993) the concept is even replaced by the notion of 'current employment' defined as 'all generally accepted work a worker is able to perform'. Activation policies thus involve a clear tendency to widen the notion of 'suitable employment'. In terms of equity there is less protection of 'rights' of workers which flow from training, previous work experience *et cetera*. In terms of market efficiency one might conclude that flexible involvement in the labour market is apparently valued higher than the surplus value of workers' training and previous experience.

5 Conclusions

In this chapter we have argued that activation policies are not as new as is often suggested and taken for granted since the Eighties. In the introduction we discussed four means of realising an activating welfare state. We showed that these four means can also be retraced in earlier periods, although the context and the use of words are different. A good concrete example of the institutionalization of facilities which promote coping abilities was the initiative taken by the Baptist minister Ris in 1777. The other means (strengthening financial ties between citizens and facilities, confronting users with their responsibilities and delegating responsibilities to actors indirectly involved) concern matters that were normal practice till the beginning of the twentieth century. Only just after 1920 things changed slowly, but during the Eighties the government partly retraced her steps again. The four characteristics of an activating labour market policy, also mentioned in the introduction, are to a higher degree rooted in the structure and values of modern society. The important concepts of an activating labour market policy, like labour mobility, flexible labour relations, tripartite administration and employment-finding are mainly based upon ideas developed in the course of this century.

Since the eighteenth century fundamental changes, of course, have taken place in society, among which are the decreased meaning of religion in daily life and the changes of production processes and technologies. Nevertheless there are striking similarities in the approach of unemployed and poor citizens as well as in the arguments given in favour of and against activation. The economic situation seems, among others, to be decisive in the approach to activation. Usually a low economic trend is reflected in the height of unemployment. The conclusion that activating policies flourish best in times of a low economic trend, therefore, should not surprise.

---

[22] Kamerstukken II 1985-1986, 19 261, p. 141.

Above all the parallels between the end of the eighteenth century and the last quarter of the twentieth century are striking. Unemployment and internationalization of the economy go together. It proved to be just these two periods, as well as the Twenties and the Thirties of the twentieth century, that were heydays for activating policies. We noticed that two kinds of motivation were given for activating measures. On the one hand there are financial reasons. During an economic crisis characterised by high unemployment figures the costs of welfare quickly get out of hand. It is argued that by activating the unemployed and by creating employment the costs can be lowered. Moreover the idea that people make themselves useful mainly by working is always an argument in favour of activation. In the eighteenth century it was the Enlightenment conception of labour as a wholesome duty by which man can make himself useful for society, which was adopted. Nowadays earning one's living by having a job is more or less considered a prerequisite of preventing social exclusion. Financial and social considerations nowadays go together.

The question whether the morality and physical condition of the long-term unemployed would be sufficient for them to be reintegrated into the labour market later, if unemployment were to decrease, is not a recent concern either, as we showed. While the concern for their well-being may have been sincere, at the same time here too economic motives played a part. Especially in the long run it might be economically damaging if a substantial group of people were excluded from the labour force.

Also arguments against activation correspond in different periods. It is doubted whether activation will indeed lead to a lasting integration into the 'real' labour market. If someone is doing subsidised work for some time but eventually falls back into unemployment, the measure is afterwards considered to be a waste of (public) money. Furthermore the possibility of employers abusing the regulations is always pointed out. Sometimes it seems too simple to get subsidy for a job which the employer would have commissioned without subsidy anyway. Finally the reward for the work often is very low, most of the time in between welfare and minimum wages in the market sector. This is necessary on the one hand to lower the costs and to maintain the incentive to accept work. On the other hand it means that people involved stay in a poverty situation. This could be demotivating.

Thus, equity does not seem to play a major part in decision-making about activation. Even more so activation is disliked explicitly for equity reasons. Nevertheless, we could show that not *only* financial-economical arguments play a part. It might be doubted if, in the eighteenth century, fulfilling this 'wholesome duty' was considered to be equitable by everyone. At most, we would say, by those people who thought it important themselves to live up to this duty. For the present, however, the proposition can be defended that there is a group of people who thanks to activation get the opportunity to escape from (further) social isolation. Finally, it was argued that the application of the criterion of 'suitable employment' is no guarantee for equity. The criterion can easily be stretched, by which it rapidly loosens its value, certainly if at the same time sanctions become more severe.

References

Eerenbeemt, H.F.J.M. van den, Armoede en arbeidsdwang, 's-Gravenhage 1977.

Commissie-Van Rhijn, Sociale Zekerheid. Rapport van de Commissie, ingesteld bij Beschikking van de Minister van Sociale Zaken van 26 maart 1943, met de opdracht algemeene richtlijnen vast te stellen voor de toekomstige ontwikkeling der sociale verzekering in Nederland, 's-Gravenhage 1945

Damme, D. van, Armenzorg en de staat, Gent 1990.

Dercksen, W.J., Het schip van zorg (oratie Rijksuniversiteit Utrecht), Utrecht 1993.

Handelingen II 1961-1962, 6796, bijlage, nr. 3 (Memorie van Toelichting), Algemene Bijstandswet.

Handelingen II 1964-1965, 7171, bijlage, Wet op de Arbeidsongeschiktheidsverzekering.

Handelingen II 1964-1965, 7736, bijlage, Wet Werkloosheidsvoorzieningen.

Handelingen II 1985-1986.

Kaar, R.H. van het, Passende arbeid, in: R. Knegt (ed.), Instituties van de arbeidsmarkt: een retrospectieve studie), Den Haag (OSA, Voorstudie 43) 1995, p. 199-201.

Kamerstukken II 1985-1986, 19 261, nr. 3, Werkloosheidswet.

Kamerstukken II 1991-1992, 22 545, nr. 3, Algemene Bijstandswet.

Roebroek, J., Sociale zekerheid, in: R. Knegt (ed.), Instituties van de arbeidsmarkt: een retrospectieve studie), Den Haag (OSA, Voorstudie 43) 1995, p. 155-208.

Rooy, P. de, Werklozenzorg en werkloosheidsbestrijding 1917-1940. Landelijk en Amsterdams beleid, Amsterdam 1979.

Staatscommissie over de werkloosheid, Verslagen, 's-Gravenhage 1914.

Swaan, A. de, Zorg en de staat, Amsterdam 1988.

WRR: Wetenschappelijke Raad voor het Regeringsbeleid, Activerend arbeidsmarktbeleid, Den Haag 1987.

Wilterdink, N., Internationalisering en binnenstatelijke ongelijkheid, in: J. Heilbron & N. Wilterdink (red.), Mondialisering, Amsterdams Sociologisch Tijdschrift, 22, 1995.

The Day-Care Efficiency, Quality and Equity Trade-off

Rudi Turksema, Jacques Siegers, Hetty van Emmerik

1 Introduction

In recent years Dutch government policy has been characterized by a withdrawal of the collective in favour of the market sector. Privatization, the rapid growth in the number of quangos[1] and the project called '*Marktwerking, deregulering en wetgevingskwaliteit*' ('The market, deregulation, and quality of legislation') on the part of the Ministries of Economic Affairs and Justice bear witness to these developments. Reasons to favour commercialization include increased (allocative and dynamic) efficiency,[2] a reduction of the government sector (including a reduction of the government budget deficit), and long term continuity of the organization.[3] The commercialization of such fields as the public utility sector has led to 'increased productivity, lower levels of inflation, more product differentiation, more (technological) innovations, and in the long term higher output and employment'.[4] However, increased competition has not led to positive developments in every sector. Liberalization of the rented housing market has not led to lower rents. Instead, prices have increased substantially.[5] Commercialization has also been introduced in the health-care and service sectors. In these sectors, an increasing demand for care and welfare services in combination with limited financial means has made it necessary to devote more attention to efficiency.[6] The health-care sector has been confronted

---

[1] Quangos are organizations that carry out a public task, are financed by the government, but do not have a direct hierarchical relation with a department or minister (see Van Thiel, Leeuw & Flap, forthcoming).

[2] Efficiency usually refers to the static allocation of resources. Allocation is efficient if 'prices and produced quantities are such that they are in agreement with the consumer's wishes and that goods and services turn up where they are supposed to, in conformity with demand and supply' (Bos, 1995, p. 44). Dynamic efficiency refers to the degree to which a market adapts to changing circumstances (see e.g. Vrancken & De Kemp, 1996, p. 40; Bos, 1995, p. 45; see also Wolfson, 1988, p. 44 & 109).

[3] Loeff Claeys Verbeke, 1994, p. 19-20.

[4] Van Hulst, 1996, p. 317, our translation.

[5] Van Schaaijk, 1996, p. 640.

[6] Van der Meijden & Kornalijnslijper, 1994, p. 1.

with budget cuts and growing demands for some time now, and the increased attention for efficiency has raised questions about the consequences for the quality and accessibility of care.[7]

'More market, less government' does not seem to have the same results all over. The question is: should the market be introduced all over? Van der Ploeg,[8] for example, noted that 'more competition cannot take place with great intensity in all fields' (our translation). According to Van der Ploeg, more competition in social security for example would lead to risk selection, so that people 'with a spot' wouldn't be insured or only at prohibitive premiums. He went on to observe that competition might endanger the accessibility of essential services for people with a low income. So in some sectors when commercialization is introduced, equity is often traded off for efficiency. Within the health-care and welfare sectors, where complex personal services[9] are supplied, quality also plays an important role. In markets for goods or services where quality is a prominent dimension, the dilemma expands into a 'trilemma'.[10] Efficiency is traded off against quality and equity, and equity is traded off against quality.

Within in the Dutch welfare sector, it is especially the day-care sector (i.e. the institutionalized child-care sector)[11] that is now confronted with increased commercialization, which seems to be typical of the developments awaiting the rest of the welfare sector. In this paper, we address two questions: (1) What elements can theoretically play a role in the day-care efficiency, quality and equity trade-off? (2) What special features of the day-care market can be distinguished and how does government policy deal with them?

In the following section, recent developments in the Dutch day-care sector will be investigated. Section 3 introduces the theoretical framework to analyse the consequences of commercialization in the day-care sector and the implications for the subsequent trade-offs between efficiency, quality and equity. The fourth section deals with the special characteristics of the day-care market and evaluates some policy alternatives on the basis of these special characteristics. Section 5 contains our main conclusions.

---

[7]   Staatscourant, October 22, 1996.
[8]   1996, p. 652.
[9]   Hansmann, 1986.
[10] Culkin *et al.*, 1991, p. 71.
[11] In this paper we confine ourselves to day care for children up to four years old, at day-care centres.

2 Day Care in the Netherlands: From the Nineteenth Century to the Present

2.1 From the Nineteenth Century to 1990

The earliest forms of institutionalized day care in the Netherlands emerged in the second half of the nineteenth century.[12] Day-care centres, then called *bewaarscholen* (nursery schools), were especially for the children of mothers who had to work and were unable to care for their children themselves. These centres were set up by associations and financed by contributions from their members, legacies, donations and contributions from the parents. These funds were insufficient to cover the expenses, and were supplemented by municipal subsidies. In 1940 these subsidies accounted for fifty per cent of revenues.[13] But it was not until the mid-Seventies that the national government really got involved in the supply of day care and introduced a separate subsidy for day-care centres in 1977: the *Rijksbijdrageregeling Kinderopvang*. The mid-Eighties heralded a new era, with policies directed at linking day care to female labour force participation.

2.2 1990-1995

The rapid rise in the Netherlands of the number of working mothers with children below the age of four in the Eighties resulted in an increased demand for day care. In 1981 there were 97,500 married working women with children up to the age of four, but by 1991 this number had increased to 239,400.[14] The supply of day care, however, did not meet with the changes in the demand for day care. So the government decided to stimulate the supply of day care by way of three consecutive Stimulative Measures on Child Care.[15] The main objective of the Stimulative Measures on Child Care was to increase the number of day-care places (at day-care centres, guest parent projects and school-age child care). The underlying objectives were: (1) to increase female labour force participation and the economic independence of women, and (2) to involve employers in the day-care sector via employer-financed places. The introduction of employer-financed places (at subsidized day-care centres) divided child places into two types: places for working parents whose employers were willing to finance day-care places for them (employer-financed

---

[12] Van Rijswijk-Clerkx, 1981.
[13] Van Dalen, 1995.
[14] Tijdens & Houweling, 1993, p. 11.
[15] 1990, 1991-1993 and 1994-1995; Ministerie van WVC, 1989;1994.

places) and places that were in principle accessible for all other parents (subsidized places).[16]

The government's policy to stimulate the supply of day care has been successful. Table 1 shows that between 1990 and 1995, the supply of day care increased from 14,800 to 48,000 full-time day-care places, i.e. an increase of 224 per cent. This growth can be largely attributed to the newly created employer-financed places, which were responsible for 80 per cent of the growth between 1990 and 1995. In 1995, 43 per cent of the places at full-time day-care centres were employer-financed.

2.3 After 1995

On January 1, 1996 the Stimulative Measures on Child Care ended. Government tasks and responsibilities were decentralized entirely to the municipalities. The municipalities, which already were responsible for administrative matters, became responsible for financial matters as well. This decentralization was combined with an economizing measure. The total government subsidy budget of 234 million guilders was cut by 40 million guilders. A salient detail is that day-care subsidies, now in the Municipal Fund (*Gemeentefonds*), were no longer earmarked. So these subsidies do not have to be spent on day care. Furthermore, the end of the Stimulative Measures on Child Care implied a transition from the welfare sector to the market sector. In addition to subsidizing day-care organizations, the municipalities could now contract them to perform certain semi-public services via private agreements. The transition also implied a change in the distribution of child-care places. Whereas the ratio of subsidized to employer-financed places was 60:40 in 1995, the government's objective is to change the ratio to 30:70 in future.[17]

The transition from welfare to market may not be easy. Like many other non-profit organizations, day-care centres depend heavily on subsidies and have attuned their service provision to the wishes of the politicians in power. The transition might cause problems because as, Le Grand & Bartlett[18] argue, 'many people working in welfare services are not commercially or financially motivated, and find it difficult to make the shift from considering the welfare of their users to the financial state of their provider unit'.

---

[16] A third possibility is that parents finance the place themselves (private places).
[17] VOG, 1996a, p. 19.
[18] 1993, p. 14.

Table 1. Changes in Day-care Supply, 1989-1995 (as of Dec. 31)

	1989	1990	1991	1992	1993	1994	1995
Day-care places[a]	22,100	31,200	42,000	55,200	69,400	74,700	
of which full-time day-care places	14,800	21,400	28,800	34,600	41,700	45,800	48,000[c]
of which employer-financed	-	-	7,200	12,400	15,200	19,700	
Child places[b]	20,100	28,200	37,000	46,900	58,100	63,200	
Number of full-time centres	519	723	1,005	1,155	1,340	1,368	1,390[c]

[a]. Places in full-time and part-time day-care centres, company day-care centres, guest parent office, school-age child care (*buitenschoolse opvang*).

[b]. Child places: conversion of child-care arrangements mentioned in footnote a into a comparable measure: 1 child place = 1 place in a full-time day-care centre or in a company day-care centre = 1.5 places in school-age child care or in a part-time day-care centre = 2.5 guest parent couplings (see CBS (1995, p. 28) for details).

[c]. Preliminary figures (CBS, 1996, p. 27).

Source: CBS, 1995, p. 6.

These developments regarding child places at day-care centres since 1977 have been summarized in Figure 1. Assuming that the number of children using day care is a good indicator for the supply of day care, we can see that there was not much of a day-care supply before 1990, although it had increased rapidly since about 1985. As of 1989 the supply is indicated by the number of child places. From Figure 1 it can be seen that when the Stimulative Measures on Child Care were effective, the number of child places continued to increase, but that growth slowed down during the last years the Measures were in force. What direction will the supply of day care develop in after 1995, i.e. after commercialization and after policy decentralization from the national government to the municipalities? As we will show in the next section, efficiency, quality and equity trade-offs play an important role in this process.

Figure 1. Changes in the Supply of Day Care Between 1977 and 1995[a, b]

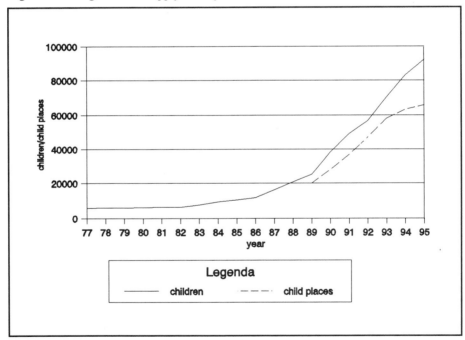

[a]   Children: number of children in full-time day-care centres.
[b]   Child places: conversion of child-care arrangements mentioned in footnote a of Table 1 into a comparable measure: 1 child place = 1 place in a full-time day-care centre or in a company day-care centre = 1.5 places in school-age child care or in a part-time day-care centre = 2.5 guest parent couplings (see CBS (1995:28) for details).
Sources: CBS, 1989 & 1997.

3 Trilemma: Efficiency, Quality and Equity Trade-off

To explain the changes in the supply of day care, it is not enough to assume a direct relation between two macro phenomena, in this case the developments in day-care supply and the transition from welfare to market sector combined with policy decentralization. Rather, we will have to go to the level of the individual day-care centre, which is where relevant decisions about supply are made (by the day-care centre decision-makers: the site managers and their directors). The explanatory scheme in this section is focused on this micro level. The multi-dimensional nature of day care (in terms of quantity, price, quality and client mix, *cf.* Walker, 1991) is important to keep in mind in this context. It means that, as we argue below, decisions about the supply of day care imply decisions with regard to the efficiency, quality and equity trade-offs. To explain this micro level decision-making, the point of departure is the assumption that people strive to maximize certain goals and, since they are restricted by the available resources, they have to make choices on how to reach these goals. The confrontation of goals with restrictions leads to the resulting behaviour,[19] in this case to choices that have to be made with regard to the supply of day care at individual firm level. Changes in supply are, analogously, assumed to be the resultant of changes in restrictions.

In his social production function approach, Lindenberg[20] gives an indication of what these goals and restrictions are. Two universal ultimate goals are distinguished by Lindenberg: physical well-being and social approval. Both of them can be achieved via lower level, intermediate goals. Production functions relate goals at different levels. As such, production functions operate as a restriction. Other restrictions are time and budget restrictions. The important budget restriction in this case is the fact that the trading result has to be positive. Social approval can be produced via status, affect and behavioural confirmation. Affect may be derived from a partner and from one's own children. However, affect is not assumed to play an important role in the decision-making of the site manager at a day-care centre. Status and behavioural confirmation can, in turn, be achieved via goals lower in the goal hierarchy. So status production factors for the site manager may be the size of the day-care centre,[21] the number of employer-financed places and the trading result. The decision-maker produces behavioural confirmation by conforming to the (trading result, quality and equity) norms of significant others. An important aspect of the production function of behavioural confirmation is that, in the Netherlands, the relative weights of the

---

[19] Siegers, 1992, p. 537.
[20] 1991, 1992.
[21] *Cf.* Hoxby, 1995, p. 7.

norms of significant others have been altered by the commercialization and decentralization of day-care subsidies.

Factors at individual decision-maker level are not the only ones relevant to explain changes in the supply of day care at firm level. Factors at the day-care centre and day-care centre surroundings level are relevant too. Firstly the individual decision-maker is embedded in a day-care centre. The day-care centre and the people who work there have their own standards and values concerning day care.[22] This is indicated by factors such as the age of the organization (older day-care centres were set up in periods when quality and equity were important goals and can be assumed to adhere to these goals more than newer day-care centres), and whether it has a private or a public agreement with the municipality. Secondly, the day-care centre itself can be embedded in a larger organization. Part of the decision-making with respect to the supply of day care may be located at this level. This is indicated by such factors as the extent of delegation of administrative responsibilities, whether there is a central bureau, and the diversity in tasks. Thirdly, demographic characteristics of the municipality such as its size, and population density and the number of pre-school children, reflecting the demand side of day care, influence the supply of day care.[23] Also the composition of the Town Council and the kind of companies in the vicinity of the day-care centre influence how many child places the decision-maker can hire out. A Town Council with numerous female councilors and leftist politicians is apt to subsidize more public day-care places.[24] Additional effects on a day-care centre's supply (lower prices, higher quality) can be expected from local competition from other day-care centres and alternative forms of day care.[25]

The factors at the three levels that have an effect on the supply of day care are presented in Figure 2.

---

[22] *Cf.* James & Rose-Ackerman, 1986, p. 51; Van der Meijden & Kornalijnslijper, 1995, p. 19.

[23] Van Dijk *et al.*, 1993.

[24] Gustafson & Stafford 1992; Van Dijk *et al.*, 1993.

[25] Blau, 1989; Chipty, 1995, p. 423.

Figure 2. Explanatory Model

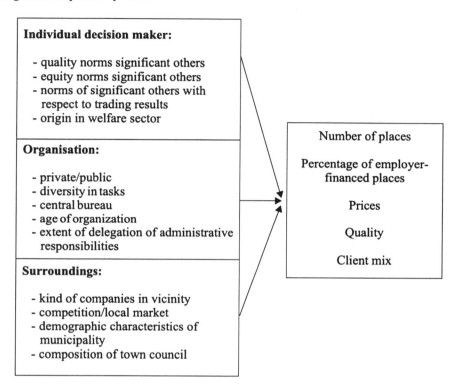

The restrictions at the level of the organization and of the surroundings combined with the decision-maker striving for a maximum trading result, quality and equity create a 'trilemma'[26] for the decision-maker. Given the restrictions, she has to find an optimal mix between trading result, quality and equity. Providers 'have to make enough money to remain economically viable'.[27] They also have to provide high-quality care if they are to attract clients and keep their own employees, board and fellow professionals satisfied. And if they want to promote equitable access to and use of care, they should also have sufficient day-care places open to the public (i.e. not mainly employer-financed places).

The choice behaviour of the individual decision-maker, given the demand for day care, leads to a certain supply of day care at firm level (in terms of quantity, quality, price, client mix and percentage of employer-financed child places). These individual

---

[26]   Culkin *et al.*, 1991, p. 71.
[27]   Hofferth & Phillips, 1991, p. 5.

supplies can be aggregated to macro level, i.e. the aggregated supply of day care in the Netherlands.

Just like *differences* in the supply can be explained by *differences* in restrictions, *changes* in the supply of day care can be explained by *changes* in the restrictions. In the Netherlands the day-care sector has moved from the welfare to the market sector and day-care subsidies have been decentralized. Since day-care subsidies are no longer earmarked, day-care centres are no longer certain of a fixed budget. And due to the change from the welfare to the market sector, there is increased dependence on employers. Whether or not there are enough companies in the day-care centre's surroundings that are willing to hire day-care places for their employees is more important to the day-care centre that operates mainly in the market than the day-care centre that is mainly subsidized. Both of these changes also affect the decision-maker's social production functions. More specifically, the weights attached to the production factors in the production function of behavioural confirmation will change. A trading result will be traded off against equity and quality.[28] These changing restrictions will lead to changes in the supply of day care.

4 Day-Care Centres between Market and Government

In this section, we go into the performance on the day-care market. In Section 4.1, some sources of market imperfection, hampering an efficient market, are distinguished. Section 4.2 deals with the normative aspects of the day-care market (equity): how is day care distributed among parents? Market imperfections can be partly resolved and inequalities can be reduced by government policy. In Section 4.3 we evaluate recent government policies based on how they deal with market imperfections and how they affect distributional issues.

4.1 Market Imperfections[29]

Two kinds of efficiency are important in this field: allocative and dynamic efficiency. Allocative efficiency implies that 'prices and produced quantities are such that they are in agreement with the consumer's wishes and that goods and services turn up where they are supposed to, in conformity with demand and supply'.[30] Dynamic

---

[28] E.g. Chipty, 1995; Hofferth & Phillips, 1991, p. 5-6; Hoxby, 1995, p. 3-4; Moret Ernst & Young, 1995, p. 7; Rose-Ackerman, 1983 for comparable trade-offs.

[29] See also Siegers & Turksema (1996).

[30] Bos, 1995, p. 44 (our translation).

efficiency, refers to the degree to which a market adapts to changing circumstances.[31]

Allocative Efficiency

Whether or not a market is efficient can be evaluated on the basis of three conditions (see also Walker, 1991):

(1) there is full competition (firms and households act as price-takers, there are no monopolies);

(2) all the buyers and sellers are completely informed (no information asymmetry);

(3) there is a full set of markets (no externalities).

In this section, we address the degree to which the day-care market meets with these three criteria.

The day-care market is neither characterized by full competition nor by monopoly. Rather, we can speak of monopolistic competition, as the supply of a large number of providers is somewhat different in terms of price, convenience for the parents, proximity of the location, availability and quality. Each provider is a monopolist of its own variety, but also has to deal with competition because consumers can easily turn to another variety. Compared to a market with full competition, the monopolistic element causes the supply to be lower and the price to be higher, but this may be compensated for by the fact that the diversity of modes meets the widely varied demand for day care.

The second source of market imperfections, incomplete information, causes more concern. There is incomplete information because providers and consumers do not know each other;[32] this leads to inefficiency. And in itself, the nature of the services causes an information problem. Day care is not a search good, i.e. a good whose quality can be assessed in advance, nor is it an experience good, i.e. a good whose quality can only be determined after consuming it. It is a trust good, because parents cannot monitor the provider's efforts and have to trust the provider to take good care of their child and offer quality care.[33] This kind of information asymmetry leads to a tendency toward moral hazard and adverse selection.[34] Moral hazard means that the provider, due to the lack of quality control, has no incentive other than a moral one to supply the quality agreed upon. This has a downward effect on the quality of

---

[31] See e.g. Vrancken & De Kemp, 1996, p. 40; Bos, 1995, p. 45; see also Wolfson, 1988, p. 44 & 109.

[32] Kagan, 1991, p. 92; Chipty, 1995, p. 419.

[33] Wielers, 1991, p. 69, 76; see also Van Binnebeke, 1996.

[34] Walker, 1991.

care in the day-care market.[35] Adverse selection means that information asymmetry causes consumers to not want to pay a higher price than the average quality in the market justifies. This may mean that only the sellers of lower than average quality goods can make a profit and survive in the market.[36] Providers of higher than average quality care have better opportunities outside this market, and will leave the market. Therefore, moral hazard and adverse selection both lead to a reduction in the supply and a decrease in quality.

The third source of market imperfections is market incompleteness. This also applies to the day-care market. Firstly, it is impossible for parents to reserve a place at a day-care centre in advance other than for a few months. So there is no trade across time periods. In as far as this has a downward effect on fertility, there is a downward effect on the future demand for day care and, thus, on the supply of day care. Secondly, there are externalities involved in the day-care market. Day care leads, for example, to increased female labour force participation, as propagated by the Dutch government, and to economic independence for men as well as women. Since individual decision-makers are not necessarily guided by such macro objectives, it can be expected that less day care will be supplied than is desirable from society's point of view.

Dynamic Efficiency

Allocative efficiency should be juxtaposed to dynamic efficiency, and seems to be stimulated by the introduction of the market. In the day-care sector, dynamic efficiency manifests itself in new developments such as product innovation, in the form of flexibilization. This seems to be helpful in solving a problem that comes up frequently in the welfare sector, namely that organizations have a strategic policy that is not orientated externally long term. Van der Meijden & Kornalijnslijper[37] call welfare management 'not innovative, not anticipative, not directed at "pioneering", but defensive, static and reactive' (p. 19, our translation). The fact that managers of day-care centres do not see an increase in price as feasible could be seen as an indication of this attitude.[38] According to Van der Meijden & Kornalijnslijper, in welfare work and care centres insufficient attention is being devoted to the exploitation of new products and markets. Commercialization may focus more attention on dynamic efficiency.

---

[35] Cf. James & Rose-Ackerman, 1986.
[36] Weimer & Vining, 1992, p. 74.
[37] 1994.
[38] VOG, 1996b, p. 37.

4.2 Equity

In the case of the day-care market, equity pertains to two things: accessibility and an equitable distribution (client mix). Two critical remarks have to be made with respect to the accessibility of day care. Firstly, leaving the choice of whether or not to offer day care to employers means day care will mainly be offered in sectors where employers are dependent on women, like the health care sector.[39] This makes these sectors even more attractive to female workers, which reinforces the existing segregation between men and women in the labour market instead of reducing it. In sectors where employers are not as dependent on female workers, less day care will be financed for employees, and only for certain employees. Employers will finance day-care places to keep or recruit highly skilled female employees, but will not do so for their less skilled employees.[40] This enlarges existing social inequality, since earnings and other terms of employment are usually more favourable in primary jobs than in secondary jobs. Furthermore, the supply of day care by employers may be cyclically sensitive. As the need grows for employers to hire additional women when the economy is in an upswing, they will be inclined to make more facilities available, but when the business cycle turns down again, these facilities will be just as easily withdrawn. Secondly, policy decentralization to the municipalities causes accessibility differences between the municipalities. This way, the availability of day care is dependent on whether day care has priority on the particular Town Council's political agenda.[41]

4.3 Evaluation of Government Policy

In the two previous subsections, we concluded that several market failures and equity concerns apply to the Dutch day-care market. A number of policy solutions can be used to correct market and government imperfections and equity concerns. Each of these policies addresses different combinations of market and government imperfections and distributional issues. In this subsection, we evaluate the Dutch government policies used to correct the defects of the day-care market in recent years.

1990-1995: Supply-side and Demand-side Subsidies
Supply-side subsidies are appropriate to address the third source of market imperfections, externalities. Positive externalities brought about by these subsidies

---

[39] Cf. Schippers & Siegers, 1992; Teulings, 1993, p. 1126.
[40] Schippers & Siegers, 1992.
[41] See Gustafsson & Stafford, 1992; Van Dijk et al., 1993.

99

include the increase of women's labour force participation and economic indepen-dence (the underlying objectives of the Stimulative Measures on Child Care, see Section 2). Within the framework of the Stimulative Measures on Child Care, supply-side subsidies in the form of matching grants[42] were used to increase the supply of day care. As we noted in Section 2, the Measures were successful in the sense that there was a substantial increase in the supply of day care. However, this increase in efficiency was at the expense of equity in terms of the client mix. This was mainly the consequence of the introduction of employer-financed places (to involve employers in the day-care sector, one of the other underlying objectives of the Stimulative Measures on Child Care, see also Section 2 and Subsection 4.2). A study by Maassen van den Brink & Groot[43] gave an indirect indication of the change in client mix (measured in terms of the distribution of women over income categories) after employer-financed places were introduced in 1990. Their survey (on the demand side of day care: among women) showed considerable shifts in the distribution of women over income categories between 1991 and 1995: the share of women in the highest income category (more than Dfl 1,400 a month) increased from 22.9 to 55.4 per cent, whereas the share of women in the lowest income category (no income of their own) decreased from 31.4 to 12.9 per cent.

From 1996: Demand-side Subsidies and Regulation
With the transition from the welfare to the market sector, supply-side subsidies for employer-financed as well as subsidized places have ceased to exist. Subsidized places have been replaced by places reserved for target groups (minorities, one-parent families, etc). Together with the introduction of employer-financed places under the Stimulative Measures on Child Care, this implies that for all practical purposes, accessibility to day care has been denied to parents who work for an employer who is not willing to finance day care for its employees and for parents who do not belong to a target group (unless they can afford an expensive private place). The introduction of places reserved for target groups has introduced a further distinction between consumers (parents) and buyers (employers and municipalities). This may have consequences for the price and quality of day care, because employers and municipalities can be assumed to have other goals than parents. Government

---

[42] According to Weimer & Vining 'an appropriately designed per unit subsidy to the supplier generates an increased supply of the good, reducing the undersupply caused by the externality and thereby increasing social welfare' (1992, p. 158).
[43] Maassen van den Brink & Groot (1996).

intervention is now limited to the still existing demand-side subsidies for employers[44] and a 'general administrative measure' (AMvB). The introduction of this general administrative measure in the day-care market runs parallel with the transition from the welfare to the market sector. This can be done by occupational licensing, which provides a standardization of skills and knowledge, or on the basis of quality standards. Both of them address the second source of market imperfection, i.e. information asymmetry between consumers and providers. Licences and quality standards become even more important when the general administrative measure (AMvB) expires in a few years and a system of self-regulation develops.

5 Summary and Conclusions

In this paper, we have developed an explanatory model to analyse the day-care sector's transition from the welfare to the market sector. We theoretically identified elements that play a role in the efficiency, quality and equity trade-off in the day-care market. Within a day-care centre, factors at three levels (the level of the decision-maker, the level of the organization, and the level of the day-care centre's surroundings) influence the decision-maker's choices with respect to the supply of day care in terms of price, quality and accessibility.

We also gave an indication of the special features and concerns of the day-care market. Several market imperfections such as monopolistic competition and information asymmetry obstruct full competition in the day-care market. Dutch government policies have been evaluated on the basis of these special features and concerns. This evaluation showed that the government's efforts to correct existing market failures or reduce inequalities have only been partly successful. The supply of day care has increased from 14,800 to 48,000 full-time day-care places between 1990 and 1995, but at the expense of the accessibility of day care. The answer to the question in which direction the supply of day care will develop after the transition from welfare to market sector (see Section 2.3) may be: downward – the first day-care centres have already gone bankrupt. However, this possible decrease in the supply of day care may be prevented if day-care centres are given an opportunity to complete the transition from infant industry to normal enterprise.[45] An example of this can be found in the Dutch city of Maastricht, where the local day-care

---

[44] Although now via fiscal arrangements, instead of via the Stimulative Measures on Child Care.
[45] Loeff Claeys Verbeke, 1994, p. 27.

organization and the municipality agreed upon a transitional period of five years, in which the transition to normal enterprise could be gradually completed.

References

Blau, D.M. (1989), The child care labor market (Working paper 89-7), Chapel Hill, NC: Department of Economics.

Blau, D.M. (1991), The quality of child care: An economic perspective, in: D.M. Blau (ed.) The economics of child care, (p. 145-173), New York: Russell Sage Foundation.

Bos, D.I. (1995), Marktwerking en regulering. Theoretische aspecten en ervaringen in Nederland en het buitenland, The Hague: Ministry of Economic Affairs.

CBS (1989) – Centraal Bureau voor de Statistiek, Kindercentra 1986, The Hague: SDU.

CBS (1994) – Centraal Bureau voor de Statistiek, Kindercentra 1993, The Hague: SDU.

CBS (1995) – Centraal Bureau voor de Statistiek, Kindercentra 1994, The Hague: SDU.

CBS (1996) – Centraal Bureau voor de Statistiek, Statistisch jaarboek 1996, The Hague: SDU.

CBS (1997) – Centraal Bureau voor de Statistiek, Kindercentra 1995, The Hague: SDU.

Chipty, T. (1995), Economic effects of quality regulations in the day-care industry, American Economic Review, papers and proceedings, 85(2), 419-424.

Culkin, M., J.R. Morris & S.W. Helburn (1991), Quality and the true cost of child care, Journal of Social Issues, 2, 71-86.

Gustafsson, S. & F. Stafford (1992), Daycare subsidies and labor supply in Sweden, Journal of Human Resources, 27, 204-230.

Hansmann, H.B. (1986), The role of nonprofit enterprise, in: S. Rose-Ackerman (ed.), The economics of nonprofit institutions, (p. 57-84), New York: Oxford University Press.

Hofferth, S.L. & D.A. Phillips (1991), Child care policy research, Journal of Social Issues, 47(2), 1-13.

Hoxby, C.M. (1995), Is there an equity-efficiency trade-off in school finance? Tiebout and a theory of the local public goods producer, NBER Working paper 5265, Cambridge: NBER.

James, E. & S. Rose-Ackerman (1986), The nonprofit enterprise in market economics, Chur: Harwood Academic Publishers.

Kagan, S.L. (1991), Examining profit and nonprofit child care: an odyssey of quality and auspices, Journal of Social Issues, 47(2), 87-104.

Le Grand, J. & W. Bartlett (1993), Quasi-markets and social policy, London: Macmillan.

Lindenberg, S. (1991), Social approval, fertility and the female labour market behaviour, in: J.J. Siegers, J. de Jong-Gierveld & E. van Imhoff (eds.), Female labour market behaviour and fertility, (p. 32-58), Berlin: Springer.

Lindenberg, S. (1992), The explanation of preferences, in: H. van Goor (ed.), Empirische sociologie als opdracht, (p. 49-66), Groningen: MB-boek.

Lindenberg, S. (1996), Continuities in the theory of social production functions, in: H. Ganzeboom & S. Lindenberg (eds.), Verklarende sociologie. Opstellen voor Reinhard Wippler, (p. 169-184), Amsterdam: Thesis.

Loeff Claeys Verbeke (1994), Nederland privatiseert, The Hague: SDU.

Maassen van den Brink, H., S. Gustafsson & W. Groot (1995), Kinderopvang tussen markt en overheid, Amsterdam: Welboom.

Maassen van den Brink, H. & W. Groot (1996), Monitoring kinderopvang. Veranderingen in het gebruik van kinderopvang 1991-1995, Amsterdam: University of Amsterdam.

Ministerie van WVC (1989), Kinderopvang geregeld: advies over de besteding van 130 miljoen aan kinderopvang vanaf 1990, Rijswijk.

Ministerie van WVC (1992), Stimuleringsbeleid Kinderopvang 1990-1993. Resultaten over 1990 en 1991, Rijswijk.

Ministerie van WVC (1994), Stimuleringsmaatregel kinderopvang 1994-1995, Rijswijk.

Moret, Ernst & Young (1995), Een betere bedrijfsvoering van de kinderopvang, Utrecht: MEY.

Petersen, C. (1996), Marktwerking en de doelmatigheid van verzekeraars, Economisch Statistische Berichten, March 7, 1996, 603-605.

Rose-Ackerman, S. (1983), Unintended consequences: Regulating the quality of subsidized day care, Journal of Policy Analysis and Management, 3(1), 14-30.

Schippers, J.J. & J.J. Siegers (1992), Public day-care centres, company day-care centres, and segregation between men and women in the labour market: The case of the Netherlands, Labour, Review of Labour Economics and Industrial Relations, 6, 151-168.

Siegers, J.J. (1992), Interdisciplinary economics, De Economist, 140(4), 531-547.

Siegers, J.J. & R.W. Turksema (1996), De markt voor kinderopvang, Mens & Maatschappij, 71(4), 355-361.

Staatscourant, October 22, 1996, Kwaliteit van de zorg verdient meer beleidsmatige aandacht.

Teulings, C. (1993), Een doelmatige organisatie van de kinderopvang, Economische Statistische Berichten, 1124-1130.

Tijdens, K & J. Houweling (1993), Geschiedenis van de kinderopvang, in: K. Tijdens & S. Lieon (eds.), Kinderopvang in Nederland, Organisatie en financiering (p. 11-27), Utrecht: Jan van Arkel.

Van Binnebeke, L. (forthcoming), Regulering van en door de advocatuur, Ph.D. Dissertation, Utrecht University.

Van Dalen, R. (1995), De collectieve zorg voor jonge kinderen, Jeugd en samenleving, 10, 595-605.

Van der Meijden, R.R. & N. Kornalijnslijper (1994), Doelmatig welzijn. Een onderzoek naar aangrijpingspunten voor een doelmatiger bedrijfsvoering in welzijnsinstellingen, The Hague: VNG Uitgeverij.

Van Dijk, L., A.H.E.B. Koot-du Buy & J.J. Siegers (1993), Day care supply by Dutch municipalities, European Journal of Population, 9, 315-330.

Van Dijk, L. & J.J. Siegers (1996), Sociale normen, sociale netwerken en het arbeidsaanbod van vrouwen met jonge kinderen, in: H. Ganzeboom & S. Lindenberg (eds.), Verklarende sociologie. Opstellen voor Reinhard Wippler (p. 201-218), Amsterdam: Thesis Publishers.

Van Hulst, N. (1996), De baten van het marktwerkingsbeleid, Economisch Statistische Berichten, April 10 1996, 316-320.

Van der Ploeg, R. (1996), Vijf kanttekeningen bij de nieuwe mededingingswet, Economisch Statistische Berichten, July 31, 1996, 652-653.

Van Rijkswijk-Clerkx, L. (1981), Moeders, kinderen en kinderopvang, Nijmegen: SUN.

Van Schaaijk, M. (1996), Liberalisering van de huurwoningmarkt, Economisch Statistische Berichten, July 31, 1996, 640-644.

Van Thiel, S., F.L. Leeuw & H.D. Flap (forthcoming), 'Quangocratisering' in Nederland?, Beleid en Maatschappij.

VOG (1996a), Gemeenten en kinderopvangorganisaties: een paar apart, Rijswijk: VOG.

VOG (1996b), Kostprijsanalyse in de kinderopvangsector, Rijswijk: VOG.

Vrancken, P.H.J. & A.A.M. de Kemp (1996), Marktwerking in het secundair en tertiair beroepsonderwijs, The Hague: Ministry of Economic Affairs.

Walker, J.R. (1991), Public policy and the supply of child care services, in: D.M. Blau (ed.) The economics of child care (p. 51-77), New York: Russell Sage Foundation.

Weimer, D.L. & A.R. Vining (1992), Policy analysis. Concepts and practice, Englewood Cliffs (NJ): Prentice Hall.

Wielers, R.J.J. (1991), Selectie en allocatie op de arbeidsmarkt. Een uitwerking voor de informele en de geïnstitutionaliseerde kinderopvang, Amsterdam: Thesis.

Wielers, R.J.J. (1994), Opleidingen, functies en overheidsbeleid: de organisatie van de arbeidsmarkt in de kinderopvang, in: N.D. de Graaf & R.J.J. Wielers (eds.), Theorie en praktijk: verklarende modellen in de arbeidsmarktsociologie (p. 117-134), Amsterdam: Siswo.

Wolfson, D.J. (1988), Publieke sector en economische orde, Groningen: Wolters-Noordhoff.

Zwier, B. (1989), Schets van de ontwikkeling van de kinderopvang in Nederland, in: B. Zwier and E. Mostert (eds.), Kinderopvang (p. 13-26), The Hague: Sdu.

Flexible Labour and Social Security

Yvonne Konijn

1 Introduction

The current government's motto is 'Flexibility in labour relations must be stimulated'. For modern society the standard labour pattern of 40 hours a week for 40 years is no longer sufficient, it rather demands an alternation of work and other activities, and a flexible use of labour. In order to stimulate this process solutions are looked for within labour law. The dismissal laws which many consider too rigid, must be changed, working hour regulations have to be liberated and there should be no more obstacles impeding temporary work or any other form of flexible labour. In view of the necessity of flexibilisation the government is now faced with the problem of how to choose from the many instruments available those that will prove economically and socially most efficient. A number of options to achieve a balance between flexibility and security in labour law were proposed in the memorandum *Flexibiliteit en Zekerheid* (flexibility and security) which was published in December 1995. Meanwhile the *Stichting van de Arbeid* (Labour Foundation) has supported most of its proposals,[1] and a bill has been put forward in Parliament. A number of changes as regards flexible labour relations in labour law are therefore anticipated. In the same memorandum the Minister has indicated that the relationship between social security and flexibilisation will also have to be reconsidered because 'as is obvious, a dynamic and (re)activating social security cannot be missed in an employment system that adapts to new circumstances'.[2]

Flexibility and social security are the key issues of this contribution. Focussing on the central theme of this collection flexibility in employment may be considered an efficient use of labour capacity – both in order to achieve the best possible business results and to increase employment –, and social security a contribution to social justice. The key note here is the description of efficiency as obtaining the best possible result given the cost. Social justice is taken to stand for the guarantee of equal opportunities in work and income for every worker while trying as much as possible to combine work and other activities of the worker.

---

[1] Ministry of Social Affairs and Employment, 1996.
[2] Ministry of Social Affairs and Employment, 1995, p. 2.

An important reason for flexibilisation is the need for companies to be able to meet changes in production.[3] Temporary and stand-by workers are then the likeliest candidates. Using these categories of workers is supposed to achieve the most efficient production situation because only work actually done will have to be paid for.

Another motive for stimulating flexibilisation is the government's aim of more employment. Besides continuing to restrict wage costs and reduce social premiums, as well as increasing the quality of the labour available by means of education, the government considers flexibilisation of labour and the labour market necessary in order to achieve an increase in employment in the market sector.[4]

A further argument presented is that workers wish to adapt their working pattern to other activities. It appears, though, that in doing so workers do not opt for flexible contracts because of the insecurities attached to such contracts. Workers usually only accept such contracts if 'nothing better is offered'.

The wish for flexibilisation, therefore, seems to be born out of different and even opposing motives. An employer requires flexibilisation from a business-economical point of view and wants to make as efficient as possible a use of available labour. The government wishes to increase employment which would reduce the numbers of unemployed claiming benefits. And finally, employees want flexibilisation of labour relations in order to be better able to combine work with care tasks or other activities but without hazarding their job or income security.

It remains to be seen whether flexibilisation of labour can be achieved in such a way as to meet all these requirements.

This seems impossible at first sight. From a point of view of cost reduction the use of flexible labour relations, if used to the full, seems an appropriate means because work will then only have to be paid if actually done. In such a system business risks are then for the employees' account. Any form of job or income protection will result in an increase in costs. However, employees appear to find this protection important. They will only accept flexible labour if forced to. Thus, efficiency in the form of a company policy that meets the demands of the market, and equity will be poles apart.

The basic assumption of this article is that efficiency and social justice should not be opposing but concurring factors. Only then will we come to the point where

---

[3] Other reasons are: preliminary phase before a permanent contract, reduction of number of regular workers either to achieve a flexible organization or because of insecurity as regards the continued existence of the job, and temporary replacement. See Bolhuis, 1996.
[4] Sociale Nota 1996, TK 1995-1996, 24 402, no. 2.

flexible labour is considered a valuable part of the labour market. Changes in social security will contribute to this process.

Flexible Labour

Though at first a new and unfamiliar phenomenon, flexible labour is now a common aspect of the labour market. Statistics Netherlands previews of 1995 show that more than 50% of employees have a flexible labour relation; 35% are internally flexible labour relations and 18% are externally flexible labour relations.[5]
Other research has shown that 43% of small companies, 79% of average-sized companies and 97% of large companies employ people on the basis of flexible labour contracts.[6]

Flexibility can be achieved in various ways. It comprises in short the enhancement of labour patterns that have been adapted to the labour demand of companies (and possibly the need for employees to combine work with other activities). In realising this a distinction is made between internal and external flexibilisation. Internal flexibilisation aims at employees with 'fixed' contracts who may be deployed flexibly within the company by broadening their functions, by overtime and variable working hours. External flexibilisation aims at hiring people on the basis of contracts other than permanent labour contracts.
The form of such a flexible contract defines the degree of social protection. Flexible labour contracts mostly comprise labour agreements for specified periods, temporary contracts and stand-by contracts. These contracts offer a decreasing degree of social protection.
Those who are least protected (stand-by employees) actually form a rather large group. Of all companies 29% employs short-time workers, 17% uses temporary workers and 16% uses stand-by workers. The nature of the company is furthermore also of influence. Thus, for example, trade, catering and agriculture businesses employ far larger numbers of stand-by workers.[7]
In this paper therefore I will concentrate on that group of flexible workers where the rift between efficiency and social justice seems largest: stand-by workers.

From an efficiency point of view stand-by workers seem to be *the* solution. And yet, they too have some disadvantages.

---

[5] Baenen and Bosch, 1996.
[6] Bolhuis, 1996.
[7] Bolhuis, 1996, p. 13.

First, due to current legislation there is a large gap between permanent and flexible workers. Social security legislation is for the most part written for permanent workers. This division entails not only socially undesirable effects, such as marginalization of a certain group of employees,[8] but also the fact that stand-by work is not considered very valuable. Therefore, workers will accept flexible work if 'there is nothing better', but they will quit flexible work the moment they can get a permanent contract. And workers with a fixed contract are less likely to give up their position for fear of being worse off. Thus, this division also increases the immobilization of workers.

Secondly, the chances of industrial accidents are larger with flexible workers than with permanent workers. Because the relationship with the company is minimal the worker has little knowledge of the production process and the inherent dangers. This means that flexible workers will always need to be well instructed for the performance of their tasks. This is not always possible and thus the chance of an accident increases. This in its turn not only increases the losses of the company but also the social costs involved because there are no adequate arrangements for flexible workers.

Thirdly, flexible labour may entail loss of quality. Production costs can indeed be cut by employing stand-by workers but this will come at a price, namely loss of quality. The question is whether employers (especially in Europe) can afford that.[9]

Fourthly, current social security regulations lead to complicated procedures because in each individual case it will have to be investigated whether a flexible worker may or may not claim social benefits. Research shows that the determination of social security rights for flexible workers is far more complicated, intricate and therefore expensive than those of other labour relations.[10]

The above-mentioned disadvantages make it clear that the use of stand-by workers is not as efficient as is sometimes argued. In order for flexible labour to become more efficient I consider a number of changes necessary. The gap between permanent and flexible workers needs to be closed. A mere strengthening of the position of flexible workers seems less desirable as this would only lead to a more rigid labour market. Far better be it to look for a system where permanent workers become more flexible and flexible workers become more permanent.[11] It is furthermore necessary for flexible workers too to develop a relationship with the company or companies

---

[8]   See also Ministery for Social Affairs and Employment, 1995, p. 8.
[9]   See on this also: Van der Staay, 1996, p. 55 ff.
[10]   KPMG, 1995, p. 181.
[11]   The Memorandum Flexibiliteit en Zekerheid offers a number of proposals to this effect.

where they work. This may be achieved if the employer regularly hires them on such conditions as to form an incentive for the employee to remain willing to work for the company on a more flexible basis. Thus the quality of production will be easier to maintain and the chances of industrial accidents is reduced. As far as regulations are concerned, it is necessary that these should be organized in such a way that they offer not only adequate protection but are also phrased in simple and lucid terms. Such regulations not only result in more efficiency but also in increased social justice. Until now solutions have mostly taken the form of labour law regulations. I feel that further changes in social security are necessary in order to gain an adequate system of flexible labour relations that is acceptable to all parties.

Social Security

Considering legislation in the field of social security it appears that that too has until now only catered for permanent labour relations.

For flexible workers the main obstacles are benefit qualification criteria and conditions. To be able to claim benefits there is the criterion of a certain reference period (WW, Unemployment Insurance Act) or certainty about the times when the worker was actually employed (Article 7:629 Civil Code, ZW (Sickness Act) and WAO (Disability Insurance Act)). Most flexible workers cannot or only with difficulty meet these conditions. Then there is also the question whether flexible employment can be considered appropriate employment.[12]

With the various revisions of social security legislation until today little or no attention was paid to the (desired) changed work patterns. As regards disability legislation for example the aim is towards reduction of sick-leave and reintegration of employees. The actual measures taken seem to aim at employees with a 'permanent' labour contract. And even when a new act[13] was drafted the consequences of this act for flexible workers were hardly considered. It is true that some haphazard regulations have been introduced but there has been no structural consideration of the specific problems that face flexible workers in case of illness.

Due to this lack of adequate social security amenities flexible workers as compared to their permanent colleagues depend more heavily on actual work in order to earn

---

[12] The government also mentions these obstacles in the memorandum Werken aan Zekerheid, Bouwstenen voor een modern en houdbaar stelsel, which was presented to the Lower House together with the budget for 1997 of the Ministry of Social Affairs and Employment. See Ministry of Social Affairs and Employment, 1996, p. 53.

[13] Wet uitbreiding loondoorbetalingsplicht bij ziekte (Act on duty to continue paying wages in case of illness), Stb. 1996, 134.

an income. If they are unable to work due to disability or unemployment these risks are not always covered by the regulations of Article 7:629 CC, the ZW, the WAO or the WW. Their dependence on the employer this way only increases.

However, social security not only aims to provide some income protection but also to prevent people from losing their place in the labour process. Futhermore, reintegration of employees has become an ever more important goal of social security.[14] If social security were to include measures which would also cover flexible workers the chances grow of flexible labour taking a more permanent place within the labour system then has been the case until now.

Besides, a proper social security system is important from a social point of view. The very same worker is also a consumer and is thus part of the economy. Better income security enables the employee better to partake in that economy.

I think there is ample reason to critically review the present social security system with a view to flexible workers. What obstacles and problems does the flexible worker face? What possibilities might a changed social security offer as regards a system of flexible labour relations that is both efficient and socially just? These questions form the subject of this contribution. Reviewing the entire social security system, however, is beyond the scope of this paper. I have therefore opted to discuss the regulations on sickness and unemployment, as the main guarantees for a steady labour relation.

2 Claims During Illness

General

Income protection during the first 52 weeks of illness has since 1 March 1996 become primarily the employer's responsibility. Pursuant to Article 7:629 CC the employer is obliged to pay 70% of the employee's wages if the employee is, due to illness, incapable to do his job.

For those who have no (longer) an employer, the ZW acts as a safety net. This act is intended primarily for employees whose short-term labour contract ended while they were ill, for employees with trial periods, temporary workers and those for whom it is uncertain whether there is an employment contract (the so-called 'equals and rarities'). The government thought it irresponsible and also counter-productive

---

[14] Noordam, 1996; see also Klosse and Schippers, 1997.

to leave this group, which is too large and socially too important, uninsured.[15] In case of illness these groups are paid by the industrial insurance board.

The legislator's policy aims at a stricter distribution of costs among all parties involved in social security. As a consequence of the system chosen for the *Wet Uitbreiding Loondoorbetalingsplicht by Ziekte* (WULBZ; Act on the Extension of the Obligation to Continue Paying Wages in Case of Sickness) the arrangements in case of illness have become more individualized. The responsibility is no longer carried by a collectively established body (the industrial insurance board) but by the individual employer.

This choice has a number of consequences.

Firstly, the number of possible conflicts between employer and employee increase. The employer, especially as he now has to cover the costs of sick-leave himself, will check more strictly whether he is the one obliged to pay the wages. As he is only obliged to pay if there is an employment contract at the time the employee falls ill, he will deny the existence of such a contract in case of flexible workers. The risk of uncertainty about whether a flexible worker is entitled to either wages or sick-benefit lies primarily with the employer. If the employer refuses to pay wages in case of illness one will first have to determine whether or not the employer is obliged to pay. The industrial insurance board applies the rule of thumb that in case of doubt there will be no pay. This means that the employee either has to initiate proceedings against his employer or accept that he will receive no wages nor any sick-benefit. Initiating proceedings against the employer on whom you depend anyway is not a very attractive option. That is the more so for flexible workers. During the discussion of the bill in parliament it was proposed to unambiguously indicate who is responsible in case of doubt. Another suggestion was to charge the industrial insurance board with claiming the sick-benefit from employers. Neither proposal was adopted.

A second consequence of the legislator's choice is that it is now more attractive for employers to employ workers as much as possible on flexible contracts so that in case of illness they only have to pay wages for a short time or not at all. The government ministers three solutions which would have at least some restrictive effect as a remedy against such escapes:[16]

Firstly, the employer must mention to the industrial insurance board the nature of the contract at the start of the contract. This obligation will, according to the govern-

---

[15] TK 1995-1996, 24 439, no. 3.
[16] Explanatory Memorandum p. 43.

ment, provide important initial information for the industrial insurance board about the nature of the labour relation. Discrepancies between the initial announcement and the claim for sick-benefit may lead to further investigations. This could form a first restriction.

A second restriction is sanctioning. It is statutorily laid down that the industrial insurance board is authorized to entirely or partially refuse to provide sick-benefit if the employee's acts are prejudicial as regards the industrial insurance board. Actively or passively contributing to the end of his employment contract or pretending to have relationship other than an employment relationship may be regarded as such.

A third restriction is that flexibilisation is by its nature limited. An employer cannot allow himself too many flexible workers.

These proposals too indicate where the risk lies. The first one does not prevent the possibility that in case of further investigation the flexible worker may end up empty handed. The second proposal brings the responsibility even more directly to the employee's door and the third one does not solve anything for those nevertheless employed on a flexible contract.

A third consequence is that the regulation may increase unequal treatment of workers. Some employers will be more strict than others. There is no central authority that determines by means of more or less fixed policy rules whether the employee in question is entitled to sick-benefit during illness. It is the individual employer who sets out a policy as regards sick-leave in his company, which increases the chance of differences in treatment. Here too workers and especially flexible workers have little or no say in the matter.

All in all the flexible worker's position has not changed for the better. The more so because there are loopholes in the legislation which were dealt with rather carelessly in parliament. One of the reasons for that is the lack of special knowledge of the flexible worker's social security law position.[17]

Specific Problem Areas

a. Claims on the Employer

Article 7:629 CC provides a claim to continued payment of wages for 52 weeks in case the employee has not performed his agreed work because he or she was incapable to do so due to illness or pregnancy or birth. This stipulation applies only in as far and for as long as there is an employment contract between parties. As the

---

[17]   See also Olbers, 1996, p. 85.

employer's obligation to pay wages will be most important in case of illness the first thing to determine is whether there is an employment contract in force at the time the employee falls ill. In order to conclude whether or not a flexible worker is entitled to wages one will have to check whether any work has been contracted and, if so, what that agreed work *in casu* consists of. After all, the claim to continued wages only exists if the employee is unable to perform the agreed work due to illness.

For those who have had a regular labour pattern for several years it is possible to indicate what the agreed work consists of. The past few months or years are reviewed and thus the average number of working hours per week or month can be calculated. It must be assumed that that number will also apply in future. In fact this amounts to a part-time contract for the average number of hours. And if a minimum number of hours has been agreed on there is at least a claim to that number.

If a stand-by worker has only just begun working or is employed on the basis of irregular working hours where it is uncertain when he will be working, one cannot simply assume a claim to wages based on Article 7:629 CC.

During the parliamentary discussions in the Senate a guideline was offered as regards this one problem: in case of flexible workers with irregular working hours the reference period used in the ZW to determine daily wages may be used.[18]

Furthermore, a stand-by worker is entitled to wages if he has been called and cannot refuse or if he is already at work and it is clear for what period he has been employed.

In all other cases where it is impossible to determine whether the stand-by worker would go to work and there is no average working pattern the claim to wages is uncertain despite the existence of an employment contract. And, of course, no employer will be overly eager to acknowledge his duty to pay wages.

In these cases the first thing necessary is to get the situation clear to all parties. In case the employer denies the wage claim and the stand-by worker claims otherwise the court will have to decide the matter.

In the mean time the worker has no right to sick-benefit. Therefore, here too, the risk is entirely the stand-by worker's.

As the new regulation of Article 7:629 CC was construed, flexible workers were hardly taken into consideration. This stipulation clearly aims at those with regular working hours. It is uncertain whether people who lack such regularity can invoke

---

[18]   Handelingen EK 6 February 1996, p. 20-952 ff.

the article. Not only do they have to prove that there was an employment contract at the time they fell ill, they also need to indicate what were the agreed tasks.

b. Access to Safety Net Regulation

The government is of the opinion that:'Whoever falls within the scope of the insurance and cannot claim continued payment of wages is entitled to sick-benefit.'[19] If that were truly the case the ZW would have to include a provision that would grant sick-benefit to everyone with an employment contract but no right to continued wages. This is not the case.

An appeal to the safety net provision of the ZW is open only to the categories mentioned in Article 29 paragraph 2 ZW.

The ZW is based on employees that have no (longer) employment contracts in the sense of Article 7:629 CC. In paragraph 1 of Article 29 ZW it is stipulated that no more sick-benefit is granted if the employee is entitled to wages as mentioned in Article 7:629 of Book 7A CC because of a contract pursuant to which he or she should be working.

Workers engaged on the basis of an employment contract and not entitled to continued wages on the basis of Article 7:629 CC, are left in the lurch. The safety net provision of the ZW does not apply here because this possiblity is not mentioned in Article 29 paragraph 2 ZW.

c. Insurance Pursuant to the ZW

Article 29 paragraph 2 under a states that those insured under Articles 4 and 5 ZW, barring a few exceptions, may claim sick-benefit. These are temporary workers, homeworkers who earn more than 40% of the minimum wages and stand-by workers who work at least two days a week. These are workers without a 'normal' employment contract.

However, whether they will actually receive sick-benefit very much remains to be seen. That depends on Article 6 ZW as well. The current version of that article was written when the WAO was drafted which contains a similar stipulation.[20] The intention of the article was to prevent that an 'empty' employment contract where no (more) work was done and no (more) wages were paid, would still grant a right to sick-benefit.[21]

Pursuant to Article 6 paragraph 2 ZW an employment contract only exists on days when the employee is actually working or when he earns half or more of his normal

---

[19] Explanatory Memorandum p. 34.
[20] Therefore what will be said below about the ZW also holds true for the WAO.
[21] TK 1962-1963, no. 7171, 3, p. 36.

114

wages. This rule contains exceptions (under d and e for example) that may be of importance for flexible workers. The exceptions mean that if the employment contract covers either only part of the week or not regularly every calendar week an employment contract is nevertheless assumed to exist. In the latter case, by the way, it is assumed to exist only for the week when the work is actually done or would have been done if the employee had not fallen ill. This is called a week insurance.

The Central Appeals Court's interpretation of these stipulations offers little consolation to the flexible workers. The Central Appeals Court apparently thinks it important that there is a continuous labour relation. This is only the case, according to the Court, if it is a part-time contract or a contract that the employee must heed.[22]

And that is exactly the category of workers that now have to turn to their employers in case of illness because they will usually have a regular employment contract.

As it is hardly feasible that there are flexible workers who, failing an employment contract, will meet the conditions set by the Central Appeals Court the exceptions included under d and e of Article 6 paragraph 2 ZW will prove of little avail to flexible workers.

And that in its turn means that those workers are only insured on the days they actually work (also called day insurance). In fact, what it boils down to is that they are obliged to pay premiums but are in most cases not entitled to sick-benefit.[23]

d. Start of ZW Benefits

Another stipulation not very well thought over with a view to flexible labour relations is Article 29, paragraph 2, under c ZW. According to this clause sick-benefit is paid to the person whose employment contract ends before the ZW benefit stops. The insured is entitled to sick-benefit from the first day of incapability to work following the end of his contract but no earlier than the third day of incapability to work. Which flexible worker will meet that requirement?

Not the ones working on a permanent employment contract, for the condition is that the contract has ended.

This concerns flexible workers who are regularly called to work, or who work temporarily or at home pursuant to a prior agreement and who fall ill during a period

---

[22] Central Appeals Court 17 July 1995, PS 18 October 1995, no. 788, p. 1483.

[23] The interpretation of article 6 paragraph 2 ZW not only has its repercussions on insurance based on the ZW but also on those based on the Ziekenfondswet (National Health Act). Insured under the Ziekenfondswet are employees in the sense of the ZW. That means that flexible workers may be either in or out of the Ziekenfondswet. Uncertainty and insecurity prevail here as well.

when they are actually working. These workers are entitled to sick-benefit the moment the agreed period of work has ended. The employer will try to limit the duration of his duty as much as possible so that the flexible workers can be dropped in the safety net. If in such a case fake constructions are used the flexible workers run the risk that the industrial insurance board will consider that a prejudicial act and will subsequently reduce or stop the benefit (Article 44 para. 2 under j ZW).

Flexible workers who work irregular hours on the basis of a prior agreement will not so easily come under the safety net provision. There will be separate employment contracts for each period of actual work and they will all in turn end. There is no insurance coverage during the periods in between contracts.

Conclusion

Regulations on income protection in case of illness have quite some loopholes as regards flexible workers. It appears that the legislator has been inconsistent and has failed to consider the question whether these regulations offer adequate protection to flexible workers. All too easily it has been assumed that those who cannot rely on their employers will come under the safety net regulation. In that assumption the legislator has ignored the problems a flexible worker will have in enforcing continued payment of wages, the problems caused by the rules of the ZW and the consequences of the choice that the employee is the one to bear the risks.

3 Unemployment

As is the case with the regulation on sick-benefit, the rules of the *Werkloosheidswet* (WW, Unemployment Insurance Act) do not always guarantee an income substituting benefit in case the insured risk materializes either. The problems faced by flexible workers under this act are not caused by whether or not they are workers according to the definition of the WW. The WW contains no stipulation such as Article 6 paragraph 2 ZW and WAO.

There are, however, other stipulations which usually deny the flexible worker his or her right to unemployment benefits.

a. Loss of Working Hours
The first problem is the condition of Article 16 paragraph 1 WW which says that in order to qualify for benefits the worker must lose at least five hours or at least half the number of working hours per calendar week. Article 16 paragraph 2 WW stipulates that working hours per week means the average number of hours per week

for which the worker has been employed during the 26 weeks immediately preceding the loss. These stipulations too indicate that the assumed basis is steady employment. For flexible workers working irregular hours it is difficult to pinpoint when loss of working hours occurs.

b. Entitlement to Continued Wages

Another problem is that the condition of Article 16 paragraph 1 WW does not entitle the worker to continued payment of wages. In case of stand-by contracts it is not always clear whether or not such a right exists. The first thing to determine is whether the stand-by contract is an indefinite labour contract. If that is the case then the stand-by worker does under circumstances have a right to continued payment of wages pursuant to Article 7:628 CC unless it has been mutually agreed to exclude this clause in a written agreement. Here too it is up to the flexible worker to, if needs be, confront his employer on the matter. If he fails to do so because he thinks his employer is not obliged to pay wages and if the industrial insurance board misinterprets this failure as a prejudicial act it will temporarily or definitely refuse to pay part or all of the worker's benefits (Art. 24 in conjunction with Art. 27 WW). An example of this is the case of a driver who according to his employment contract worked as a 'stand-by driver'. He had desisted from claiming wages because in his employment contract Article 7:628 CC was explicitly excluded. At some time in the past, however, the Supreme Court had decided[24] that an employer cannot invoke such an exclusion clause in case of invalid dismissal. The driver, therefore, had wrongly desisted from claiming wages. By forfeiting his wage claim he committed a prejudicial act.[25]

c. Reference Period

The reference condition of Articles 17 and 17a WW is the worst problem for most flexible workers. This condition states that of the 39 weeks immediately preceding the first day of unemployment the worker must have worked at least 26 weeks. Besides this condition the so-called employment-history-condition also applies: during the five calendar years immediately preceding the first day of unemployment the worker must have received wages for at least 52 days per year in at least four calendar years. This latter condition does not apply for so-called short-term benefits. The Secretary of State acknowledged that introduction of this stricter reference condition (previously it was only 26 weeks in the year preceding unemployment)

---

[24] NJ 1959, 588.
[25] CRvB 1 December 1992, RSV 1993, 135.

would hit temporary and stand-by workers mostly, but he stuck with the assumption that income protection pursuant to WW is and should be better as the employment history is longer. Remarks from Members of Parliament that this assumption is a breach of the government's policy to improve flexibilisation and that this rule would reduce the workers' willingness to work flexible hours were more or less discarded.[26]

Conclusion

As was the case with the regulations on sick-benefit, the flexible worker is often insured and therefore has to pay premiums but due to the nature of his employment he cannot claim benefits. Particularly the reference period condition denies the flexible worker access.

4 Appropriate Employment

The various social security regulations oblige the employee to accept appropriate work under penalty of (partial) reduction or complete refusal of benefits. However, legislation is not entirely clear as to what is appropriate employment.

The ZW and Article 7:629 CC only mention appropriate employment without indicating what that would be. The ZW obliges the employee capable of doing appropriate work to try and find such work and, if given the opportunity, to do such work. Article 7:629 CC third paragraph under c stipulates that the employee is not entitled to continued wages if he refuses to accept appropriate employment offered to him by the employer while capable of doing it. Appropriate employment has the same meaning in both stipulations. During discussions in parliament the Secretary of State suggested that all depends on whether the employee is capable of reassuming his own work. If that is the case then the interpretation of the term must aim at that. If a return to the original job is deemed impossible then it will involve a wider orientation. However, it must be work that the employee can in all reasonability be requested to do, with regard for his past employment, training and physical condition.[27]

The WW does provide a definition of appropriate employment: all work fitting the capabilities and expertise of the employee unless acceptance cannot be required for

---

[26] TK 1994-1995, 23 985, no. 5, p. 8 ff.
[27] EK 1996-1997, 24 439, Explanatory Memorandum p. 64.

reasons of a physical, mental or social nature. Employment pursuant to the *Wet Sociale Werkvoorziening* (Social Employment Act) is not considered appropriate (Article 25 para. 3 WW). Whether employment can be considered appropriate will have to be determined in each individual case in view of the specific circumstances of that employee.[28]

In determining the degree of disability for work the WAO takes all generally accepted employment that the employee with his capacities and expertise is capable of performing as criterion (Article 18 para. 5 WAO).

The question now is whether flexible work or the refusal of such work by the employee should be the employee's responsibility. Or, as the government phrased it in its memorandum, to what extent may such forms of employment be deemed to come under the concept 'appropriate'. What requirements must be met by the form and duration of the contract?[29]

These questions have not yet been subject of case law. At most, in relation to the WW, the question has come up whether an employee may be required to accept temporary work, and in another case the employment offered by an agency was considered appropriate for the employee in question.[30]

As flexible employment becomes a more familiar concept, attention must be given to the question whether and to what extent flexible employment can be appropriate and this may also have to be codified.

5 Possible Solutions

For flexible labour to be accepted as valuable labour and in order to avoid the situation where all risks lie with employees or social insurance funds, labour law and social security law will have to be regarded as two sides of the same coin. The priorities are work and the employer's responsibility as regards all related risks. However, such an attitude can only be succesful if social security plays the role of safety net.

A system will have to be developed where it is clear when the employee, the employer or the social insurance funds have to bear the risks of illness or unemployment. To determine this it is unwise to simply take the employment contract as a basis.

---

[28] CRvB 2 February 1995, RSV 1995, 161.
[29] Ministry of Social Affairs and Employment, 1996, p. 53.
[30] CRvB 16 July 1991, RSV 1992; CRvB 30 September 1996, RSV 1996, 70.

At the moment the employment contract functions as a 'ticket' to employment and social security provisions. In practice this means investigating whether the criteria as mentioned in Article 7:629 CC have been met. This has led to fake constructions structuring the labour relation in such a way as to avoid an employment contract. The original goal, protection of economically dependent workers, thus got lost. A criterion which honours this goal rather better and is furthermore much easier to apply can be found in the BBA. Everybody who personally works for someone else deserves protection unless he usually does such work for more than two people or if he is helped in doing this work by more than two other people not being his spouse or blood relations, family members or adoptive children living with him, or if this work is only incidental for him. Perhaps the scope of incidental labour can be further explained by indicating how much the minimum number of hours for an employment relation is. The advantage of this criterion is not only that the person deserving protection comes within its scope but also that whoever does not need this protection need not be bothered with social security legislation.

Another point is that at present labour law and social security law are too much seen as two separate issues. Thus it may happen that actions under labour law are punished under social security law.[31] Rights and obligations following from the employment contract as it is in force between parties cannot be regarded separate from those that apply under social security legislation.

It is furthermore necessary to attune legislation better to the existence of flexible relationships.

In the memorandum *Flexibiliteit en Zekerheid* the Minister assumes that the older the labour relation the stronger the claim the employee has on the employer. This has resulted in a number of proposals in the field of labour law. Below I will make some suggestions concerning the changes in social security.

Regulations on Sick-Benefit

Bearing in mind the above-mentioned key notion, the following primary condition could apply to flexible workers: the first 13 weeks of illness are covered by the social safety net and only after that period will the employer be obliged to pay wages. Such a system will also solve the problem of uncertainty as regards the extent of the wage claim on the employer: if the employee falls ill there is a wage claim

---

[31] The employees of Fokker personally experienced this. Because they had agreed to temporary lower wages in an attempt to save the company they were in the end confronted with lower WW benefits than would otherwise have been the case.

for the average number of hours worked during the thirteen weeks preceding the illness.

In order to make such a system statutorily possible a number of legislative changes will have to be made. The government has announced that it will investigate whether it is possible to make the ZW more easily accessible for flexible workers by changing week insurance into month insurance. In itself this will be an improvement on the current situation but for this proposal to work it is also necessary to gain certainty on the question of whether the proposed month insurance still requires a permanent labour contract. If that is the case flexible workers will not be greatly helped by this measure.

To my opinion Article 6 paragraph 2 ZW should be abolished. The goal of this article – prevent empty employment contracts that may give right to benefits – can also be achieved by including further conditions in Articles 4, 5 and 6 ZW such as a minimum number of hours in order for an employment contract to come under the ZW. Incidental short-term employment may thus be excluded from the insurance. Such employment would then entail neither premiums nor benefits, unlike the current situation where premium duty is easily established yet never results in a valid claim for benefits. This new system would also prevent having to determine when day or week insurance applies. Employment contracts that meet the requirements for insurance will be permanently covered.

Another point that needs clarification is who the flexible worker has to address in case of illness: the employer or the industrial insurance board. As it is the flexible worker with an employment contract has no right to sick-benefit when ill. A more balanced system will have to be introduced where it is clear whom the incapacitated flexible worker will have to address. The Sickness Act will have to stipulate very clearly that entitlement to sick-benefit exists if there is no obligation to continue paying wages pursuant to Article 7:629 CC. Article 7:629 CC will have to state very clearly in what cases such an obligation exists for the employer and when not.

These measures will help to create a simple and lucid system which will prevent a number of conflicts between employers and flexible employees. This in its turn will reduce transaction costs which will contribute to higher efficiency in execution and thus result in a reduction of the tension between efficiency and social justice.

Unemployment

As far as the WW is concerned, the government has announced that it will investigate whether another structure of the WW with building blocks and savings elements will better suit the labour market. According to the administration one possible solution is a system where the worker builds up rights during each period that he works and which may be invoked the moment he becomes unemployed.[32]

In this it links up with the proposals of the FNV in its memorandum *Tijd voor nieuwe zekerheid*. In this memorandum the introduction of a so-called build-up-WW is advocated. Under that system flexible workers may build up a right to benefits without having to meet reference demands as is now the case under the WW. The build-up-WW would be a sort of entrance hall to the ordinary WW. The idea is that for each week worked a right to WW is created and after 130 weeks worked the worker is entitled to WW benefits of 70% of the last earned income for a period of 6 months. After those 6 months the worker is entitled to 70% of the statutory minimum wages for another two years.[33]

These proposals also honour the idea that the longer a person has worked the more rights he should have. They are all proposals I think deserve attention. They are attractive because of their simple construction, as regards both legislation and execution, and there is a clear link with past employment without cutting flexible workers short.

Appropriate Employment

As regards appropriate employment the Ministry for Social Affairs and Employment has made some suggestions in the past. The suggestions all concerned appropriate employment in the context of the WW. It is accepted that employment with irregular working hours can in principle be considered appropriate employment. However, certain minimum requirements will have to apply:
− the employment has to be more definite than merely incidental; therefore, the work has to comprise at least 5 hours a week or 20 hours a month according to the contract;
− payment will have to be at least minimum wages according to the collective agreement or proportionate minimum wages;
− the contract has to stipulate how and at what times/moments the employee may be called.[34]

If these requirements have been met the employment can be considered appropriate. This would also fit in with the idea that flexible employment is not inferior. The requirements meet the demand in the market for efficient use of labour without

---

[32] Ministry of Social Affairs and Employment, 1996.
[33] FNV, 1996, p. 43 ff.
[34] Ministry of Social Affairs and Employment, 1987, p. 90 ff.

completely sacrificing social justice for the ever increasing group of people who have or have to accept flexible employment.

Conclusion

If a system is designed in which it is clear who is responsible for income and job security with more coherence between labour law and social security law the chances will increase that flexible employment will be more socially acceptable. This requires improved solidarity between workers in the sense that employees in permanent jobs will have to relinquish their securities to some extent in favour of flexible workers. This also requires the insight of employers that offering more security to flexible workers is in the end more efficient. Furthermore, the willingness of employers to provide more guarantees for flexible work will probably increase if in social security legislation such measures are taken with which to achieve an even distribution of risk.

For flexible workers such a system will offer better prospects as regards improvement of their position and maintaining employment.

The more flexibility and protection of the employee are combined the better the wish for improved efficiency can be met in a socially just way. Efficiency and social justice are not mutually exclusive but rather mutually supplemental.

References

Baenen, N., and L. Bosch, Flexibilisering van arbeid en individuele sociale zekerheidsrechten: blijft Katrijn afhankelijk van Jan?, Paper for the WESWA Conference of 13 November 1996.

Bolhuis, M. van, Externe flexibilisering, een onderzoek bij bedrijven, Inspectiedienst SZW, Ministerie van Sociale Zaken en Werkgelegenheid, May 1996, p. 6.

FNV, Tijd voor nieuwe zekerheid, 15 April 1996.

Klosse, S. en J.J. Schippers (red.), Met zekerheid naar de toekomst. Sociale zekerheid in Nederland op de drempel van de 21ste eeuw, Maklu, Antwerpen/Apeldoorn 1997.

KPMG, Bureau voor Economische Argumentatie BV, Niet-reguliere arbeid en werknemersverzekeringen, December 1995.

Ministerie van Sociale Zaken en Werkgelegenheid, Flexibele inzet van arbeidskrachten, November 1987, p. 90 ff.

Ministerie van Sociale Zaken en Werkgelegenheid, Flexibiliteit en Zekerheid, December 1995, p. 2.

Ministerie van Sociale Zaken en Werkgelegenheid, Flexibiliteit en Zekerheid, 3 April 1996, no. 2/96.

Ministerie van Sociale Zaken en Werkgelegenheid, Werken aan Zekerheid, PS 21, 2 October 1996.

Noordam, F.M. Inleiding Sociale Zekerheidsrecht, Deventer 1996.

Olbers, M.M., Geen Wulbz meisje maar een sloddervos, SR 1996, p. 85.

Sociale Nota 1996, TK 1995-1996, 24 402, no. 2.

Staay, A.J. van der, De plaats van de arbeid, ESB 17-1-1996, p. 55 ff.

36-Hours Working Week in Banking:
Efficient or Socially Justified?

Tineke Bahlmann, Maaike Lycklama à Nijeholt, Stella den Uijl, Bart Verkade

1 Introduction

Opinions with respect to the reduction of working hours differ. Supporters of reduction of working hours are of the opinion that the introduction of reduced working hours is a solution to the unemployment problem, whereas opponents of reduction state the opposite.

The collective labour agreement for banking was one of the first collective labour agreements in the Netherlands in which a 36-hours working week was agreed upon. The agreement was concluded on April 1st, 1995. By means of exploratory research, this paper investigates to what extent the 36-hours working week in banking is efficient or socially justified.

The central research question can be formulated as follows:
How do efficiency and social justice relate to each other with respect to the 36-hours working week in banking?

In order to answer the central research question, the following questions will be discussed:

* Why was the 36-hours working week in banking introduced? Do motives with respect to efficiency or social justice underlie this decision?
* How is the 36-hours working week in banking organized?
* To what extent is the 36-hours working week in banking efficient?
* To what extent is the 36-hours working week in banking socially justified?
* What possible changes could be made in order to improve the efficiency or social justice of the 36-hours working week in banking?

First of all, a description of the terms 'efficiency' and 'social justice' will be given in section 2. Section 3 deals with the attitude with regard to the reduction of working hours at macro level. Two visions with respect to the policy that the government should adopt on the labour market will be discussed, i.e. the free market vision and the redistribution vision. It will also be considered whether one of the above-mentioned visions can be applied to the policy of the Dutch government with respect to labour market issues. Furthermore, attention will be paid to the extent to which the reduction of working hours can be seen as efficient and/or socially justified at macro level.

Section 4 deals with the reduction of working hours at meso level. At this level, the answer to the first question will be given. The points of view of the trade unions and employers' organization concerning the reduction of working hours in banking at the time of collective bargaining will be looked into. Why did negotiators and the parties they represented finally agree on a 36-hours working week? Did motives with respect to social justice or rather efficiency underly this decision?

Section 5 discusses the reduction of working hours at the micro level. This paragraph provides an answer to the remaining questions. Finally, section 6 contains the conclusions. The central research question will also be answered in this section.

The nature of this research is exploratory. In order to answer the various questions and the central research question, seven interviews have been taken at three different types of bank: a cooperative banking society, a commercial bank and a savings-bank. In addition to this, two trade union leaders, who were closely involved with the collective bargaining in banking have been interviewed: Mr De Leeuw den Bouter (service sector CNV) and Mr Hamaker (FNV service sector). Furthermore, a literature research on the reduction of working hours has been carried out. Newspaper articles were frequently used in order to optimize the level of current events. Due to the limited number of interviews, general statements cannot be made. The aim of this research is to obtain a first impression of the relation between efficiency and social justice with respect to the 36-hours working week in banking.

2 Market Efficiency Versus Social Justice: A Description

Before we elaborate on the reduction of working hours, we present a definition of the terms market efficiency and social justice.

When deciding on the functioning of certain market types, three criteria[1] that help us with defining both concepts can be applied in economics. First, it is investigated to what extent a specific market type functions technically efficient. Is there for

---

[1]   See for instance Schöndorff *et al.*, p. 15.

126

instance waste of material? The level of *technical efficiency* is investigated by this first criterion. This type of efficiency can be described as "the extent to which, given the objectives, the final state that is to be reached, is reached at the sacrifice of as little means of production as possible".[2] The second criterion is the extent to which the allocation of the means of production to the possibilities of production corresponds to consumers' preferences. This is the degree of *economic efficiency*. Finally, the third criterion looks into the *equal opportunities* and *justice* of the division of means, income, knowledge and power for various market types.

With this description it is possible to speak of market efficiency if the first two criteria i.e. technical efficiency and economic efficiency have been fulfilled. We assume social justice if the third criterion has been met: equal opportunities and justice with respect to means, income, knowledge and power should be present.

According to Hessel[3] market efficiency is characterized by an individualistic exchange relation between the parties, in which these parties strive for their own interest. With social justice, it is recognized that this individualistic exchange relation is not sufficient in reality. Consequently, parties should take the interests of others into account to a certain extent. He states that the notion of social justice or social solidarity presumes an involvement in the interests of others that exceeds individualism.

If we apply the concepts market efficiency and social justice to the reduction of working hours, we come to the following descriptions.

The reduction of working hours is efficient if the introduction results in an increase in market efficiency, i.e. the balance of economic and technical efficiency. In this case, the reduction of working hours leads to a more efficient use of the means of production like labour and/or corresponds better to consumers' preferences.

The reduction of working hours is socially justified with respect to employees and outsiders[4] if its introduction leads to a higher level of equal opportunities. We do not only refer to the preservation and the redistribution of labour, but also to the extent of full employment qualitatively. Moreover, social justice surpasses one's work situation; the personal situation of the employees, including their personal choices, also plays a part.

---

2   Keuning *et al.*, p. 26.
3   Hessel *et al.*, p. 318.
4   Think about the unemployed labour force, for instance.

127

3 Macro Level: Two Visions With Respect to the Fight Against Unemployment and the Labour Market Policy in the Netherlands

3.1 Introduction

Measures to control unemployment have been a point of special interest in Dutch government policy since the Seventies. The growth of the working population and the rising productivity are two factors that are responsible for the high level of unemployment. At this moment, approximately 500,000 workers are without a job in the Netherlands. Is the reduction of working hours a solution to this problem?

3.2 Two Visions: The Free Market Vision and the Redistribution Vision

De Beer[5] mentions two visions with respect to the interference of the government on the labour market: the free market vision and the redistribution vision.
According to the free market vision the solution to unemployment can be sought in abolishing the interference of the government. This vision states that by removing the impediments on the labour market, the free market mechanism will be activated. Demand and supply on the labour market will balance each other in a natural way. As a result, full employment quantitatively will come into being. Anyway, forced unemployment will disappear: anyone who is willing to work should be able to find work. The free market mechanism can be stimulated by measures such as deregulation, flexibilization and decentralization. As concrete measures De Beer mentions the abolition of:
* minimum wages;
* mandatory collective labour contracts;
* the law on working hours;
* the law governing the hours of trading ("*winkelsluitingswet*");
* employment protection, and
* regulation of mediation and temporary employment.

Besides, by considerable budget cuts on social security expenditures premiums may be reduced in order to keep the wedge between gross labour costs and net income as low as possible. The economy will get more room to breathe[6] due to lower tax rates and decreased social security contributions.

---

[5]   De Beer, p. 64 *et seq.*
[6]   Crince Le Roy, p. 115.

Advocates of the redistribution vision acknowledge that the free market vision possibly leads to full employment quantitatively. However, they point out that because of the free market mechanism/laissez-faire mechanism no full employment qualitatively will arise. By simply laissez-faire a labour market might arise with a strong dichotomy between rich and poor. Jobs with unfavourable working conditions and wages that are too low to make a decent living could appear. Supporters of the free market vision defend themselves by claiming that everyone should be able to profit from the free market in case of persistent economic growth. However, those in favour of redistribution are of the opinion that the economic growth will not be high enough for this purpose.

De Beer states that the redistribution vision holds nothing against dynamics and flexibility per se, however, it would like to organize these concepts. Therefore, the redistribution vision argues in favour of a "revitalization of the institutions." According to this vision, the remission of employment is structural. Only by reorganizing labour, it is possible to create a sufficient level of employment (measured in persons!). In order to obtain good results, a consensus should be reached between trade unions, employers and government resulting in an agreement. According to De Beer, employees should agree to the flexibility demands of employers in exchange for shorter working hours. Employers on the other hand should not increase the pressure of work. They have to provide those employees who have care tasks with a full labour market position at work. According to De Beer specific government regulations in this respect consist of: making the shorter working hours financially more attractive by means of premium differentiation, introduction of legislation on part-time work and by positive discrimination in favour of employees with part-time jobs in collective labour agreements. This consensus is a prerequisite for the success of such a policy. In this way, full employment qualitatively and quantitatively can be realized. When no consensus is reached, full employment qualitatively is only left to a small number of employees. The others lose out. In this case, we are dealing with full employment qualitatively but not quantitatively.

3.3 Labour Market Policy in the Netherlands

Dutch labour market policy lies somewhere between these two visions. Depending on the spirit of the age, the policy inclined towards redistribution (Seventies) or towards free market (Eighties). At this moment, the government pursues the following lines of policy[7] to reduce unemployment:

* reinforcement of the economic structure;
* reduction of labour costs;
* subsidies with respect to labour costs and employment plans for the long-term unemployed.

Moreover, the government publicly prefers agreements on the reduction of working hours in collective labour agreements.[8] However, the government omits to make shorter working weeks more attractive financially. Furthermore, a new law on working hours ("*Arbeidstijdenwet*") became effective on January 1st, 1996. With this law, the government offers employers and employees the opportunity, within specified limits, to lay down[9] working hours by mutual agreement at company level. By doing so, the government tries to increase internal numerical flexibility.[10] Therefore, the labour market policy embodies ideas of both the free market vision and the redistribution vision.

3.4 Reduction of Working Hours: Efficient or Socially Justified?

The Central Planning Bureau[11] argues that reduction of working hours is an artificial limitation of the supply of labour, which is bound to have a negative effect on production and employment in the course of time. In the end more people will find a job. However, the total labour productivity expressed in working hours will diminish. The Central Planning Bureau predicts that a reduction of working hours towards 36 in the year 2000 will result in an employment growth of 83,000 persons

---

[7] Heij, p. 23.
[8] Hamaker, interview September 11th, 1996.
[9] Ministry of Social Affairs and Employment, February 1996.
[10] A definition of flexibility should be given here. Flexibility can be divided into internal and external flexibility. In case of internal flexibility, the regular workforce caters for the need of the variability of labour. In case of external flexibility, the needs are met by workers who do not belong to the organization. Futhermore, a distinction can be made between numerical and functional flexibility. Numerical flexibility relates to the adaptability of the workforce to variations in the volume of capacity demanded, whereas functional flexibility refers to the adaptability of the workforce to meet the task and job specifications. Internal numerical flexibility therefore concerns the adaptability of the labour of the regular workforce to variations in the volume of the capacity demands. (E. de Haan, *et al.*, p. 56). Whenever we refer to flexibility in the course of this article, we refer to internal numerical flexibility.
[11] C.E.P., p. 253 *et seq.*

at best and 21,000 at worst, provided there are pay cuts. The unemployed working population will then decrease with 73,000 and 19,000 persons respectively.[12] Without pay cuts, employment will increase with 38,000 persons at best and 1,000 persons at worst. The unemployed working population subsequently decreases with 29,000 or 0 persons, respectively. In any case, the employment/working hours ratio decreases.[13]

The opinions with respect to the results of the research performed by the Central Planning Bureau differ.

Vogelaar[14] for instance argues that the calculated employment increase of 83,000 persons at best by the Central Planning Bureau is rather poor. By combining the reduction of working hours with a prolongation of the hours of trading (by keeping the shops open during the evenings and on Saturday), better use can be made of capital goods. In this way, machinery could be kept going for a longer period of time. As a consequence, efficiency will improve and employment will increase more sharply than was estimated originally.

In the same article, Rinnooy Kan observes that the calculations of the Central Planning Bureau are based on a hidden surplus labour as a result of which shorter working hours will lead to an increase in productivity. However, in his opinion surplus labour has already been out of existence. Moreover, a reduction of working hours will mostly take place without pay cuts. Consequently, labour costs per hour will increase and harm employment. As a result, the competitive position of the Dutch business community will be jeopardized.

---

[12] The unemployed working population decreases less compared to the extent to which employment increases, due to the fact that the jobs created are not only filled by people who were formerly unemployed.

[13] The Central Planning Bureau presumes that, as a result of the bottlenecks in the introduction of the 36-hours working week, in the year 2000 a decrease in productive capacity in the market sector will occur of 15% at best and 30% at worst, expressed as a percentage of the reduction of working hours. At the same time, a productivity gain of 10% or 33% per working hour in relation with the reduction of working hours will occur. The Central Planning Bureau has taken two scenarios into account: one with a capacity loss of 15% and a productivity increase of 10% and one with a capacity loss of 30% and a productivity increase of 33%.

[14] *NRC Handelsblad*, 20-03-1996.

Kalma[15] points out that the labour costs per product unit only amount to 10% of the cost price in the industry and 5% in internationally competing enterprises. An increase in labour costs of 10% as a result of the introduction of the 36-hours working week without pay cuts will lead to a 1% increase of the cost price of the product in the industrial sector and to a 0.5% increase in internationally competing enterprises. According to Kalma, this increase can amply be compensated by an increase in productivity and/or a decrease in costs of public health due to a reduction of absenteeism. He does not mention a loss of capacity in relation with the reduction of working hours.

All this shows that the opinions with respect to the effects of the reduction of working hours differ. At present, it remains unclear to what extent the reduction of working hours increases efficiency and to what extent it enhances social justice. The future will reveal how these aspects relate to each other. In order to give an indication, we investigate whether and to what extent the introduction and implementation of a reduction of working hours will improve the efficiency and social justice in banking.

4 Meso Level: Reduction of Working Hours in Banking

4.1 Employment in Banking

Employment in banking is subject to pressure. Until 1990 employment continued to increase. However, since the beginning of the Nineties a reduction of the number of employees has been standing out. Mergers, reorganizations and the automation of payments contributed to this. Up until now, the decrease in workforce took place without dismissals. This was possible due to expensive redundancy schemes, the mobilization of outplacement agencies and by not renewing temporary employment contracts.

At present about 100,000 employees are employed in banking. However, a further reduction of the workforce is anticipated. Banking deals with fierce competition. The external competition is for instance caused by insurance companies, investment companies, lease and finance corporations.[16] The banks also compete among each other for a market share in niches, like for instance the market of the people of

---

[15] Kalma, *NRC-Handelsblad*, 7-5-1996.
[16] Coolen, p. 25.

substance. Finally, the competition with foreign banks increases further due to internationalization. Increased competition causes a reduction in costs policy,[17] which leads to a further decrease of employment. Dutch banks employ many people, compared to foreign banks. Due to automation processes, jobs of unskilled workers disappear. Especially back office acitivities are concerned here. At the same time, an important instrument in the competitive struggle is the quality of the supplied services and products[18] and the market activities. As a consequence, more jobs in the commercial front office and in the internationally operating sectors become available for highly-skilled workers. It is obvious that there is also a great demand for automation experts due to ever increasing automation. These employees are primarily recruited externally. This is caused by the discrepancy between the required level of qualification for new jobs and the level of education of current employees. Therefore, the banks deal with both an inflow and outflow as far as personnel is concerned. On average employment diminishes. It is to be expected that, all in all, at least 20,000 jobs will be lost in banking the next five years. As a consequence of the uncertainty, the percentage of union members has increased considerably. In 1988, only 9% of bank employees were members of trade unions, at present this percentage has increased to approximately 25 to 27.

4.2 The Points of View of Trade Unions and Employers' Organizations

Both trade unions and employers' organizations protect the interests of their members as best as they can. Per branch of industry, trade unions strive for good terms of employment and fringe benefits for the employees and for preservation of as many jobs as possible. In addition to this, the boards of the trade unions aim at social goals such as promotion of employment, environmental protection and encouragement of emancipation. Employers' organizations aim at as high a level of efficiency as possible for enterprises. Besides, their members have an interest in motivated employees and social ease among the workforce. Labour costs are a special point of interest on the agenda of employers' organizations. In general, labour costs should be reasonable: as low as possible, but high enough to motivate employees.

Employers' organizations are cautious with respect to a 36-hours working week. They only agree to a 36-hours working week, if this increases efficiency in the company. However, they fear an increase in labour costs if the introduction of a

---

[17] Tijdens, p. 188.
[18] Coolen, p. 25.

shorter working week is not coupled with pay cuts. Moreover, they argue that extra personnel has to be recruited, which leads to a further increase in costs. Furthermore, they foresee organizational problems as well as communication problems, as a result of which the overhead expenses will increase. They also point to the dangers of introducing the 36-hours working week for the entire workforce. According to the employers' organizations a 36-hours working week is not suitable for particular functions, such as those jobs where employees are being rewarded on the basis of certain job responsibilities and not on the basis of the number of hours that they have to be present in the company, or those jobs that are scarce on the labour market. Therefore, the employers' organizations consider the 36-hours working week as an instrument that decreases efficiency. They look upon the introduction of a shorter working week as the 'distribution of poverty'.

On the other hand, trade unions advocate the 36-hours working week. They view the shorter working week as a means to create additional employment or to prevent redundancies. In their opinion, a desired effect of the introduction of the 36-hours working week as a 4-days working week, is the fact that more leisure time becomes available that could, among other things, be spent on care for children or education. They point out that high wage claims could be prevented by entering into an agreement on the 36-hours working week. Furthermore, the productivity in companies that have surplus labour as a result of the introduction of the 36-hours working week can increase. Moreover, according to the trade unions a decrease in absenteeism might occur due to the extra leisure time.

Whereas efficiency is an important motive during collective bargaining for the employers' organizations, social justice is the basis for the trade unions. In the past, both parties fought for their own interests during the negotiations. Nowadays, mutual understanding grows.[19] The parties think along and together they try to find a solution which is based on increased efficiency as well as on social justice so that many interests of the parties can be realized.

Van Hoof[20] argues that employers' organizations will agree to the proposal to reduce working hours as long as they see an opportunity to fit it in with their own purposes. For instance, they could use the reduction of working hours to push back internal surplus labour and to increase flexibility in working hours. According to Van Hoof, flexibility in working hours could considerably save labour, because the

---

[19]   De Leeuw den Bouter, interview 26th August 1996.
[20]   Van Hoof, p. 165-166.

deployment of workers can be better geared to fluctuations in production. Further-more, within the service industries business hours can be adapted to the consumers' wishes.

In current collective bargaining the exchange between the reduction of working hours and flexibility of working hours is often made. Possibly, an improvement in efficiency as well as an improvement in social justice may ensue from this exchange.

4.3 Collective Bargaining in Banking

The most important task of the trade unions[21] as far as collective bargaining in banking is concerned, was to prevent as many redundancies among employees as possible.[22] As mentioned before, banking deals with an outflow of unskilled personnel (especially administrative staff in back office functions) as well as with an inflow of skilled personnel, commercial staff in particular. Overall, employment decreases. In order to maintain employment, trade unions demanded a 34-hours working week for the entire staff, preferably scheduled in 4 days per week. Later on in the negotiations, they demanded a 36-hours working week, again preferably spread over 4 days. The shorter working week was asked for the entire staff, and not only for unskilled workers. The reason for this lies in the fact that the trade unions did not want to mark these unskilled workers as superfluous. In their opinion, the morale of personnel could decrease. Moreover, during the spare time thus created, unskilled workers could be trained and afterwards move on to functions that became vacant due to reduction of working hours and which did not suffer from a personnel surplus before reduction of working hours. According to the trade unions, the loss of jobs for unskilled workers could not be prevented due to automation processes that increased the level of efficiency. By introducing a shorter working week for the entire staff, the moment when redundancies for the unskilled workers become inevitable can be postponed. This can be viewed as an extension of the brake path.[23] Until 1998, there will be no redundancies. Unskilled workers could use this time to study in order to meet the requirements of positions inside or outside banking. Therefore, trade unions asked for education for their employees, so that they could attend training courses or be retrained for internal or external functions. In exchange, the trade unions offered the employers' organizations to agree to a pay freeze for three years and an extension of business hours and consequently the working hours

---

[21] FNV, CNV, BBV, VHP and UNIE.

[22] De Leeuw den Bouter, interview 26th August 1996; Hamaker, interview 11th September 1996.

[23] De Leeuw den Bouter, interview 26th August 1996.

of employees. Furthermore, demands with respect to the mobility of employees would no longer constitute a problem.

The trade unions looked upon the offer of 'a shorter working week and greater flexibility' as a package deal; only the entire package was under negotiation. It was impossible to proceed with only one part of the deal.

The primary concern of the employers' organization[24] was to guarantee efficiency for the banks. In other words, the aim of the organization was to strive for the maintenance of 'commercial strength'[25] both nationally and internationally.[26] In addition to this, it is very important for the banks to keep up their reputation as a solid sector, as it provides a high level of security to the customers. Therefore, the banks cannot afford unrest among their personnel as a consequence of possible redundancies due to automation and bad publicity.[27]

The employers' organization offered a 32-hours working week for unskilled personnel only. This way, redundancies could be avoided for the next three years. In the meantime, employees could prepare themselves for another job inside or outside banking by means of training. Later on in the negotiations, the employers' organization offered a 36-hours working week, provided that the hours did not necessarily have to be put into 4 days and provided that the employers could determine which employees could be excepted from the 36-hours working week.

Initially, the employers' organization did not want to agree to a generic reduction of working hours, since commercial customer-oriented consultancy functions and functions in the internationally operating sectors are scarce. Besides, the organization offered career training and courses by means of an interbanking vocational-training scheme.

Furthermore, the employers' organization asked for more flexibility, meaning flexible working hours to extend the hours of business.

In March 1995 the parties came to an agreement.
The basic principles of the new collective labour agreement[28] were:
* preservation of employment by means of reorganization;

---

[24] WGVB.
[25] Commercial strength is understood to mean the capacity to keep on fighting the commercial battle.
[26] De Leeuw den Bouter, interview 26th August 1996; Hamaker, interview 11th September 1996.
[27] For this reason, the unions reached for newspaper publicity a number of times, in order to strengthen their negotiating position.
[28] Klijn, p. 11.

*   flexibilization;
*   decentralization of labour relations.

The spearheads of the collective labour agreement that became effective on April 1st, 1995 are: not later than October 1st, the 36-hours working week will in principle be introduced for the entire staff. After the 36-hours working week has been introduced, the employer has the possibility to extend the hours of business. Only for working on Saturdays, the employees will receive a bonus of 25% of the hourly wage. The division of individual working hours is decided by mutual agreement. The preferences of the employee are taken as a starting point, unless organizational impediments are present. If the latter is the case, the employer has to account for the impediments.[29] The reduction of working hours has to be accompanied by recognizable spare time for the employee. This means that the employee minimally ought to get half a day off per week or one day off every fortnight. From a business point of view, the employer has the possiblity to determine deviant working hours for groups or individual employees. This rule can only be applied in exceptional cases and should be presented and substantiated to the works council. Deviant working hours may not exceed 40 hours per week on average. The hours in between the 36th and 40th working hour can be saved up. These individually saved hours can be used for special activities preceding early retirement, to raise income during the early retirement or pension scheme, to study for a certain period of time as agreed with the employer. They can also be paid out in part at 116.33% with a maximum of 128 hours and/or the use of maximally 80 extra spare hours per year. On October 1st, 1997, the entire workforce will get a pay increase of 2%.

The motives of trade unions with respect to a 36-hours working week in banking originated from the pursuit of social justice: a 36-hours working week for the entire staff, to prevent inequality on the one hand and to reduce unemployment on the other hand. The motives of the employers' organizations can be traced to the promotion of efficiency interests of their members: the members agreed, because the reduction of working hours was accompanied by an extension of business hours. Furthermore, it is very important for the banks to keep up their reputation as a solid sector. Therefore, the banks cannot afford unrest among their personnel as a result of possible redundancies. Both parties have an interest in an extension of the 'brake path'.

---

[29] In case of disputes, individual employees can invoke the internal right of complaint. Groups of employees and their executives can settle their disputes in consultation between the manager and the works council.

During the negotiations, parties sympathized with each other. The trade unions recognized the fact that some of the unskilled workers lacked motivation for education.[30] In conclusion we can say that the reduction of working hours went hand in hand with flexibility, and consequently, the pursuit of social justice was accompanied by the pursuit of efficiency in the collective labour bargaining. The interests of employers' organizations in efficiency and those of trade unions in social justice could both be accounted for in the collective labour agreement.

5 Micro Level: The 36-Hours Working Week in Three Different Types of Bank

5.1 Introduction

As mentioned above, the concluded collective labour agreement leaves much room for case-specific interpretation per bank. The collective labour agreement allows employers to determine varying working hours for individual employees or groups of employees of maximally 40 hours per week, if it is in the interest of the company. However, the collective labour agreement intends to allow as few exceptions as possible to this rule. The purpose of this paragraph is to give an idea as to how the 36-hours working week was introduced in three different banks: a cooperative banking society, a bank that used to be a commercial bank and a bank that used to be a savings-bank. Besides, for all three banks the level of efficiency and social justice of the 36-hours working week will be investigated, as well as possible improvements that can be made. In order to investigate this seven employees were interviewed: in the cooperative banking society, a district manager and a member of the working group that implemented the collective labour agreement were interviewed; in the former commercial bank, a district manager, an account manager and a cash manager were interviewed and finally, an account manager and the chairman of the central works council were interviewed on behalf of the former savings-bank. The number of bank employees that were interviewed is limited. As a consequence, it is not possible, and in our opinion quite useless, to rank the answers for various groups of employees. However, we strove to interview those employees that were closely connected to the introduction of the collective labour agreement, and who consequently have a clear insight in current matters with respect to the 36-hours working week. The 36-hours working week was not yet introduced

---

[30]   De Leeuw den Bouter, interview 26th August 1996.

at the work stations of two of the persons who were being interviewed[31] at the time the interviews took place. As far as the other interviewed persons are concerned, they had been dealing with the 36-hours working week for a couple of months. Therefore, the opinions of the interviewees with respect to the extent of efficiency and social justice of the 36-hours working week in banking concern first impressions and/or expectations. The interviews were taken on the basis of a questionnaire (see appendix). Some time before the interviews took place, the persons involved received an explanation with respect to the research. The explanation contained a description of efficiency and social justice, as mentioned in section 2.

Besides the above-mentioned interviews, this section also made use of interviews with Mr Hamaker (FNV) and Mr De Leeuw den Bouter (CNV). Finally, in order to find out how the 36-hours working week was introduced we used the collective labour agreement in banking itself as well as newspaper acticles and research reports of the FNV.

5.2 Ways in Which the 36-hours Working Week was Introduced in Banking[32]

Of the three investigated banks, the cooperative banking society introduced the 36-hours working week for almost the entire staff. Only members of the board of directors were exempted. In some cases, the employees were free to choose whether they wanted to work 36 hours a week or whether they wanted to be exempted from this rule. This especially holds for specialist functions. In the summer of 1995, the bank started with a number of pilot projects.

Also, the original savings-bank introduced the 36-hours working week for almost the entire workforce. Again, as few employees as possible were excluded from the 36-hours working week, in order to prevent an outflow of personnel. The employees had to ask for exemption if they wished to be excluded from the 36-hours working week.

---

[31]   The interviewed employees of the cooperative banking society are being referred to here. However, these persons are closely involved in the implementation of the 36-hours working week, and have, as a result of this, a very good idea of the effects of the shorter working week.

[32]   At the moment of writing this paper, not all branch offices of the above-mentioned banks have introduced the 36-hours working week. However, a large number of outlets did introduce the 36-hours working week. The preparations for introducing the 36-hours working week in all branches are at an advanced stage. Therefore, a good impression can be obtained as to how the 36-hours working week will be introduced in various types of bank.

Both in the cooperative banking society and in the savings-bank, 5% to 10% of the employees were exempted from the 36-hours working week. It is striking that this percentage is much higher for the commercial bank. Here, 22% of the employees have been excluded from the 36-hours working week.

Whereas the cooperative banking society and the savings-bank introduced the 36-hours working week for as many employees as possible, the commercial bank exempted a substantial percentage of its employees from the shorter working week. Mr. De Leeuw den Bouter argues that there is a connection between the origins of the different banks and the way in which the 36-hours working week was introduced. As far as the origin of the banks is concerned, De Leeuw den Bouter makes a distinction between banks that originate from 'Dutch clay' and banks that originate from the 'tea plantation.' The cooperative banking society has its origins in 'Dutch clay.' The bank started out as a cooperation of farmers for farmers. The members could and still can draw their strength from this financial cooperation. The organizational structure of this bank is decentral due to the cooperative background. The investigated savings-bank is a savings-bank for the people from way back and can therefore also be considered a bank with a 'Dutch clay' background. The commercial bank has its origins in the 'tea plantation.' This bank focuses on commerce, aims at as high a level of efficiency as possible and is characterized by a strong hierarchical structure. In the meantime, the banks grow more and more towards one another as far as their activities are concerned. At present, the banks also have to focus on as a high a level of efficiency as possible to beat the competition. To give an example, the cooperative banking society has just recruited several external directors in order to increase the efficiency mentality in the company. It may be clear that sometimes a difference of opinion occurs between the directors that are strongly oriented towards efficiency and the general management. However, according to Mr. De Leeuw den Bouter, the original background of the banks determines the way in which the 36-hours working week is introduced for their personnel.

5.3 The Level of Efficiency and Social Justice of the 36-Hours Working Week in Banking

One of the questions that was asked during the interview was whether there would be any efficiency improvements as a result of the 36-hours working week. The following answers were given (the answers are ranked in order of importance; the answers that were given most frequently are at the top. All answers are mentioned[33]).

* The introduction of the 36-hours working week coincides with an extension of business hours. As a result of this extension, people can work more customer-oriented, which increases efficiency. Moreover, during off hours, like Monday mornings, (a part of) the office could be closed, which reduces costs.
* The level of absenteeism possibly decreases, because employees are better able to visit a doctor or a dentist in their own time. Moreover, due to the extra spare time employees rest better and as a result, they probably become ill less quickly.[34]
* As a result of the reduction of working hours, employees have to be able to perform the tasks of their colleagues. Because of this, the interchangeability of personnel is expected to increase.
* Extra spare time that arises as a result of the reduction of working hours can be used for self-education.
* Due to the high level of absence as a result of the 36-hours working week, the cash department of the commercial bank has opted for an extra means of communication: the cash employees are informed as to what happened during the previous week by means of a circular letter. Part-time employees, who until recently were less informed about current events, take advantage of this. The overview with respect to the work that is or has to be done has improved by this.
* In case the 36-hours working week is introduced for employees, who in reality work many more hours per week, introduction of the shorter working week can be seen as a form of restraint of the costs of hourly wages. We will come back to this later on in this section.
* As a result of overcapacity of especially unskilled workers productivity has been improved by the 36-hours working week.

The question 'will the level of efficiency change for the worse' resulted in the following reactions.

---

[33] This also applies to answers on the questions below.

[34] Apart from that, the director of a chain of banks of the cooperative banking society argues that the level of absenteeism has been extremely low the last few years. He suspects that this emanates from fear of dismissal. A further decrease of absenteeism has not been perceived yet, nor does he think it desirable.

* As a consequence of the absence of employees due to the reduction of working hours, internal gearing and communication problems occur.
* The absence of employees, due to the reduction of working hours results in a deterioration of their accessibility for the customers. As a consequence, a loss of 'commercial strength' might occur.
* Due to the reduction of working hours, it is necessary to recruit extra (often unskilled) staff short term. As a result, labour costs will increase for the banks.
* As a result of the generic introduction of the 36-hours working week, even for those function groups that do not have overcapacity, a shortage of available knowledge occurs in certain fields.
* As a consequence of the reduction of working hours, the involvement in work decreases. This has a negative effect on productivity.
* Because people work less, they also learn less.

The following positive effects of the 36-hours working week on social justice were mentioned.

* As a result of the reduction of working hours, redundancies among superfluous workers come at a later stage. In the meantime, employees that are threatened with dismissal are enabled to increase their job opportunities inside or outside banking by means of education.
* The generic reduction of working hours increases job opportunities for super-fluous staff within their own company, provided that people actually work 36 hours and that no loyalty hours will be made.
* Due to the reduction of working hours short term employment increases in banking. As far as the lower function groups are concerned, the growth in employment will only be temporary.
* The reduction of working hours might improve the family situation as well as emancipation: more time arises for child care and household work.
* The extension of the hours of business that coincided with the reduction of working hours can have a positive effect on emancipation: by chosing different working hours the partners are able to share child care and household work.
* As a consequence of the reduction of working hours, the employees are able to use the extra spare time they get every week or fortnight for self-development. As a result, their welfare increases.
* The reduction of working hours makes mutual agreements with respect to working hours and job responsibilities necessary. The obligatory communication that is required may lead to an improvement of mutual understanding.

Certain aspects of the introduction of the 36-hours working week are considered to be socially inequitable.

* The generic introduction of the 36-hours working week is thought of as unjust, if it is applied to employees who have a much longer working week in practice and whose job responsibilities are not made easier.
* Because not all banks introduced the 36-hours working week for the entire staff, the danger arises that employees that are allowed to work 36 hours in one bank are being pinched by other banks where they are allowed to work 40 hours per week.
* Due to the fact that the employees are less present at work, social contacts decrease.[35]
* The extension of business hours that coincided with the reduction of working hours might have a negative effect on the employee's social life, because he sometimes has to work evenings or Saturdays.

A number of the answers are incompatible. As far as efficiency is concerned, the advantage of extra time to study is opposed to the fact that one learns less because one works less. The restraint of the costs of hourly wages seems contradictory to the fact that it is necessary to recruit extra personnel in the short term. However, the former refers to higher personnel, whereas the latter refers to lower functions.[36]
As far as social justice is concerned, it is striking that the extension of business hours is considered both an advantage and a disadvantage. On the one hand there might be a positive effect on the employee's family situation (improvement of emancipation), on the other hand the employee's social life might be subject to pressure. In our opinion, the prevailing point of view depends on the specific situations of the employees and whether the 36-hours working week is introduced by mutual agreement.

The advantages and disadvantages with respect to the 36-hours working week as far as efficiency and social justice are concerned, are based on expectations or experiences over a couple of months. Therefore, it is not possible to determine how these aspects relate to each other. However, it may be observed that efficiency and social justice need not be mutually exclusive.

---

[35] The fact that not everybody is able to visit the Friday afternoon gathering anymore was given as an example.
[36] For a further explanation, see also paragraph 5.4 on the difference between job culture jobs and hour culture jobs.

5.4 Recommendations to Improve the 36-hours Working Week

The question 'which changes should be made in order to limit or prevent certain disadvantages of the 36-hours working week' primarily resulted in solutions with respect to efficiency.

It was suggested that the internal gearing and communication problems could be mended:
*   by having the employees take their extra spare time off per week or fortnight on fixed but different days, so that it becomes clear when they will be absent;
*   by determining a daily period per week on which all employees should be present in order to hold meetings, *et cetera*;
*   by making sure that the employee can be reached even when he is absent.

Furthermore, it was suggested that the accessibility for customers could be improved:
*   by assigning more than one contact per customer;
*   by making sure that the employee can be reached even when he is absent.

Finally, the following solution was given with respect to the problem of the shortage of available knowledge as a result of lacking overcapacity for introducing the 36-hours working week: let the part-time employees in those functions temporarily make more hours. However, in our opinion this solution is not applicable to higher functions, because these functions are rarely performed by part-timers.

Two disadvantages of the 36-hours working week can be traced to the generic introduction of the shorter working week, i.e. a disadvantage concerning efficiency and a disadvantage with respect to social justice. The former is caused by a shortage of available knowledge that arises in those function groups that lacked overcapacity before the 36-hours working week was introduced. The latter is caused because part of the employees actually work more than 36 hours per week.

If one takes a closer look at the situation in banking, two different types of job can be distinguished. The distinction is determined by the way the jobs are organized. The first type of job concerns those functions in which the employees have to be at the office for a specified number of hours per day, on the basis of which the employees are being paid. Examples would be an operator or a cash employee. It often concerns functions of unskilled personnel. There is talk of a so-called hour culture. In the second type of job, the employees have certain job responsibilities. The employees are being rewarded on the basis of their responsibilities. Examples of these functions are an account manager or a director. Often functions of highly-skilled workers are involved here. This is the so-called job culture. Whereas the hour culture is suitable for the 36-hours working week, the job culture is characterized by a far more complex situation.[37] The generic introduction of the 36-hours working week is a bitter pill for job culture employees who often work more than 36 hours per week. Especially these employees refer to the social unjustice of the introduction of the 36-hours working week. As far as the problem of the shortage of available knowledge due to the generic introduction of the 36-hours working week concerns job culture jobs, the employees continue to work the old number of hours in order to perform their tasks, despite the 36-hours working week. This seems an improper solution for the problem. In this respect, the position of the commercial bank which excluded 22% of the staff from the 36-hours working week can be defended from the point of view of social justice as far as the job culture employees are concerned.

However, the line of reasoning that advocates a generic introduction of the 36-hours working week can easily be followed as well. If the 36-hours working week would only be introduced for hour culture employees, the possibilities for superfluous personnel to be transferred to higher functions decrease. The danger of a so-called double labour market within banking will arise: a market that is on the one hand characterized by scarce job culture jobs and on the other hand by superfluous hour culture jobs. In that case a clear dividing line can be perceived. The employees of the hour culture jobs are expected to show solidarity and share labour. The above results in a dichotomy of the labour market with little transfer possibilities from the hour culture market to the job culture market. This does not favour social justice.

In our opinion, the reduction of job responsibilities of job culture jobs provides a solution for the problem: a 36-hours working week can actually apply to skilled personnel. Before the reduction of job responsibilities can actually take place, it is necessary to have sufficient skilled workers available to take over the tasks that become free. For this reason we think that the reduction of responsibilities cannot take place immediately. Therefore in our view, a formal 36-hours working week for the entire staff of the job culture is not socially justified in the short run. However, in our point of view one should nevertheless work towards an actual 36-hours working week. This cannot be realized immediately. The cooperative banking society and the former savings-bank have already formally introduced the 36-hours working week for employees of the job culture. Even though this is not socially justified for

---

[37]   Van Bergen, 1996.

job culture employees in the short term, from a social justice point of view it is the best option for all employees in the long term. In the case job culture employees, the 36-hours working week should be accompanied by a reduction of job responsibilities in the future. The skilled workers that were interviewed admitted that a reduction of job responsibilities might be a solution. However, in their opinion, the reduction of job responsibilities remains a problem for small banks with relatively few employees. They emphasize that the reduction of job responsibilities also requires a change in mentality of the public: for instance, people should be willing to deal with two directors.

Apart from that, it should be remarked that transfers of superfluous unskilled workers to higher positions are not always possible. Promotion is not possible for those employees who have already reached the height of their powers, despite extra training.

6 Conclusions

The main reason why the 36-hours working week was introduced in banking had to do with the fact that employers saw a possibility to increase efficiency. In exchange for the 36-hours working week an extension of business hours, which leads to a more customer-oriented approach, was agreed upon by collective bargaining. Furthermore, it is of the utmost importance for the banks to keep up their reputation as a solid sector, as it provides a high level of security to the customers. Therefore, the banks cannot afford unrest among their personnel as a result of possible redundancies due to automation. As a result of the 36-hours working week dismissal of employees is off for the moment and industrial peace has returned.

The most important motive of the trade unions with respect to the introduction of the 36-hours working week as regards social justice: the trade unions wanted to prevent as many redundancies as possible.

The way in which the 36-hours working week has been introduced in different banks strongly depends on the background of those banks. Although all the banks, due to fierce competition, focus on an efficiency increase and grow more and more towards one another as far as their activities are concerned, it appears that two of the banks that we investigated which had a 'Dutch clay' background introduced the 36-hours working week for almost the entire staff, whereas the bank that originated from commerce exempted 22% of its employees from the 36-hours working week.

From the interviews with the employees it may be concluded that the introduction of the 36-hours working week might result in changes for the better and for the worse as far as efficiency is concerned. One of the efficiency improvements is the extension of business hours that coincided with the introduction of the 36-hours working week. An efficiency deterioration that was often mentioned concerned the gearing and communication problems that occurred as a result of the absence of employees. According to the persons that were interviewed, these problems could partially be solved by assigning a fixed absence day for every employee as well as a day on which all staff have to be present.

As a result of the introduction of the 36-hours working week, the moment when dismissals become inevitable can be postponed. This extension of the brake path is one of the socially justified aspects of the 36-hours working week. In the meantime, employees can attend training courses or can be retrained, so that they can possibly move on to another job. The generic introduction of the 36-hours working week is sometimes looked upon as socially inequitable for those employees who actually work many more hours per week. The problem of job culture versus hour culture becomes apparent here. However, if job culture employees would be excluded from the 36-hours working week, the danger of a double labour market arises. In our opinion, this is also socially inequitable. A solution for this problem can be found in reducing job responsibilities of job culture jobs.

In our view, reducing job responsibilities cannot occur immediately; undercapacity may occur since these functions often lack overcapacity. Other workers have to be adequately trained first before they can take over these tasks. At present, generic introduction of the 36-hours working week has already taken place in the cooperative banking society and in the former savings-bank. In our view, this is not socially justified for job culture employees in the short term. In the long term it will help social justice, provided that the shorter working week is accompanied by a reduction of job responsibilities. The job culture employees of the commercial bank are often excluded from the 36-hours working week. In the short term, this is socially justified for these workers, however, it is not socially justified for the entire staff. Interviews with higher personnel of all banks show that a 36-hours working week for job culture employees can take place not only formally but also actually. However, a change in mentality of the public (including the customers) is necessary then.

Due to the limited number of interviews, no general conclusions can be drawn. The aim of this paper is to obtain an impression as to how efficiency and social justice relate to each other with respect to the 36-hours working week in banking. Because the 36-hours working week in banking is combined with flexibility it can increase the level of efficiency and be socially justified at the same time, provided the introduction is implemented correctly. Here, efficiency and social justice are not opposed to each other, but next to each other.

Appendix. Questionnaire 36-hours Working Week in Banking

1. What has been the reason for your bank to introduce the 36-hours working week?

2. In terms of market efficiency and social justice, what motives did prevail when the 36-hours working week was introduced? Can these motives be qualified as efficient or socially justified?

3. What was the attitude with respect to the introduction of the 36-hours working week from the side of the
    – employers/board of directors
    – employees
    – higher personnel
    – lower personnel
    – employers' organizations
    – trade unions?

4. What demands did the above-mentioned parties make with respect to the introduction of the 36-hours working week?

5. * In what way has the 36-hours working week been introduced/did you introduce the 36-hours working week (how many hours per day, how many days per week, for which personnel)?
    * What were the reasons to introduce the 36-hours working week in this specific way?
    * What were the advantages/disadvantages thereof?

6. As far as efficiency is concerned, what are the benefits of the introduction of the 36-hours working week?

7. What are/were the disadvantages with respect to efficiency when your company introduced the 36-hours working week (accessibility for customers, problems with respect to communication or coordination, *et cetera*)?

8. Can/could these disadvantages be solved while preserving the 36-hours working week?
    If so, how?

9. In your opinion, do the advantages of the 36-hours working week counter-balance the disadvantages?

10. * Has the 36-hours working week been introduced for the entire workforce?
    * If yes/no, can this be seen as advantageous or disadvantageous?

11. * If the 36-hours working week has only been introduced for part of the workforce; do you think there is a chance of dividing the workforce in two groups, i.e. a group that is being paid on the basis of their presence and a group that is being paid for finishing certain tasks (hour culture jobs vs. job culture jobs)?
    * If this is the case, what about:
      – mobility between the two groups?
      – motivation of the employees that belong to one of the groups?
      – relations between the two groups?

12. Do you think that a strict introduction of the 36-hours working week is possible for higher personnel and members of the board of directors? If so why, if not why not?

13. Do you think the employment situation of highly-skilled female personnel is improved by a strict introduction of the 36-hours working week, compared to that of the male workforce?

14. In your opinion, is the introduction of the 36-hours working week socially justified or socially inequitable
    – with respect to the prevention of unemployment among the current work-force?
    – with respect to higher vs. lower personnel?
    – in any other way?

15. In your opinion, do the advantages balance the disadvantages as far as social justice is concerned?

* * *

References

Beer, P. de, De Filosofie achter het werkgelegenheidsbeleid, in: F. Huijgen, A. Glebbeek, N. van den Heuvel, R. Kunnen, W. Salverda, J. Siegers, Naar volwaardige werkgelegenheid? SISWO publikatie 394, Amsterdam 1995, p. 57-79.

Bergen, A. van, Winnen bij 36 uur, Elsevier, 13 April 1996, p. 66-71.

Bergen, A. van, CAO-onderhandelingen, Elsevier, 4 May 1996.

Centraal Planbureau, Centraal Economisch Plan 1996, SDU uitgevers, Den Haag 1996.

CNV, Medicijn of miskleun?, CNV-opinie, no. 4.

Coolen, S.E., De 36-urige werkweek in het bankbedrijf, thesis under the authority of the FNV, vakgroep personeelswetenschappen, Katholieke Universiteit Brabant, February 1996.

Correia, I.H., Efficiency and equity: is there a trade-off?.

Crince Le Roy, E.A.W. en L.J. Emmerij, Het nieuwe herverdelingsvraagstuk, Economische Statistische Berichten, 1 February 1995, p. 114-116.

Danko, Q, Korter werken, meer banen?, Financieel Economisch Management, 19 August 1995, p. 52-53.

Delsen, L., atypical employment: an international perspective, Groningen 1995.

FNV, Korter werken voor meer banen, third edition, April 1983.

Haan, E. de, P. Vos en P. de Jong, Flexibiliteit van de arbeid: op zoek naar zekerheid, Welboom Bladen, Amsterdam 1994.

Hessel, B., J.A. den Hertog, C.E.M. Schutte, F.K. Sprik en J.B. Wezeman, Sociaal en Economisch recht: grensvlak van markt en overheid, Wolters Noordhoff, Groningen 1995.

Heij, J.J., Kabinet is ATV vergeten, Intermediair, 29 September 1995, p. 23-25.

Hoof, J. van, De arbeidsmarkt als arena: arbeidsmarktproblemen in sociologisch perspectief, Uitgeverij SUA, fifth edition, January 1994.

Inspectiedienst SZW, CAO-afspraken 1996, eerste interim rapportage, May 1996

Inspectiedienst SZW, Flexibilisering van de Arbeid: een onderzoek naar flexibilisering in CAO's, May 1996.

Jong, O. de, De Harde strijd van FME, Elsevier, 6 January 1996, p. 60-61.

Kalma, D.R., Korter werken betekent niet minder produceren, NRC-Handelsblad, 7 mei 1996.

Klijn, A., De invoering van de 36-urige werkweek in het bankbedrijf: onderzoek naar het proces van implementatie van de 36-urige werkweek en de uitkomsten van dit proces, thesis under the authority of the FNV, vakgroep algemene economie, Universiteit van Amsterdam, August 1996.

Ministerie van Sociale Zaken en Werkgelegenheid, Arbeidsduurverkorting onderzocht: terugblik en perspectief, Den Haag 1987.

Ministerie van Sociale Zaken en Werkgelegenheid, Ervaringen met de vierdaagse werkweek, Den Haag, March 1992.

Ministerie van Sociale Zaken en Werkgelegenheid, Arbeidstijdenwet (ATW), a new regulation for both trade and industry and the government, Den Haag, February 1996.

Pollet, I. en H. de Witte, Werknemers over arbeidsherverdeling en ADV, bijdrage voor sociaal wetenschappelijke studiedagen 1996, Sessie IOE, Katholieke Universiteit Leuven.

Sociale Zaken, VNO/NCW: Voorwaarden aan 36-urige werkweek, no. 3, 16 January 1996.

Tijdens, K., De kwalitatieve structuur van de werkgelegenheid in het bankwezen, in: F. Huijgen, A. Glebbeek, N. van den Heuvel, R. Kunnen, W. Salverda, J. Siegers, Naar volwaardige werkgelegenheid?, SISWO publikatie 394, Amsterdam 1995, p. 179-191.

Waal, L. de, Timmer vecht tegen de bierkaai, Financieel Economisch Management, p. 15-17.

The Pension Dilemma, a Matter of Efficiency Versus Equity?

Mies Westerveld

1 The Problem in its Perspective

'The relationship between market efficiency and social equity is one of the central problems of our modern welfare state. Many claim that the so called crisis of the welfare state is due to the fact that there has been too much emphasis on equity, causing the market processes which are essential to a sound economy to stagnate.'

Old age pension schemes, the subject of this article, are also affected by this crisis which the welfare state is suffering from. But here the underlying causes are, as we shall see, infinitely more complex than the afore suggested dichotomy of efficiency versus equity. The nature of this complexity affects in its turn the question of how to deal with the matter. In fact, the question of the most equitable as well as the most efficient option – or if this is not possible: the best possible mix of the two – might very well be one to which 'the' answer does not exist. More likely than not a person's preference for one option or the other is more a matter of political background or firmly rooted convictions than the result of thorough scientific research.[1] For this reason, speculations on the best or second best scheme are not the object of this article. Instead, I intend to give an analysis of what I call the pension dilemma, that is: the fact that the present scheme no longer suits our present needs, while an obvious alternative does not seem to be at hand.

I will start with a brief and, inevitably, superficial description of the history of our pension scheme, or, putting it in reverse order: where do we stand now with this

---

[1] This does not mean efforts to put the matter in a scientific perspective have not been made. Recently (spring of 1995) a doctoral thesis was published, dedicated to conceiving the optimum rate of 'efficiency' and 'effectiveness' within a pension scheme. To this end the author – an economist who works for a large company pension scheme – made an inventory of the attributes of which a pension scheme is made up and tested them to either of these two (in his opinion vital) criteria. His effort, interesting though it is, did not convince me that the objectively best pension scheme exists or can be constructed. Pension schemes are, after all, in all instances products of political choices and, as such, debatable. Breunesse, 1995.

scheme and how did we get there? This description implies an inventory of the afore suggested pension dilemma, but apart from this, I will look at the question whether this dilemma and its several aspects can be classified as a dichotomy of equity versus efficiency, and if so, how? For this classification I use both terms in their first meaning,[2] that is to say that 'equity' stands for 'the quality of being fair and reasonable in a way that gives equal treatment to everyone', and 'efficiency' for 'the quality of being able to do a task successfully and without wasting time or energy'. I will end the article with a brief conclusion on the nature of the pension dilemma and the question what is, in my opinion, needed to deal with it.

2 Charactistics of the Dutch Pension Scheme and its Role Model, the British Pension Scheme

Old age pension schemes are generally made up of three so called layers of pension, not only in the Netherlands, but in several western European countries.[3] These are: the state pension scheme, the, in many instances, obligatory occupational, or rather company schemes[4] and the personal provisions people may (or may not) buy for themselves. In the Netherlands, the first layer is part of its social insurance scheme and is obligatory for all residents; the second layer is semi-obligatory, that is only for employers, who are active within a branch of industry for which a pension scheme has been declared obligatory[5] by the minister of Social Affairs and

---

[2] Collins Cobuild English language dictionary (1992).

[3] In France and Germany the three particles are referred to as 'pillars' (*les trois pilliers*, the *3-Säulen-Prinzip*). In the Netherlands the terms 'pillars' (*pijlers*), 'steps' (*trappen*) and 'layers' (*lagen*) are used. On this, see: Dietvorst, 1994, p. 53. In this article I will use the latter, which in the Netherlands was introduced by Lutjens, as it provides a better visualisation of the present situation than its international counterpart. In the minds of most people, the three parts are supposed to add up to one net result, not stand side by side, as pillars do, carrying this result.

[4] The term 'company schemes' I have borrowed from Colin Steward (Director Parliamentary and International Affairs at the National Association of Pension Funds in London) who introduced this in his speech at the Conference Pensioenmarkt 2000 as 'a reasonable compromise' between (the British) 'occupational pension scheme' and (the Dutch) 'supplementary pension scheme'. See for the complete text: Steward, 1995.

[5] If this is not the case, the employer is free to either a) participate in the branch's scheme, if existent, b) form his own company scheme, c) buy a series of pension contracts for his workers at an insurance company or d) do nothing. Employees have considerably less choice in this. Once an employer has made up his mind as to a certain type of company pension scheme, the individual worker has no option but to participate in it.

Employment;[6] while the third is completely voluntary. In this respect the scheme somewhat resembles the British scheme, which also contains an obligatory state scheme for residents, several company schemes for workers in which participation is in many instances obligatory by law, and personal pensions people may or may not buy for themselves.[7] This should not surprise us, as the Dutch more or less copied the British state pension scheme ten years after this was constructed (in 1946, after a concept sir William Beveridge laid down in the by now world famous Beveridge Report).[8] Thereafter both countries went their own way, developing what they considered the most appropriate pension scheme for workers and other citizens. As a result, the differences between both schemes now outnumber their similarities. And although a comparison of both schemes is not the topic of this article, the developments in the UK are interesting enough for the nature of the dilemma in hand to justify a little detour along recent and not so recent developments in British legal and extra-legal old age insurances.

3 Developments in the Netherlands

The Dutch Old Age Pensions Act (*Algemene Ouderdomswet*, hereafter: AOW), 1957 was and still is a general (*algemene*) or citizens' insurance, providing people of 65 and older with a flat rate old age pension. The level of this pension has been the subject of much political debate from the day the scheme came into existence until now. Beveridge's idea was that state pensions should be sufficient for one's basic daily needs, a level which he described as 'subsistence'.[9] And although the AOW

---

[6]   This he will do, after being requested to on the grounds that a certain scheme is already effective for a large and supposedly 'representative' majority of companies within the branch. See for the procedure on this and the conditions to get permission to opt out of an otherwise obligatory scheme article 3 of the Act on Obligatory Participation in Occupational Schemes (*Wet verplichte deelneming in een Bedrijfspensioenfonds, Wet BPF*, 17.3.49, Stb. J 121 lastly changed 10.7.95, Stb. 355).

[7]   As I will show later on, this description is in its brevity not entirely correct. I will modify the presentation of the British scheme later on.

[8]   Social Insurance and Allied Services, report by sir William Beveridge, presented to Parliament by command of His Majesty, Cmnd 6404. The British reformed their complete social insurance scheme after this concept; in the Netherlands it was used only for the schemes on old age and death pensions.

[9]   Defining this level he based himself on a study of S. Rowntree about the so-called 'poverty line' (1899/1941), modifying this in such a way that in some instances he was even stingier than Rowntree. 'When Beveridge says subsistence', Kincaid, a socialist historian on British social security commented somewhat sourly, 'he means it'. KIncaid,

1957 did not as such match this ideal, it offered a fair starting point to get there: for the pensioner trying to make a living, as well as for the state aiming in the long run at sufficiency in its social insurance provision. Last but not least, it gave the several company pension schemes the opportunity to build a reasonable provision for workers on this first layer of pensions (hence the name); 'reasonable' meaning a seventy per cent provision for all participants with a contribution record of forty or more years. These seventy per cent include the state provision AOW and is in many instances related to the income earned just before retirement. In such so-called final salary schemes workers without spectacular career moves practically subsidize the pension plans of their (luckier) colleagues who do make later life careers, but this peculiar trait of the final salary concept – the less well off subsidizing the better well off, or, as Deleeck typifies it, 'perverted income redistribution'[10] – was at the time unnoticed, or, if noticed, considered irrelevant.

Meanwhile, government did its share in social income improvement. At first, it introduced a social minimum within a number of social insurance schemes, the AOW being one of them;[11] then the minimum wage level for full-time workers was legally guaranteed[12] and after that the minimum wage level for fulltimers and the AOW level for breadwinners[13] were legally tied to the development of the average wage level. By the end of the Seventies the legislation on labour and social security contained a (biannual) uprating mechanism, but this moment marked, ironically enough, the turning point in pension uprating. The Act on Periodical Uprating Mechanisms Minimum Wages and Social Benefits 1979[14] has functioned according to the book only once; then the effects of the economic recession of the early Seventies became obvious and a year by year process of lawmaking began with the sole intention of overruling the directives of this ambitious piece of legislation. All

---

1977.

[10] Deleeck, 1991, p. 25.

[11] Act on the Implementation of a Social Minimum in AOW and AWW, Act of December 10, 1964, Stb. 486.

[12] Act on Minimum Wages and Minimum Vacation Supplement (*Wet Minimumloon en Minimumvakantiebijslag*, WMM) of November 27, 1968, Stb. 657.

[13] It goes without saying (but I will say it nevertheless) that both institutions mirror the traditional outlook on the gender roles within the family of that time. As a result the AOW had to be adapted in the Eighties in order to comply with the third (social security) Directive of the EC. This subject, the ban on sex discrimination and the consequences for AOW and occupational schemes, goes beyond the scope of this article, however.

[14] *Wet Aanpassingsmechanismen Minimumloon en Sociale Uitkeringen (WAM)* of December 20, 1979, Stb. 711.

through the Eighties and Nineties state pensions and minimum wages remained frozen for several years in a row.

4 Developments in the UK

In the UK the history of Beveridge's subsistence ideal was even sadder. Here, the state pension level was allowed to wither away from the start, while no one in charge seemed to care, or at least not enough to do something about it.[15] On the other hand – or rather: as a result of this – there was a lot of pressure on politicians of either side to create a law on (additional) workers' pensions, either as a state institution or statutorily obligatory as regards its introduction and minimal contents.[16] Eventually, the several years of (political) struggle, suggestions and negotiations resulted in the introduction – under Labour but with Conservative condonement[17] – of the State Earnings Related Pension Scheme (SERPS) 1975. Under this, or rather, these acts a state minimum standard was set for the old age provision of all workers.[18] This for British standards outrageous state intrusion in private enterprise did not last long, however. Ten years later the Conservative government trimmed down SERPS substantially, but more important (for the subject in hand): restored the spirit of free enterprise by two closely connected measures. One, the introduction of the Personal Pension (PP) option; two, the abolishment, or at least the weakening of the until then hard and fast rule, that alternative pension

---

[15] Beveridge himself noted (shortly before his death in 1953) that the subsistence concept was as dead as a doornail. In a speech in the House of Lords he suggested there were but two options open to the government: either substantially raise the level of the benefits, or declare that the Beveridge report and the policy of 1946 were dropped. Needless to say, government did neither. Kincaid, 1977, p. 61. This does not mean the issue is or has been uncontroversial, though. For a (vivid) description of the parliamentary history on pension uprating, see Lines, 1985.

[16] An old and for British social insurances typical element which is, as yet, unknown in the Netherlands, is the contracting out option. Provided a company scheme is as good as (or better) than the state' scheme, an employer can get permission to 'contract out' of this scheme and invest the (otherwise state scheme) contributions in his own company scheme.

[17] Lest it be forgotten (later developments tend to efface this for British social insurance legislation remarkable fact): the major pension reform of the Seventies passed Parliament as a bipartisan agreement. On this, see: Ellis, 1989.

[18] Social Security Act (SSA) and Social Security Pensions Act (SSPA) 1975. In short: the additional pension is based on the twenty best years of one's working career, protected against inflation and can add up to 25% of this 20-best-years salary.

plans should be in effect 'at least SERPS'.[19] What remained was the prescription of a certain minimum investment in the worker's pension,[20] but it would be up to the individual worker whether this would go to the state scheme – or if the employer had contracted out: the company scheme[21] – or to an insurance company or pension fund of his own choice. Steward put it thus: 'Politically the 1980s were a period when choice became the name of the game. As far as pensions were concerned, this meant choice for the individual as to whether he joined the company scheme or not. And choice as to how he invested his money'.[22] The other side of the 'choice coin' is, as stated, that the government no longer gave a hundred per cent guarantee as to the additional (workers') pension level. Such is the price of allowing insurance companies and other private investors who, as a rule, connect benefits to profit margins instead of to a certain fixed income level, as competitors in the market of workers' pensions. In reference to this (major) difference between the two types of scheme, SERPS and 'minimal SERPS' schemes became also known as defined benefit, and MP schemes as defined contribution. This uncertainty, or perhaps better: potential hazard, of MP schemes was not considered serious enough to prevent their acknowledgement as a legal alternative for the remaining state scheme SERPS, however.

My reason for labelling SERPS 'remaining' is twofold. In the first place, it refers to the government's original intention – announced in the (opening) Green Paper – to abolish SERPS altogether. Admittedly, the suggestion was dropped the moment it became clear that practically no one, the big pension schemes and employers' organizations included, considered this a good idea.[23] But with this statement of

---

[19]   The rule remained for salary related schemes, but was dropped for the newly accepted money purchase schemes. On this: see further below.

[20]   Four per cent of the worker's salary, of which at least half must be paid by the employer.

[21]   This is something no individual worker can control. Once an employer gets permission to contract out of the state scheme, his employees automatically leave this scheme. For them the '86 reform meant more choice in that, as of 1988, they could at that point of time switch to a personal pension, leaving the company scheme for what it is.

[22]   Steward, 1995, p. 73. And for employers, one could add, it meant choice as to their contracting-out options: as of 1988 money purchase schemes would do as a state scheme alternative as well.

[23]   Green Paper: Reform of Social Security, Cmnd. 9517, 9518. Possibly – this suggestion comes from Brown in her book on British pension history – this presentation of two alternatives, one draconic, the other a little less drastic, was from the start an intended tactic to prepare the public that the state pension scheme was in for a radical change. Looking at the matter from this perspective one could say, as Brown does, that the 'achievement' of this type of presentation has been that it 'opened the way for less severe cuts in State pension provision'. Brown, 1990, p. 231.

intent the tone for the reform had been definitely set: as far as this administration was concerned, people should take their old age provision in their own hands instead of relying on the state for this. This 'tone' also speaks from the way the PP option was sold to the public: with a large, with public money sponsored publicity campaign, and with a financial stimulus for anyone trading the collective scheme (either state or company) for a personal one.[24] As a marketing campaign this part of the reform definitely was a success: by the end of 1991 over four million people had taken the step from a collective to a personal pension, about three and a half million more than had been estimated before the PP operation had begun.[25] Whether the same can be said from a perspective of social justice remains to be seen, however. Steward, an insider on company schemes, estimates that the switch from a company to a personal pension 'almost always means lower benefits'. Should this be correct – and the large difference between the estimation of 'potential PP shoppers' and the number of people who actually made the switch seems to underline its likeliness – there is not much that can be brought in against his (Stewards) second statement, 'that many people have been sold personal pensions who ought not have been'.[26]

The second reason for labelling SERPS 'remaining' is that the 1986 reform will probably finish off the state scheme as a full-blooded pension scheme.[27] At first, anyone who can (or thinks he can) get a better pension elsewhere will leave the scheme, leaving it to workers without real alternatives. After this, it will be only a matter of time before the scheme turns into the 'garbage belt' of pension insurance, that is a residu scheme for people no insurance company wants. The eventual effect of this on the level of pensions or, if this is considered inacceptable, of contributions within such a scheme may speak for itself. In the end both developments will slowly but surely make the additional state scheme go the same way as the basic scheme has gone, that is: down the drain.

---

[24] The contribution rebate, or in the words of its adversaries 'contribution bribe'. Much to the annoyance of the latter this PP bonus is financed out of the state scheme contribution fund, which may mean – 'may' as I do not have relevant data on this – that this element is the British version of 'perverted' income redistribution (the poor sponsoring the rich).

[25] Shackleton, 1995.

[26] Steward (1995) p. 75.

[27] Which would mean history repeats itself. Of SERPS' predecessor, the state Graduated Pension Scheme (GPS) it was said that 'the late and unlamented GPS came and went, suffering at its departure from pernicious anaemia induced by inflation'. Escolme et al., 1991, p. 2.

5 A Closer Look at the Pension Dilemma in the Netherlands

Returning again from the UK to the Netherlands, we see a pension scheme which, as a product of the Sixties and Seventies, reflects the working and living patterns of that day and age; patterns, which by now are considered antiquated by most people. But this is not the only reason the old age pension scheme finds itself in deep water on the brink of the 21st century. Were this the only complication, government could simply set itself the task of developing a more fitting pension scheme for new participants, while upholding the old system for pensioners and soon to be pensioners and creating some transition rules for the multitudes of workers 'in between'. Complicating factors here are the social, the economic and the demographic developments of the past and oncoming decades.

To start with the social factor, it is a by now well-known and as such much commented fact, that the relatively uniform working and living patterns of the first decades after World War II are definitely a thing of the past. Instead of just traditional (male) breadwinners with (female) dependent spouses (with or without children) and single persons without family obligations we now know a multiplicity of life styles such as: double incomes with or without children, one parent families, single people with or without a partner (living apart together), single people living alone or with (one or more) others not being their partner *et cetera*. The legislator's task to decide which level is under the circumstances 'sufficient' has, consequently, become infinitely more complex than it was before, especially since individuals have become flexible in their living situation as well. The calculating citizen of the Nineties adapts his lifestyle to the (changes in) legislation instead of it being the other way around! And it is not just citizens who have become flexible. Another revolutionary change of the past decades is the flexibility in labour patterns and relations. Partly, this trend can be ascribed to the aforementioned changes in life style, as these affect the way in which people wish to spend their working hours. But this is not the whole story. Today's flexibility is in many aspects an employer's flexibility, that is suited to the average employer's needs and not to those of his employees. The large number of flex workers – people contracted on 'zero hour', 'come as *I* call you' and other types of 'fantasy' contracts – in today's labour market is the best illustration of this phenomenon.[28] Due to their flexible nature, contracts

---

[28] And this is, in spite of all optimistic comments on this trend, for the flex worker him or herself not advantageous. As Ms Grendel, a long term flex worker, put it: 'A temporary job might be beneficial for those just leaving school, as it gives them the opportunity to orientate themselves in the labour market and have their first job experiences'. But after about a year, being a 'flex' is no longer pleasant, as it means a life full of nagging

like these are not very well suited as building blocks for a coherent pension provision, but this does not seem to be a matter of great concern to past or present administration. On the contrary. As recently as 1990 the implementation of an additional pension scheme for flex workers was judged 'unnecessary' since 'most of them are contracted at a minimum or lower wage level';[29] and for several years but especially under this administration,[30] the hiring of workers on low salary, pensionless jobs is something government not only condones, but, more than that, actively stimulates with (publicly financed) unemployment programmes, intended to improve the employment chances of the longterm unemployed.

The second relevant factor is the demographic development which took place shortly after World War II. I refer of course to the so-called 'baby boom' or population explosion, a phenomenon which changed the population landscape in several western European countries. In the Netherlands the effects of this boom were especially strong, since here it lasted a relatively long time and then stopped rather abruptly.[31] In its report 'Elderly for the Elderly' the *Wetenschappelijke Raad voor het Regeringsbeleid* (WRR) – an advisory body to the government on, among other things, longterm developments in society – describes the oncoming effects of the boom as 'a structural and lengthy process of greying due to a reduction of death as well as birth statistics'.[32]

Furthermore, and this is the third and last relevant factor, the time of continuous economic growth, when the fulfillment of practically all social wishes seemed within reach, is definitely over. In those days government could hope to and, as I illustrated, did effectively expell the 'poverty at old age'-ghost. Now the time has come that every guilder has to be turned twice and that each part of social legislation is checked suspiciously for waste. It is a time, in short, where statements as the one in the title of this article, are taken as a theme for governments, policy-makers and scientific spokesmen alike.
But how true are such statements, considering the problems government is facing with respect to the legal and extra-legal old age provisions? In order to judge this,

---

uncertainties (concerning income, insurance, living quarters, *et cetera.*) Grendel, 1996.
[29] Paper on Additional Pensions, TK 1990-1991, nro.22 167, p. 31.
[30] I refer to the so-called 'Melkert jobs', named after the present minister for Social Affairs and Employment, Ad Melkert. At this moment, there are three such programmes, each for a different segment of the labour market.
[31] Jansweijer, 1996, p. 15.
[32] WRR, 1993.

I now turn to the concrete dilemmas in respectively the state scheme AOW and the additional company schemes.

6 Dilemmas within the State Scheme

A first effort to label the pension dilemma within the AOW in terms of efficiency versus equity, leads to the following dichotomy: 'equity' (equal treatment) prescribes a pension guarantee for the working generation of today which is more or less equal to the one they have been handing out to the generation(s) before them.[33] Efficiency, on the other hand, tends to question the wisdom of upholding this social contract between the generations. This asks for some explanation. Other than company schemes the AOW is financed through PAYE (Pay As You Earn), which means the 'burden' of AOW pensions has to be carried by those of working age. If this burden is not kept within reasonable proportions – which considering the oncoming change in demographic developments asks for appropriate legislation – the (intended) financers may at a certain point try and look for ways to escape the situation, thus endangering the scheme's capacity 'to do the job'.

However, a dichotomy of this kind – where 'equity' stands for safeguarding the state pensions and 'efficiency' for their downfall – is not the whole story. In the first place, 'equity' is something all people – both the scheme's consumer (pensioner) and its supplier (tax and or contribution payer) – are entitled to and for this reason overloading the latter can be considered as unfair as underpaying the former. Another objection against the 'equity' argument is that today's working generation has had more opportunity to reserve for its old age than the now retired or about to be retired. Provided this is true, the question arises whether 'equal treatment' demands an income guarantee at old age which equals the one which was given to the former or present day elderly. But can one correctly judge collectivities like 'generations' with individual criteria as 'equity' and 'reasonableness'? This is as dubious as the generation concept itself. The only (uncomfortable) conclusion one can draw from

---

[33] The term 'generation' is used not as equivalent for a certain, precisely defined age group, but as in 'generation solidarity', a quality which is generally presented by the slogan: 'We' pay for the old age provision of 'our parents', with the tacit understanding that 'our children' will in time pay for 'ours'. Taken literally this concept is not uncontroversial, though. Some years after the generation concept was introduced (by Becker, 1992), its value was questioned by yet another sociologist (Van den Broek, 1996), who qualified the concept of 'coherent generations, marching through time' as 'charming but treacherous'.

this is, that the equity question is in this respect not just hard, but in terms of objectivity impossible to answer.

The efficiency factor raises comparable problems. True, a system which puts a too heavy load on its contributors will in the long run turn counter-productive. But the alternative of severely reducing the state pension level contains an (in)efficiency angle as well. This is the so called 'trust factor', the fact that a policy of constant devaluation will in time go at the expense of people's trust in the scheme and, consequently, of their willingness to pay for it. This is certainly no light matter, which should (and does) play an important role in the minds of all politicians, no matter what their political background. The same is true for the popularity factor of whatever measure is considered necessary. In the area of old age pensions this factor is extremely powerful, as many politicians have already experienced the hard way.[34] However, this popularity factor is not always as easy to read as one would wish, and furthermore very much a product of its age: something which is highly controversial and simply *not done* today, may very well be considered painful yet inevitable tomorrow. A good example of this complexity is, in my opinion, the outcome of a recent survey study on social security and labour opinions on this issue.[35] For this study people were asked to give their preference out of six alternatives to solve 'the AOW problem of the future' (wording as in the report).[36] Out of these, the options which – as the author of the survey put it – 'increase the load on the strongest shoulders' scored remarkably better than consumer directed measures such as a raise of the pensionable age or a decrease of the AOW level.[37] However, this willingness to 'let the richer pay' was, not surprisingly I would add, expressed mostly by people not belonging to this income group. The more well to do correspondents showed

---

[34] In the Netherlands the Christian Democratic party CDA lost the 1994 elections over (among other things) a carelessly placed remark of its chairman on the necessity to freeze the state pension level. And in Italy the at that moment very popular statesman Berlusconi fell into disgrace because he (again: among other things) had dared suggest that pension rights could and should be diminished.

[35] The Netherlands on social security and labour; first results of an extensive public opinion survey. Van Oorschot, 1996.

[36] Id. p. 83. The options are: 1) let higher income groups pay more contribution; 2) make the well to do pensioners pay contributions for the state scheme as well; 3) make people save more for their old age; 4. raise the contribution level in order to create a State Reserve Fund out of which the extra pension costs can be paid, the moment this becomes necessary; 5) raise the pensionable age from 65 to 67; 6) reduce the AOW pension level.

[37] Ibid. More concretely: 55 per cent of the correspondents favour a raise of the contribution level for higher incomes; 45 per cent is in favour of turning the better off pensioner into AOW contributor, which he is, as of now, not. Rejected were: the reduction of the AOW level (79 per cent) and a raise of the pensionable age (62 per cent).

remarkably less enthusiasm for this type of 'AOW fund raising'. It would, therefore, be a mistake to hold this willingness to uphold the AOW at all costs for solidarity, in the sense of a concern for or commitment with lower income groups. Rather, this score is a fine example of the fact that most people tend to defend their own interest. And as the same will be true for the tax and contribution payer of tomorrow, predictions about the public opinion in years to come are hard to make. What does seem safe to assume, however, is that, as of now, a drastic erosion of the state pension level such as the UK has seen, is not likely to occur here. A state policy like that would be impopular to such an extent, that it will knell the end of any politician or political party who dares to suggest it.

The final conclusion as regards the AOW is that state goals like 'equity' and 'efficiency' are not so much one anothers counterparts, pointing each in different directions, as co-operators pointing to one, or rather, several possible alternatives. Because of this, decisions to prefer one option over the other cannot correctly be labelled as a choice for more efficiency/less equity or vice versa.

7 Dilemmas within the Occupational Sector

Turning from the state to the occupational sector we see an even more complex area. To begin with, the system as it is now raises some urgent questions of (in)equity. Examples of this are the recent criticism against the concept of final salary schemes,[38] and the several claims of (in)equity company schemes are confronted with from participants as well as pensioners: women, suing for retribution of past discrimination, 'sleepers' or 'early leavers', who – as Steward put it – feel ripped off by their company scheme,[39] widows, facing the consequences of the '96 reform of the National Widows Pension Act,[40] all of them want something from their company pension scheme – more than what is officially coming to them – all are convinced that what they want is only their fair and legal share. In some instances

---

[38] Apart from the 'perverted' solidarity with career makers and the cost factor which comes with this there is the assumption that final salary schemes are indirectly discriminatory to women. On this, see: Kraamwinkel, 1995.

[39] Steward, 1995, p. 73.

[40] It would go too far to dwell on the consequences of this reform. Suffice it to say that the situations in which a survivor's pension can be claimed were diminished, that the pensions in fact granted were made income related and that survivors with pensions will face a severe loss of income in the very near future. Government has left it up to the several company schemes, whether to follow the state scheme's changes or to repair the damages in pension rights for present and/or future applicants.

the judge (the EC court) has dictated the outcome or at least the conditions of this weighing process; in others, it is up to the several Boards of Directors to decide who gets what.[41]

On top of this, the occupational sector is confronted with the same (demographic and sociographic) developments the state has to deal with. At first sight, it might seem that the oncoming change in population built up (economically speaking: the a/i factor)[42] is of no concern to company schemes, as their pension plans are funded and not like the state scheme based on PAYE. Sadly enough, this is not true: company schemes face financial hazards which are as grave, perhaps even graver than the state scheme. The reason for this is that all company schemes contain elements of redistribution (or solidarity) which are by nature unfunded. The repairment of pension breaches for early leavers is an example of this, as is the 'perverted' solidarity with late career makers, but perhaps the most important of all is the fact, that company schemes have in the past slipped into the habit of repairing each and every 'hole' that was blown into the worker's full (that is: seventy per cent) pension by state measures such as the AOW freezing.[43] Under the past demographic conditions there is nothing wrong with a certain policy of unfundedness, but the moment the balance between the number of contributors and beneficiaries changes – in that the former falls and the latter rises – this perfectly normal policy becomes risky and even hazardous.

Since there is a large common interest involved in this, government has dropped its usual policy toward workers' pensions of abstination and non-interference, and has announced legislation which will forbid the practice of unfunded obligations within the workers' pension schemes. In doing this the government accepts, as the (former) secretary of state for Social Affairs and Employment Linschoten described it, its responsibility to safeguard 'that pension guarantees of the past can and will be met in decades to come'.[44] Again, an argument like that is not so much about equi-

---

[41] These Boards are made up of representatives of labour unions and employers organizations. Much to the annoyance of the, as yet relatively young, organizations of pensioners their claim of one or more seats within the Board has been heard, acknowledged as 'not unreasonable' (by among others the secretary of state of Social Affairs and Employment), but not, as yet, honoured with concrete action.

[42] This abbreviation stands for the relationship between beneficiaries and contributors or, in economic terms: actives (a) versus inactives (i).

[43] For a more detailed description and the relevant data on this: see Jansweijer, 1996.

[44] Speech of Secretary of State Linschoten dd. March 28, 1995. PS, April 19th, 1995. A more specific description of the state's responsibility in this is given in the Paper on Additional Pensions, TK 1990-1991, 22 167, nr 2, p. 23.

ty – although that can be defended as well – as about efficiency, in that neglecting it will in time threaten the scheme's capacity to 'do the job'.

The social factor, which is relevant here, is a quality which is commonly referred to as individualization, or, rather, the way this has been interpreted by politicians and scientific spokesmen, advocating a system of 'more market' and 'less state'. In their view 'individualization' stands for the individual's wish to be freed from state ties such as obligatory collective contracts. Moreover, again: in their view, government has a real win-win situation at hand here, since answering this need will help to reduce pension costs substantially.[45]

But is this state of social freedom really 'what people themselves want'? This is at least dubious. Employers do, as a recent poll on this issue showed: a majority (about two thirds) indicated that it would welcome the chance to choose its own, most adequate pension scheme, expecting moreover a substantial drop of pension costs as a result. Employees, on the other hand, seem less inclined to part with past certainties. Of them two thirds (62%) reject the suggestion that the legal obligation to participate in a collective company scheme should be abolished.[46]

But apart from what people themselves want, the suggestion of limiting the obligatory part of workers pensions has already fallen on fertile ground with the present administration. The 1996 Paper *Werken aan Zekerheid* mentions the government's intention to 'stimulate that the amount of pension costs is reduced' with all instruments available, such as: 'the legislation on workers' obligation to participate within the company scheme and that on fiscal facilities for pension contracts'. In concrete terms the abolishment is announced of both the obligation to participate and all fiscal facilities for the upper part of pension contracts.[47]

---

[45] A well-known member of this group of 'market adherents' is the economist (and columnist) Bomhof. His outlook on the present situation is well summarized by his (recent) observation that under the present system company schemes can reign as monopolists 'unhindered by competition from insurance companies and other professional financial intermediaries'. *NRC Handelsblad*, dd. July 15, 1996.

[46] The employers' poll was organized in 1996 by the *NIPO* (a centre for opinion polls) as requested by the Union of Insurance Companies. The employees' poll stems from 1994 and was organized by the Union of Company Pension Schemes.

[47] Werken aan Zekerheid, TK 1996/97, 25 010, nos. 1- 2, p. 34. This 'upper part' (my term) is the pension guarantee over a) 70 per cent of the worker's average salary and/or b) the upper earnings level.

A state policy like that, which will put a limit to the existing solidarity between rich and poor,[48] can be in my opinion classified as resulting in less equity. And since its underlying intention is the introduction of some (market) efficiency within the scheme, this decision might very well be labelled as a choice for more efficiency at the cost of equity. There is, however, another aspect of (in)efficiency in this tendency to implement some competitive elements in an area which used to be exclusively reserved to the state; efficiency, in that it concerns the scheme's capacity 'to do the job'. This is the subject of control, or better yet prevention of market inherent risks as sloppiness, malpractice or even fraud at the side of the implementing organization. The fact that the one goes hand in hand with the other, is a well-known, as well as much studied fact for many years. In the UK this resulted in a whole set of measures, at the moment the PP option became operable and again, several years later, when the first ailments of the new scheme had become public knowledge. Measures in this respect were strict(er) state conditions under which to obtain the status of PP agent, (more) far reaching qualifications for the supervisory body, the Occupational Pensions Board, and the introduction of a state Ombudsman for Pensions. Looking in from the outside (as I do) it seems to me, that the statement about the state's responsibility 'to safeguard that pension guarantees of the past can and will be met in decades to come' is also one the British government underlines.

But how is one to do this, when at the same time adhering to the adagium that 'the market should do its job'? This question may very well become the top issue in pensions in years to come, not just in the UK but in all countries where competitive aspects are implemented in a former state social insurance scheme. A foreboding of this is in the Netherlands the recent observation of the chairman of the State Insurance Board that company pension schemes have, in his words, begun to present themselves as 'financial supermarkets, offering pensions as well as insurances'. The reason why this is, in his view problematic, is that since they tread relatively unknown ground here, they are engineered and supervised by directors who 'no longer seem to know exactly what they are doing'. The Doomsday scenario of this public official is that, if appropriate state measures to check and control this matter remain absent, it will be only a matter of time before 'the pension world will have its own Nick Leeson'.[49]

---

[48] The limit of solidarity in this is, that it will allow higher income groups to keep the top of their income away from solidarity decisions of company schemes such as, for instance, concerning wrongfully treated women or 'ripped off' early leavers.

[49] 'Directors know too little; concern over investment of pension money'. *NRC Handelsblad*, August 9, 1996. Nick Leeson, for whoever is unfamiliar with this name, was a bank employee who with his investment decisions singlehandedly ruined the renowned British

Needless to say, this subject troubles all politicians, whatever their political background. In a time when even the flooding of a house is considered something for which the individual must be reimbursed, the idea that people's investment for old age will go to waste as a result of (someone else's) sloppiness, bad investment policies or, worst, fraud is simply unbearable. Granted, so far there has been only one serious – albeit in number of victims minor – pension schandal,[50] but if there is one thing everyone concerned agrees on, it is that incidents like that should be prevented at all costs. The answer how to do this, at times when the capital of pension schemes is reaching staggering heights, is not simple, but few people doubt that a further retreat on the part of the state in order to 'let the market do its job' will be a sure and guaranteed road to disaster.

8 Conclusion

Try as I may, I am unable to qualify the pension dilemma of today and tomorrow as a conflict of equity versus efficiency. For the AOW both qualities more or less add up as arguments for one but, if approached differently, also for the other of the alternatives available. This does not mean conflicts of interests are non-existent, but where they do occur it is within the range of 'equity' or 'efficiency' itself.

In the area of company pensions a (certain) dichotomy of efficiency and equity can be spotted, but that is, to my opinion, not the main issue here. Rather, the key question of the next decades will be whether the state will be able to guarantee and safeguard both the quality and security of workers' pensions, at a time when state intrusion threatens to become equivalent to superfluous, bothersome and a nuisance to people or institutions, trying to do their job. A tendency like that may very well be fatal for the subject in hand, since the pension dilemma of today and tomorrow cannot be handled, let alone solved without a strong and consistent public, in other words government body. It is, after all, only the government, which can provide the impartiality necessary to earn and keep people's trust in the way the money which is reserved for their old age pensions is dealt with and in the reasonableness of the several redistributionary decisions which have to be taken in order to do so. Furthermore, only the government is capable to set up and maintain an institute of expert and impartial supervisors, which is another vital element for the system's

---

Barings bank.

[50] In the Netherlands, that is. I refer to the Vie d'Or (Golden Life!) scandal, where a private pension company went bankrupt, leaving many participants with expensive as well as worthless pension plans.

capacity 'to do the job', especially in view of the large amount of money which has to be kept, invested and (re)distributed.

This does not imply, however, that I have complete and hundred per cent faith in the state's capacity to guarantee that all pension claims of the past can and will be met, no matter what. This is something the state should aim for, but whether it will be able to fulfill that task succesfully, is something only time can tell. Like it or not, one hundred per cent income guarantees for life cannot be given neither by the state nor by whatever private company. This basic uncertainty about one's old age provision is something all 'generations' have had to live with, and the postwar 'generation' which so far has not endured many hardships, will not be excepted from this rule. For them the sole consolation lies in the fact that it is because of this age old truth that solidarity with and through the generations was invented in the past, and that it will for this reason always be with us.

References

Becker, H.A., Generaties en hun kansen, 1992.

Breunesse, E., Visie op pensioenen in de 21 eeuw, diss., The Hague 1995.

Broek, van den, Politics and generations, Tilburg University Press, 1996.

Brown, J.C., Social security for retirement, York 1990, p. 231.

Deleeck, H., Zeven lessen over sociale zekerheid, Acco Leven/Amersfoort 1991.

Dietvorst, G.J.B., De drie pijlers van toekomstvoorzieningen en belastingen, Deventer 1994.

Ellis, B., Pensions in Britain, 1995-1975, London, HMSO (1989).

Escolme, B. *et al.*, Hosking's pension schemes and retirement benefits, sixth edition, London 1991.

Grendel, D., The freedom of the flex worker is only make belief, *de Volkskrant*, dd. February 8, 1996.

Jansweijer, R.M.A., Gouden bergen, diepe dalen. De inkomensgevolgen van een betaalbare oudedagsvoorziening, diss. 1996, p. 15.

Kincaid, J.C., Poverty and equality, a study of social security and taxation, Middlesex 1977.

Kraamwinkel, M.M.H., Pensioen, emancipatie en gelijke behandeling, diss., Utrecht University 1995.

Lines, T., Family Income Support Part 7: maintaining the value of benefits. PSI, London, 1985.

Ministerie van Sociale Zaken en Werkgelegenheid, Werken aan Zekerheid, TK 1996/97, 25010.

Oorschot, W. van, Nederland over sociale zekerheid en arbeid. Eerste resultaten van een uitgebreid onderzoek naar de publieke opinie, Tilburg Institute for Social Security Research (TISSER), June 1996.

Shackleton, J.R., Pensions reform: the issues, Political Quarterly 1995, no. 26.

Steward, C., speech at the Conference Pensioenmarkt 2000, full text included in: Tijdschrift voor Pensioenvraagstukken, August 1995.

WRR, Ouderen voor ouderen, demografische ontwikkelingen en beleid. Rapport aan de regering nr. 43, Sdu-uitgeverij, 's-Gravenhage 1993.

From Maastricht to Amsterdam: Towards Integration of Social and Economic Policy in Europe?[1]

Inge van Berkel, Gerrit Faber, Joop Schippers, Jacques Siegers

1 Introduction

The overall objective of West-European economic integration in the period after World War II, was to improve the standard of living for the people of Europe. However, the means to bring this about were limited, and focus was on the amelioration of market efficiency. Economic progress in a narrow sense (profits, prospering industry and trades) was sought by means of integrating markets and facilitating cooperation between the Member States. Efficiency in the market for goods and for services was seen as the primary way to realize the objectives of economic integration. The creation of a welfare state providing social security and care was left to the national states.

In the Nineties three challenges can be discerned for the Member States of the European Union:

1. adapting their economies to increased competition;
2. coping with disturbingly high levels of unemployment;
3. meeting the criteria for admission to the EMU.

The question arises how a higher rate of economic growth and decreasing government expenditure can be combined with a high rate of labour participation, low unemployment and acceptable levels of income and social security. Most Member States agree that an Economic and Monetary Union will be beneficial for their economies. To meet the challenges mentioned above, many Member States tend to clear the way for market forces, by means of deregulation, privatization and flexibilization of the labour market. As a result of the attempts to strengthen economic growth and to shape government finances towards the EMU-criteria, maintaining the levels of social security is under pressure in the Member States. It is argued that factors like increased mobility of capital and production, combined with competition from non-EU-countries, makes it harder to maintain the current level of welfare for all citizens in the countries of the EU.

---

[1] The manuscript of this chapter was completed in March 1997.

This would be contrary to the first objective for the European Union, as defined in the Treaty on European Union or the 'Maastricht Treaty' (signed 7 February 1992). Also, the European Community, being one of the constituting elements of this Union, has tasks in the social and economic field as stated in Article 2 of the Treaty establishing the European Community:

> 'by establishing a common market and economic and monetary union and by implementing the common policies or activities referred to in Articles 3 and 3a, to promote throughout the Community a harmonious and balanced development of economic activities, sustainable and non-inflationary growth (...), a high degree of convergence of economic performance, a high level of employment and of social protection, the raising of the standard of living and quality of life, and economic and social cohesion and solidarity among Member States.'

One might wonder if this 'economic and social progress' will follow automatically from establishing the Common Market, the EMU and the few provisions for social and economic cohesion (Cohesion Funds, European Social Fund, Regional Development Fund) available at the European Union level. Therefore, the question to be discussed in this paper is whether extension of the stipulations on policies in the social dimension in the Union Treaty is desirable to ensure a balance between efficiency and equity in the European Community.

Efficiency and equity have traditionally been used as reasons for government intervention to bring about a more equal distribution of income and wealth. Resources that are badly utilised or not utilised at all may for example participate (more) in production if measures of regional and social policy stimulate efficient allocation. These measures, taken on the basis of efficiency arguments, are supposed to increase total welfare. Public opinion on inequality may also influence government policy: total welfare would increase when inequalities between groups and regions are removed.

The efficiency argument has also been used for government intervention independent of the argument of a more equal distribution of income and wealth, for example in the recent trend towards deregulation of markets. Both the more equal distribution of income and wealth and the redistribution in favour of the development of backward regions are then subordinate to the economic growth that the deregulated market is supposed to generate. In the present debate on the controversy between efficiency and equity the latter interpretation of efficiency (deregulation, lowering production costs) prevails.

The point of departure of this paper is that a combination of efficiency and equity is beneficial for social and economic progress in the European Union. Efficiency in production processes and in the functioning of markets depends on various factors.

A factor that is beneficial for efficiency but often forgotten in the debate, is reliability. This reliability may partly be realized by stable macro-economic and structural policies but must ideally be accompanied by policies directed at equity in the social dimension. This in order, for example, to avoid creating social unrest, resulting from loss of opportunities and decreased purchasing power, or decreased legitimacy of government policy. The notion of 'equity' in the social dimension in this paper is not absolute in the sense of equal pay or equal sharing,[2] but along the line of thought expressed by Rawls: 'social and economic inequalities are to be arranged so that they are (...) reasonably expected to be to everyone's advantage'.[3] Even though all Member States accepted the European Council's Employment Action plan,[4] no further European Community social policies seem to be developed. An imbalance may arise between policies at European Community level (with its emphasis on economic policies,[5] aimed at improving efficiency) and at national level (with its responsibility for social policy,[6] aimed at improving equity). Integration of social and economic policies at European Community level could help prevent the imbalance mentioned above. The revision of the Maastricht Treaty has taken place during the Dutch presidency of the European Union in the first half of 1997. The 'Treaty of Amsterdam' offered an opportunity for the insertion of stipulations in the social field.

After a short introduction on the history of integration of social and economic policy at European level, the focus will be on the integration of economic and social policy at European Community level since the Maastricht Treaty. Related developments in European Community legislation and the changing role of the social partners at European Community level will also be described in this second section. In the third section we will narrow the discussion down. The possibility and desirability of extending the stipulations on the social dimension in the Treaty on European Union will be compared with the existing situation. Transparency of legislation, legitimacy of policies and a restored balance between the possibilities for social policies and economic policies at European Community level that 'blends regard for equality with respect for efficiency'[7] will be used as criteria for this comparison.

---

[2] For reasons clearly demonstrated by Phelps, 1985, p. 138, 142.

[3] Rawls, (1971) as quoted in Phelps, 1985, p. 146, see also: Dietz, 1996, p. 588.

[4] Essen Presidency Conclusions, 1994.

[5] This policy, depending on the definition used, may cover any field, but usually covers topics dealing directly or indirectly with production of goods or services and with decisions on the use of scarce resources.

[6] This policy usually covers topics dealing directly or indirectly with labour, labour provision, and social security. Social policy also deals with the distribution of income.

[7] Rawls (1971) as quoted in Phelps, 1985, p. 146.

2 Integration of Social and Economic Policy at European Community Level

2.1 Introduction

At a national level, government responsibility to come to an integration of social and economic policies has become more or less evident in the postwar era. In the Netherlands, for example, five objectives for social and economic policy were formulated by the Dutch Social and Economic Council (Sociaal-Economische Raad) in 1951:
* full employment;
* a stable price level;
* equilibrium at the balance of payments;
* optimum economic growth;
* an equitable distribution of income.

In 1992, as a reaction to the changed institutional structure of the European Community, the Dutch Social and Economic Council decided to reformulate the five classical objectives mentioned before. The objective of a stable price level and equilibrium at the balance of payment are now left to 'Brussels'.[8] Member States' economic policies must be ever more in line with policies resulting from European Community decisionmaking. Social policies are mainly left to the nation, even though they are heavily influenced by these economic policies.

While the progress in the formulation of common economic policies has been evident since the first Treaty, this was not the case for social policies. Activities in the field of social policy were inspired mainly by the efficiency argument: the objective was to make the labour force more easily adjustable to the exigencies of the integrated market. For this purpose, funds were available. From the first phase of European cooperation during the early 1950s onwards, differing social legislation in the Member States is at times perceived as hampering the process of economic integration. On the one hand, differing labour costs are said to lead to social dumping or the relocation of industries to countries with the lowest labour costs. On the other hand, welfare gains from integration are largely derived from a better exploitation of comparative advantages. These are based on the relative availability of factors of production, visible in different relative prices of factors of production. Equalizing labour costs over the Member States would destroy comparative advantages and the welfare gains from integration.

---

[8]   Sociaal-Economische Raad, 1992, p. 134.

In its original text, the Treaty establishing the European Economic Community (1957) is cautious about anything resembling a common social policy, even though several ambitious objectives were formulated in the social field. Fifteen years after signing the European Economic Community Treaty the Member States in Paris jointly declared that they 'attached as much importance to vigourous action in the social field as to the achievement of an economic union' and made the provision for a first social action plan, which came into being in 1974.[9]

The adoption of the Single European Act (1986) and the time schedule for the Internal Market facilitated a solution to the resistance to further incorporation of social policies at European Community level. Until now, most of the initiatives by the European Commission to impose directives stranded where they affected the power relations between workers and management or the competence of national legislation. The Delors' concept of a 'European Social Area', rather than proposing concrete objectives for a supranational social policy, concentrated on how it should be developed. A 'Social Dialogue' between labour and capital at the European Community level would have to contribute to this European Social Area.[10]

In December 1989, the Member States adopted the Social Charter, with the exception of the United Kingdom and Denmark. This Charter of the Fundamental Social Rights of Workers, sets out twelve basic principles (see table 1).

Table 1. The 1989 Social Charter

The Charter of the fundamental social rights of workers, adopted in December 1989, sets out twelve basic principles:

1. The right to work in the European Community country of one's choice.
2. The right to a fair wage.
3. The right to improved living and working conditions.
4. The right to social protection under prevailing national systems.
5. The right to freedom of association and collective bargaining.
6. The right to vocational training.
7. The right of men and women to equal treatment.
8. The right of workers to information, consultation and participation.
9. The right to health protection and safety at work.
10. The protection of children and adolescents.
11. The guarantee of minimum living standards for the elderly.
12. Improved social and professional integration for the disabled.

Source: Nicoll, 1994, p. 170

---

[9]   Social Europe 2/95, p. 13.
[10] Hagen, 1992, p. 295-300.

The amplifications and changes in the Treaty of Rome, made in the preparatory stages of the Treaty on European Union, gave rise to new discussions on the insertion of stipulations on European social policy.

2.2 The Discussion on Social Policy at the European Summits From Maastricht to Amsterdam

European Council meetings take place at least twice a year (once during each presidency) and bring together the heads of state and government, usually accompanied by their foreign ministers.[11] These European Councils, usually indicated by the name of the host city, are the main fora for policy-making in the European Community.

Maastricht (1991)
The Maastricht Treaty amends and extends the European Economic Community Treaty, and establishes the European Union. Relevant for the social and economic policy at the levels of both European Union and Member States is the transformation of the European Economic Community into the European Community. An article of particular relevance for all policy fields is Article 3b (principle of subsidiarity). In areas which do not fall within its exclusive competence, the Community can take action only if the objectives of the proposed action cannot be sufficiently achieved by the Member States. In these cases the scale or expected effects of a proposed action may lead to Community action.[12]
In the negotiations leading to the Treaty on European Union there was strong support for the amplification of social policy, with the exception of the United Kingdom. The activities of the Community with respect to social policies now include, according to Article 3 of the Treaty on European Union 'a policy in the social sphere comprising a European Social Fund' (3.i) and the 'strengthening of economic and social cohesion' (3.j). Eleven Member States (excluding the United Kingdom) signed a Social Agreement (annexed to the Protocol on Social Policy), containing the rephrased aims of the 1989 Social Charter. The Social Protocol allows these eleven Member States to use the European Community decision-making procedures and European Community institutions among themselves. But the decisions will not be those of the Council, they will not apply in the United Kingdom, and possible costs

---

[11] Economic and finance ministers can be invited to European Council Meetings if their subjects are under discussion.

[12] 92/C 224/9.

resulting from these decisions will not be charged to the United Kingdom (see also: 3.1).

For the establishment of the Economic and Monetary Union, the Maastricht Treaty contains a timetable for individual Member States to create certain economic conditions. Targets with respect to price stability, public finance, exchange rates and interest rates are narrowly defined and limit the room for manoeuvre for Member States' fiscal and monetary policies. General instruments for national economic policies have been greatly influenced by the Maastricht Treaty. National sovereignty with respect to monetary policies has virtually disappeared as a result of the detailed stipulations with respect to the stages leading to EMU, while fiscal policies are deeply affected. As a result, priorities in the social field, especially social security, may have to bend for the economic measures necessary for entering EMU. There is no European agreement on minimum standards in the social field to prevent possible damage from this shift in priorities. The Social Agreement offers the signing Member States a possibility to set these standards among themselves. Decisions on actions with respect to delicate matters such as social security and social protection of workers require the Council's unanimity, and do not apply in the UK. In other words: the basis for ensuring a legal status for minimum standards in the social field is unstable in the Maastricht Treaty. The search for the right blend between efficiency and equity is at this stage mainly left to the Member States.

Edinburgh (December 1992)

In Edinburgh, it became evident that the Member States fear loosing their sovereignty with the clear definition of criteria for EMU set in Maastricht. The European Summit therefore brought additional statements on subsidiarity (Article 3b of the Maastricht Treaty): national powers are the rule and the Community's power is the exception. Also, when the Community acts within these principles, the means to be employed by the Community must be proportional to the object to be pursued. Furthermore, the Council declared that citizenship of the Union does not take the place of national citizenship. This statement clarifies once more that the responsibility that governments have towards citizens (for example: social security and protection) lies first and foremost with the national government.

Copenhagen (June 1993), Brussels (December 1993)

The Danish Presidency brought the fight against unemployment to the top of the European agenda. From this moment onwards the Commission has begun to develop a common European employment strategy. The Summit gave the Commission and its President the mandate to prepare the White Paper on Growth, Competitiveness and Employment. Seven points of action emerging from this White paper and the

Green Paper on European Social Policy (1993), were approved by the European Council in Brussels. These points indicated fields of action for the Member States, but it was left to the Member States to decide if and how these points should be implemented in their national policies.

Essen (December 1994)

To face new challenges for the EU, such as the realization of EMU and solving employment problems, the Heads of State and Government established a set of guidelines for short and medium-term measures in four prioritary areas. The first of these areas is 'continuing and strengthening the strategy of the White Paper[13] in order to consolidate growth, improve the competitiveness of the European economy and the quality of the environment in the European Union, and – given the still intolerably high level of unemployment – create more jobs for our citizens'.[14]

Improving the employment situation in the Member States is the first mentioned 'Economic Issue'. Possibly it was put under this economic header to avoid discussions on the competence of the Member States in the social dimension. It may also have been perceived as the perfect opportunity to give profile to 'Europe'. Larsson[15] indicated that the Essen Summit was 'a historic event when it concerns employment policy'. For the first time the Heads of State and Government could agree to a common employment strategy, underlining the role of structural measures. Also, they agreed to a procedure by which this strategy is transformed into fifteen national and multi-annual programmes. Common monitoring and follow-up by the European Commission is part of the procedure.

Five fields of action were defined to ameliorate the employment situation in the Member States. Resulting measures should be consistent within a broader context of coherent macro-economic, and structural policies and specific labour market policies.

---

[13] In these priorities, the Council refers to the White Paper on Growth, Competitiveness and Employment (1993). This is the 'economic' of the two White Papers issued in 1993 and 1994. The White paper "European Social Policy, A way forward for the Union" (COM(94)333, 1994), the follow-up of the 1993 Green paper on Social Policy was less debated and less influential.

[14] Presidency Conclusions European Council Essen, 1994.

[15] Director-General of DG V, the Directorate-General for Employment, Industrial Relations and Social Affairs of the European Commission, at the opening speech of the Dutch Post-Essen Follow-up Seminar, which took place December 1995 in The Hague.

Table 2. Essen Employment Action Plan

The measures should include five key areas:

1. Improving employment opportunities for the labour force by promoting investment in vocational training. To that end a key role falls to the acquisition of vocational qualifications, particularly by young people.
2. Increasing the employment intensiveness of growth, in particular by:
   * more flexible organization of work in a way which fulfils both the wishes of employees and the requirements of competition;
   * a wage policy which encourages job-creating investments and in the present situation requires moderate wage agreements below increases in productivity;
   * finally, the promotion of initiatives, particularly at regional and local level, that create jobs which take account of new requirements, e.g. in the environmental and social services spheres.
3. Reducing non-wage labour costs far enough to ensure that there is a noticeable effect on decisions concerning the taking on of employees and in particular of unqualified employees. The problem of non-wage labour costs can only be resolved through a joint effort by the economic sector, trade unions and the government.
4. Improving the effectiveness of labour market policy: the effectiveness of employment policy must be increased by avoiding practices which are detrimental to willingness to work, and by moving from a passive to an active labour market policy. The individual incentive to continue seeking employment on the general labour market must remain. Particular account must be taken of this when working out income-support measures.
5. Improving measures to help groups which are particularly hard hit by unemployment:
   * specific efforts are necessary to help young people, especially school leavers who have virtually no qualifications, by offering them either employment or training;
   * the fight against long-term unemployment must be a major aspect of labour market policy. Different labour market policy measures are necessary according to the very varied groups and requirements of the long-term unemployed;
   * special attention should be paid to the difficult situation of unemployed women and older employees.

Source: Commission des Communautés Européennes, Secretariat General, 1994

Economic recovery is one of the tools to solve the problems of employment and unemployment in Europe: further efforts are needed to solve the structural problems. According to the European Council, in this process an important role will be played by dialogue between social partners and politicians.[16]

---

[16] Presidency conclusions, European Council, 1994.

Madrid (December 1995)

The Essen re-employment strategy gave Europe an agenda, not only for 1995, but also for the years ahead as was emphasized in the Madrid Summit which took place in December 1995. The first paragraph of the summary of the Madrid conclusions reads: 'The European Council considers that job creation is the principal social, economic and political objective of the European Union and its Member States and declares its firm resolve to continue to make every effort to reduce unemployment.' This declaration on employment as the principal objective goes far beyond the phrase in the 1991 Treaty and also brings a new dimension when compared to the conclusions from the latest Summits. This may play an important role in the debate on the revision of the Treaty.

The Madrid Summit confirmed the Essen strategy, and approved the Single Report from the Ministers of Finance and Labour. This report includes new commitments on youth, on long-term unemployment and on equal opportunities, which means that for the first time a convergence of views has been achieved on the approach to be followed to ensure that the current economic recovery is accompanied by a more thorough going improvement of the employment situation. The Madrid Summit confirmed that the new process of multi-annual programmes and common follow-up and monitoring is a permanent process; the Summit requested the Ministers of Labour and the Ministers of Finance to come back at the end of 1996 with a report on a common employment policy.

From the side of the Commission, there seems to be increased attention for employment systems as a whole: the interplay of taxation, welfare, the organization of training and education, regulation and other policies. Even though the Member States are responsible for the fight against unemployment and the creation of jobs, the European Community institutions have the responsibility to develop a common strategy, reach agreement on objectives and commitments, support the Member States in the implementation of the strategy through the structural funds and – finally – to take responsibility for a qualified follow-up.[17]

Turin 1996

On the eve of the Intergovernmental Conference, the president of the European Commission (J. Santer) pointed at the importance of reconciling economic and social objectives, adding that 'the social dimension is not a cost or a burden, but rather a source of dynamism which will enable us to take on the challenges of the future,

---

[17] Larsson, 1995.

including that of international competition'.[18] The most recent initiative launched by the President of the European Commission is 'Action for Employment – A European Pact of Confidence'.[19] The purpose of this pact is to mobilise all actors, at European, national and local level, to make their full contribution to a new employment orientation of all policies. The initiative includes four elements: the macro-economic framework, completion of the Single Market, reform of employment systems and, finally, use of the structural funds.

The objective of the Intergovernmental Conference on the revision of the Maastricht Treaty, starting at the European Summit in Turin, was to discuss the institutional reform of Europe. However, employment turned out to be one of the major subjects of discussion for the Council of Ministers of the European Union in the beginning of 1996. It was agreed that promotion of employment is a major theme on the political agenda of the EU.

Amsterdam 1997?

Debate on the 'social' dimension since the Maastricht Summit has increasingly focused on employment. Suggested approaches for tackling unemployment and improving the employment situation are laid down in the five Employment Action Plan-points decided upon in the Essen Summit. Member States agreed upon the need to work on these European Community action points, with the cooperation of the social partners. The negotiations on the revision of the Maastricht Summit will determine how much of this increased attention for social policies, especially employment, will be brought into the Treaty on European Union. Extending policies in the social dimension or enlarging the funds available may prove to be sensitive issues in the light of a possible enlargement of the European Union.

2.3 Related Changes in the European Community

Discussions on European Community social policy often raise debate on the limits of European Community influence on Member States' labour costs and their social security systems. Meanwhile, the Social Dialogue and European Community legislation increasingly influence Member States' policies.

---

[18] European Foundation for the Improvement of Living and Working Conditions, 1996, p. 9.

[19] European Foundation for the Improvement of Living and Working Conditions, 1996, p. 9.

European Community Legislation

Legal provisions in the social dimension have been put in place over a long period. In the European Community, legislation has rarely been used to prescribe specific actions in the social policy sphere. But it is considered to be one of the tools at the Community's disposal to give shape to European Community social policy, by itself or as a complement to other instruments.

In the Green Paper on Social Policy,[20] the amount of legislation is called 'relatively small in relation to other instruments' (such as financial support and agreements between social partners). Yet it has also 'furnished a sound basis for the guarantee of fundamental social rights for *workers*' (authors' emphasis). Legislation in the social dimension can be divided into three categories: facilitating freedom of movement of workers, equal pay for men and women and working conditions (labour law and working conditions and health and safety at work).

The first regulations ever adopted in the social field related to free movement of workers, and coordination of social security systems for migrant workers. Stipulations in Title III regard free movement of persons, services and capital. Workers are free to accept work (except employment in the public service) in any of the Member States, and under certain conditions to stay there after having been employed, by the end of the transitional period at the latest. Discrimination based on nationality between workers of the Member States as regards employment, remuneration and other conditions of work and employment is consequently to be abolished (Article 48). Only recently this led to commotion in international football: the Bosman-case on the transfer-system was won on the basis of this Article 48.

The second area of Community legislation in the social field is equal treatment of men and women. Article 119[21] has been able to serve in practice as a basis for a comprehensive policy combining rights and the promotion of equal opportunities for women. In accordance with community legislation, judges in the Member States must interpret national legislation in the light of community legislation. For example the Barber-arrest (17 May 1990), confirmed the classification of pensions and supplementary pensions as pay in the sense of this Article, thus indicating a right on equal treatment. Pension funds, insurers and employers in the Member States argued that a retroactive effect of this arrest would lead to unacceptable financial consequences. This held especially true for the Netherlands and the UK. The Dutch Government formulated a proposal for a protocol preventing the retroactive effect. During the Maastricht Summit this protocol was accepted as an Annex to the Treaty: '[B]enefits

---

[20] COM(93)551.

[21] 'Member States shall ensure and maintain the application of the principle that men and women should receive equal pay for equal work.'

under occupational social security schemes shall not be considered as remuneration if and in so far as they are attributable to periods of employment prior to 17 May 1990.' One of the Dutch trade unions 'was not amused' and successfully started a procedure for one of its members. The resulting Vroege judgment, in which the European Court stated that exclusion of women from pension plans through eligibility rules since 1976 has been contrary to article 119, seems to overrule this protocol.[22]

A third area of more recent legal developments concerns the protection of workers with respect to health and safety at work. Several Council Directives exist, for example to assure approximation of the laws of the Member States, or on minimum safety and health requirements in the Member States, or on the minimum requirements for improving safety and health protection in the Member Sates etc.[23] The Dutch government calls these European Community obligations 'sometimes impeding for deregulation on the national level'.[24]

Limits of European Community policy in the social dimension on the basis of the body of the Treaty on European Union are not always clear, as the European Community directive on working hours demonstrates. According to the British government, this directive cannot apply to the UK; not signing the Agreement on Social Policy would have provided them exemption from European Community social policy. According to the European Court, however, the directive follows from European Community legislation and therefore applies to all Member States.[25]

Member States' and Social Partners' comments on the Green Paper on Social Policy showed diverging opinions concerning the desired influence of legislation. Representatives of trade unions, women's organizations and disabled, but also the French Ministry of Labour, Employment and Vocational Training and the Italian government stress that advantage should be taken of the new legislative framework to create a 'Social Europe' where rights are protected by law and social dumping is avoided. The Dutch Ministry of Social Affairs and Employment and the German Labour Ministry suggest that legislative proposals should take account of the different economic strengths of Member States, for example by basing legislation on minimum standards. 'Where large differences exist, recommendations are preferable to binding regulations.'[26] The German Labour Ministry indicates that minimum standards should be set for workers' rights, but these standards should not be too detailed. They

---

[22] Kraamwinkel, 1995, p. 180.
[23] COM(93)551, p. 89-90.
[24] Ministerie van Sociale Zaken en Werkgelegenheid, 1996, p. 91.
[25] De Volkskrant, 13 November 1996.
[26] COM(93)551, p. 84.

should include equality of treatment for part-time and temporary workers, equality between men and women, protection in the event of dismissal, *et cetera*.[27]

Social Partners

The Social Agreement annexed to the Treaty on European Union provides reinforced structures for social dialogue. Not only is the Commission obliged to consult management and labour on the possible direction of Community action, also it must consult management and labour on the content of the envisaged proposal. If the European Community Social Partners 'so desire, the dialogue between them at Community level may lead to contractual relations, including agreements'. In the Agreement this is further defined for eleven Member States.[28] These agreements may be implemented either in accordance with the procedures and practices specific to management and labour and the Member States. When it concerns matters named in Article 2 of the Agreement measures may, at the joint request of the signatory parties, be implemented by a Council decision on a proposal from the Commission. The Council acts by qualified majority, except where the agreement in question contains one or more provisions relating to one of the more sensitive areas of social policy referred to in Article 2(3) of the Agreement (see also: 3.1). Especially the option of implementation through contracts between management and labour at European Community level 'illustrates the ways and means by which the Community intends to promote the development of social policy: concertation, negotiation and consensus'.[29] But cautiousness about the influence of the European Community Social Dialogue shows in the Declaration on Article 4.2 in the Agreement: this arrangement implies no obligation for the Member States to apply the agreements directly or to work out rules for their transposition, nor any obligation to amend national legislation in force to facilitate their implementation.

Employers' organizations UNICE (Union of Industries of the European Community) and ETUC (European Trade Union Confederation) welcomed the new role of the social partners. ETUC wisely phrases that 'the social dialogue to date has been a sort of apprenticeship and now needs to be developed and strengthened in the light of the Maastricht Treaty'. The Danish, German and Swedish Ministries of Labour and the Austrian Government indicated that the social partners at national level should have more influence on the implementation of Community instruments.[30]

---

[27] COM (93)551, p. 84.
[28] Article 4 of the Agreement on Social Policy.
[29] COM(93)551, p. 12.
[30] COM(93)551, p. 85.

In their comment on the Green paper on Social Policy, European employers' organizations expressed their concern about the multiplicity of pending Commission initiatives concerning employee participation, information and consultations. One of these pending Commission initiatives was accepted by the Council in 1994: the European Works Council Directive.[31, 32]

Despite their differing opinions on some of the matters mentioned above, the European Social Partners produced several common documents in the Social Dialogue. For example in their first annual review of Essen, they request the heads of states to do three things:

* ensure coherence between labour market policies, and macro-economic and competitiveness policies: an appropriate mix of macro-economic and competitiveness policies is seen as necessary in particular for sustaining higher rates of investment;

* take the national experiences in the follow-up to the five Essen points into account: Social Partners in the Member States agree on these action points and play an important role or – in the case of labour market policies – 'are ready to play their role';

* authorize a first review of the Essen procedures to ensure effective implementation, to measure progress and to assess the need for further action.

The social partners state that 'it is in particular important to ensure that the Economic and Monetary Union goes together with an active employment strategy: the economic guidelines exercise and the Essen employment process should be seen as a whole'.[33]

3 Towards a Social Paragraph in the Union Treaty?

3.1 Introduction

In the present Treaty and its Annexes many aspects of social policy are covered in some way (see table 3).

---

[31] The idea is to set up transnational works councils to be informed on a firm's general situation.
[32] Social Europe 2/95, p. 7.
[33] European Social Dialogue, 1995, p. 3.

Table 3. European Community Social Policy Stipulations in the Maastricht Treaty

Title III: Free movement of persons, services and capital
Restrictions on the freedom of establishment of nationals (especially workers) are to be abolished by progressive stages.

Title VIII: Social provisions and the European Social Fund
The Commission must play an intermediary function in that it 'shall have the task of promoting close cooperation between Member States in the social field' (Article 118), 'shall endeavour to develop the dialogue between management and labour at European level' (Article 118b). Strongest responsibilities for the Member States are found in Articles 118a and 119. In Article 118a, Member States not only agree to encourage improvements in the working environment as regards the health and safety of workers, but also to adopt minimum requirements for gradual implementation by majority voting. Article 119 clearly states: 'Each Member State shall (...) ensure and (...) maintain the application of the principle that men and women should receive equal pay for equal work.'

Title XIV: Economic and Social Cohesion
Article 130a states that: 'in order to promote its overall harmonious development, the Community shall develop and pursue its actions leading to the strengthening of its economic and social cohesion. In particular, the Community shall aim at reducing disparities between the levels of development of the various regions and the backwardness of the least-favoured regions, including rural areas'.[34] Article 130b further specifies that 'Member States shall conduct their economic policies and shall coordinate them in such a way as, in addition, to attain the objectives set out in Article 130a'.

Means to achieve social policy goals as summarized in Table 3, until now have consisted of partial redistribution of finances through the Social Fund and the Structural Funds and of legislation on the basis of the Treaty (see also 2.3). For the objective of economic and social cohesion, the procedure for monitoring the 'conduct' of Member States with respect to their economic policies, and the coordination of these policies, shows little opportunities for European Community level actions.

In the Social Protocol, annexed to the Treaty, the twelve High Contracting Parties agree to authorize the eleven Member States that wish to continue along the path laid down in the 1989 Social Charter to use the institutions, procedures and mechanisms of the Treaty among themselves. Resulting acts and decisions may also be applied in the countries that signed the Agreement. The UK shall not take part in the

[34] C92 224/50.

deliberations, and neither the resulting Acts nor their financial consequences shall be applicable to the UK. According to this Agreement the Community shall support and complement the activities of the Member States in virtually all fields of social policy. There is a distinction between fields on which the procedure described in Article 189c applies (for example: improvement of the working environment to protect workers' health and safety, working conditions, information and consultation of workers). Directives allowing for adoption of minimum requirements for gradual implementation of these activities require qualified majority voting. More sensitive issues, such as social security, social protection, representation of interests and extra financial contributions for the promotion of employment and job-creation (Article 2.3) continue to require unanimity of the Council.

Curtin (1993) analyses the status of the Protocol of Social Policy and the Agreement. Among the possible interpretations are: considering the Protocols annexed to the Treaty as an integral part of it. A highly controversial part of the Protocol, if one accepts the argument that it forms an 'integral part' of Community law, is the provision that acts adopted by the Council in accordance with the non-participation by the UK shall not be applicable to the UK. This provision appears to institutionalize the possibility of the differentiated application of Community law. If the Protocol has the effect of conferring the status of 'Community social policy' on the social policy pursued by the eleven, the result will be not only that the Community then has two social policies, but that, for the future, the social policy of the eleven will have to be considered as part of the *acquis communautaire* for the purposes of enlargement.

In the Maastricht Treaty, the seedbed for coordinated European Community social policies has been designed. What keeps the discussion on a 'Social paragraph' alive are the unfavourable growing conditions, like for example the opt-out of the UK, the requirement of unanimous voting for many aspects of social policies and the fragmentation of the field over the various Titles.

3.2 Possible Contents of a Social Paragraph

Since the first Treaties, only little progress has been made towards common social policies. A maximum seems to have been reached by the formula used for the Maastricht Treaty: an Agreement on social policy for all Member States but one.

As indicated in section 3.1, the legal status of the Agreement and possible actions following from this agreement, leaves a lot to be desired. Which means that there are hardly any possibilities at European Community level to counterbalance the stipulations on economic policies that are firmly based in the Treaty. All policy recommendations and procedures in the social field that can be brought into the body of the Treaty will be safe from the legally instable status of the Protocols. Three possible options will be described.

1. Devising a chapter on social policies, including minimum standards and a timetable

The contents of a chapter on the broad field of social policies would probably be based on the present Protocol on Social Policy, with the same or more requirements on unanimity in the decision-making process. Elaboration of the present text with the ILO Conventions that were selected as minimum standards for labour at the UN Social Summit in Copenhagen would be an option (see table 4).

Table 4. ILO Conventions selected as minimum labour standards at the UN Social Summit in Copenhagen (1995)

Convention no. 87:	Concerning Freedom of Association and Protection of the Right to Organize (1948);
Convention no. 98:	Concerning the Application of the Principles of the Right to Organize and to Bargain Collectively (1949);
Convention no. 138:	Concerning Minimum Age for Admission to Employment (1973);
Convention no. 111:	Concerning Discrimination in Respect of Employment and Occupation (1958);
Convention no. 29:	Concerning Forced or Compulsory Labour (1930);
Convention no. 105:	Concerning Abolition of Forced Labour (1957);
Convention no. 155:	Concerning the Protection of Safety and Health at Work (1981)

Source: Waart, P. de, 1996, p. 257

Besides these generally approved ILO minimum labour standards, criteria could include minimum standards for wages and social security benefits or the objective of a reasonable distribution of income. 'Policy competition' between the Member States could not lead to lowering social norms and guarantees below a certain level in case of such minimum standards. A timetable would enable Member States to adjust national policies to meet the new demands in the social field and facilitate evaluation of the consequences: Member States would remain responsible for the design and execution of policies to reach the common goals.

This EMU-like option of setting out a timetable and fixed criteria for a 'social union' could include possibilities for 'opting-out'. This option may seem highly unlikely for European Community social policies: welfare arrangements in the Member States differ widely. Minimum standards that are set too high or too low, for matters that affect the government budget and related welfare state arrangements or business investments, will lead to social and political unrest in Member States.

2. Including a chapter on employment

Improving the employment situation for various reasons seems to be an acceptable common objective. It has already been used to develop common employment strategies: all Member States have agreed upon the five Essen Action points and upon the monitoring procedures of their multi-annual programmes. Specifying the structural goals for the employment policy in a separate Article, in the terms of the Single Report[35] of the ECO/FIN Council and the Social Council (integration of all young people, prevention of long term unemployment and mainstreaming equal opportunities in all employment policies) may meet with little resistance. The following statement indicates what needs to be done: '[T]he key to this employment strategy is the development of an integrated approach, whereby all the relevant policies – macroeconomic and structural policies – have to contribute, and have to support each other in the fight against unemployment.'[36] This was also included in Santer's idea on a European Employment Pact: this Pact would have to lead to European and national agreements on job-creation, reduction of labour cost, deregulation and schooling and training. The five Essen Points, the Member States' multi-annual reports and the monitoring procedures could be integrated in such a chapter on employment.

3. Emphasizing the relationship between economic and social progress

An option that has been chosen for other non-economic topics in the Treaty is to point at the relation of this policy field with other policy fields. For example environmental policies, development policies, and cohesion policies are based on this construction:

* In Article 3 development cooperation is mentioned as an activity of the European Community for the purposes set out in Article 2 (see section 1). Article 130u confirms the fact that development cooperation is an objective aiming at 'sustainable economic and social development of the developing countries', 'smooth and gradual integration of the developing countries into the world economy' and to 'campaign against poverty' in developing countries. The formulation pointing at the relation between development policy and other European Community policies is found in Article 130v: '[T]he Community shall

---

[35] Approved by the European Summit in Madrid, 1995.
[36] Larsson, 1996.

take account of the objectives referred to in Article 130u[37] in the policies that it implements which are likely to affect developing countries.' The Council can act in accordance with the procedure referred to in Article 189c to adopt measures in this field.

* Title XVI, Article 130r on Environment is linked to Article 2 ('sustainable and non-inflationary growth respecting the environment') and Article 3 ('a policy in the sphere of the environment'). Not only does Article 130r.2 state: 'Environmental protection requirements must be *integrated* into the definition and implementation of other Community policies', but also that Community policy shall be 'based on the principles that preventive action should be taken, that environmental damage should as a priority be rectified at source and that the polluter should pay'. The Council can act in accordance with Article 189c (and consulting the Social and Economic Committee) to decide what action is to be taken by the Community in some cases. For most matters however, unanimity is required.

* For economic and social cohesion, Title XIV states: 'Member States shall conduct their economic policies and shall coordinate them in such a way as, in addition, to attain the objectives set out in Article 130a.' Definitions of these objectives (economic and social *cohesion* and reducing the disparity between the levels of regional *development*) are not part of the Treaty, but in practice this Article mainly aims at reducing regional disparities in the European Community.

This option would require similar links to objectives of policies in the social field. Translating objectives for economic and social progress (Article B and Article 2) in terms that could be operationalised, like 'poverty' for development cooperation and the definition of rules like 'the polluter pays' for environmental policies would mean a great leap forward. Use of terms is now vague in Article 130a (only the general term 'development' is used), and there are no simple rules like: 'In formulating and implementing economic policies, the EC and the Member States take into account the effects of these policies on the income distribution and regional inequalities.' If equally applied and controlled throughout Europe, the investment climate in Europe may benefit from this kind of rules. This in terms of a socially, economically and politically stable Union with high participation levels of the labour force.

---

[37] An important part of Community development policy, namely the cooperation with the African, Caribbean and Pacifc countries (Lomé Convention), is excluded from the provisions of Article 130u.

3.3 Advantages and Disadvantages of a Social Paragraph

As indicated in section 3.2, there are several possibilities to make social policies more visible in the Treaty. The first option consists of creating a new chapter on social policy containing the larger part of the Agreement on Social Policy, elaborated with minimum standards on a number of topics. A second option consists of adding a section on employment. The third option consists of underlining the relationship between social and other policies. All options are based on insertion in the main body of the Treaty.

Any of these options obviously would enhance the transparency of legislation: all Member States would be bound by the Treaty and the Directives resulting from the Treaty stipulations. Any addition or clarification of the way to attain the primary goals ('economic and social progress') of the Union in the main body of the Treaty is bound to have the advantage of transparency of legislation. The feasibility of the insertion of such a Chapter, however, is highly unlikely given the continued EMU-scepticism. Arguments now used against EMU are probably based on the same fears of loosing national autonomy and comparative advantages that occur as regards common social policies. Transparency of legislation is only one of the factors contributing to an effective functioning of legislation.

Legitimacy is another reason for paying more attention to the social dimension in the Union Treaty, as mentioned above. The level on which the rules for efficiency and equity are established may contribute to their acceptance. On the one hand it could be argued that agreement on more balanced regulation of the social dimension when compared to the economic dimension at European Community level would be beneficial: it could contribute to the acceptance of legislation directed at a more efficient functioning of markets. On the other hand, increasing the stipulations on social policies could be said to lead to a further decrease of national governments' manoeuvring space, which may have negative effects on the solidarity with European Community economic policies. And solidarity with the objectives is a *sine qua non* in an era of (public) deregulation.

Finally, assigning responsibilities to meet certain norms and control them to stakeholders, seems in many cases to be able to virtually make obsolete government legislation or intervention (for example in the case of covenants on environmental issues that function better than punitive public legislation).[38] European Social Dialogue has already led to a number of sectoral agreements, mainly related to health and safety issues (for an overview: see Social Europe 95/2). In December 1995 the

---

[38]   Hessel e.a., 1995, p. 361.

first Framework agreement (on parental leave) has been drawn up by the Social Dialogue. If this indicates a trend towards more encompassing agreements by the social partners at European level, legislation should be formulated accordingly.

4 Conclusion

Debate on European social policies in recent years tends to stress the relation between economic and social policies. Employment related issues have always been positioned between those fields. At European Community level, despite the broad objectives already formulated in the European Economic Community Treaty, the focus has always been on efficiency: for a better functioning of the Internal Market, but also for a more efficient allocation of resources over the regions (see section 2.1). Member States have always remained responsible for the equity part: for the distribution of income and most other social policies in the field of labour and social security. The present shift in focus, towards a more social European Community, is not only due to fear of social unrest, alienation of European citizens or other possible negative side effects of an unequal distribution of work and income. There is also recognition of the fact that, even though there can be no social progress without economic progress, 'conversely, economic wealth cannot be built in a social desert'.[39] Notions like the maximin principle seem to shine through in the sections on economic and social cohesion (cohesion funds directed at reducing disparities between the levels of development of the various regions and the backwardness of the least-favoured regions, including rural areas). However, the budget to realize these goals may vary over the years, and a principal statement on the coherence between social and other policies would highlight the importance the Member States attach to these goals.

Emphasis on improving the employment situation, being one of the main prerequisites for social policies, may prove a sensible route for attaining economic and social progress. Employment is after all the best insurance against a fading social security system. But there will always be people whose 'employability' at certain times cannot be upgraded, and this argument does not only apply to low-skilled workers. Some attention for non-workers, even for those non-workers who are not registered as unemployed would contribute to the profile of a 'Social Europe'. The search for the right blend between efficiency and equity at European Community level has

---

[39]   Santer, 1996, p. 9.

already brought a Social Protocol and a Social Agreement into the Treaty. Perhaps this construction is indeed a Trojan horse: it may bring the victory for those who plead for the integration of social and economic policies.

References

Commission des Communautés Européennes, Secretariat General, (1994), Conceil Europeen – Essen, 9 & 10 décembre 1994, Conclusion de la Presidence (SN 300/94), Commission des Communautés Européennes, Bruxelles.

Commissie van de Europese Gemeenschappen (1994), Groei, Concurrentievermogen, Werkgelegenheid. Naar de 21e eeuw: wegen en uitdagingen. Witboek. Bulletin van de Europese Gemeenschappen, Supplement 6/93. Bureau voor Officiële Publikaties der Europese Gemeenschappen, Luxembourg.

Curtin, D.M., (1993), The Constitutional Structure of the Union: a Europe of Bits and Pieces, in: K. Hellingman (red), (1993), Europa in de steigers: van Gemeenschap tot Unie, Kluwer, Deventer.

Delors, J. (1986), The Single Act and Europe: a moment of truth (Ninth Jean Monnet Lecture), Office for Official Publications of the European Communities, Luxembourg.

Directie Arbeidsmarkt, Ministerie van Sociale Zaken en Werkgelegenheid, Directoraat Generaal V, Werkgelegenheid, Industriële Betrekkingen en Sociale Zaken van de Europese Commissie, Economisch Instituut/Centrum voor Interdisciplinair Onderzoek van Arbeidsmarkt- en Verdelingsvraagstukken, Universiteit Utrecht, European System of Documentation on Employment (1995), Post-Essen Follow up: Nationale Dialoog Nederland, Den Haag, 20 december 1995, Verslag, Economisch Instituut/CIAV, Utrecht.

European Commission (1992), Treaty on European Union, together with the complete text of the Treaty establishing the European Community, Official Journal of the European Communities, Information and Notices 92/C 224, Volume 35, 31 August 1992, Office for Official Publications of the European Communities, Luxembourg.

European Commission, Directorate-General for Employment, Industrial Relations and Social Affairs, Social dialogue – The situation in the Community in 1995, in: Social Europe 2/95, Office for Official Publications of the European Communities, Luxembourg.

European Commission, Directorate-General for Employment, Industrial Relations and Social Affairs (1993), Green Paper. European Social Policy. Options for the Union. Consultative document. Communication by Mr. Flynn, 17 November 1993. COM(9 3)551, Office for Official Publications of the European Communities, Luxembourg.

European Foundation for the Improvement of Living and Working Conditions, European Commission, Directorate-General V, Employment, Industrial Relations and Social Affairs (1996), Working on European Social Policy: A report on the forum, Office for Official Publications of the European Communities, Luxembourg.

European Social Dialogue (1995), Joint declaration of the Social Partners on Employment, Brussels.

Europese Commissie, Directoraat-generaal Werkgelegenheid, Industriële Betrekkingen en Sociale Zaken (1994), Europees Sociaal Beleid. Toekomstige acties voor de Unie. Een Witboek, COM(94)333, Bureau voor Officiële Publikaties der Europese Gemeenschappen, Luxembourg.

FNV (1996), De sociale uitdaging voor Europa. Naar een actief sociaal beleid voor de Europese Unie, Stichting FNV Pers, Amsterdam.

Hagen, K., in: Z. Ferge and J.E. Kolberg (eds.) (1992), Social policy in a changing Europe, Westview Press, Boulder.

Institute of European Affairs (1995), 1996 Intergovernmental Conference. Issues, Options, Implications, Institute of European Affairs, Dublin.

Hessel, B., J.A. den Hertog, C.E.M. Schutte, F.P. Sprik, J.B. Wezeman (1995), Sociaal en economisch recht. Grensvlak van markt en overheid, Wolters-Noordhoff, Groningen.

Kraamwinkel, M. (1995), Pensioen, emancipatie en gelijke behandeling, Uitgeverij fed, Amsterdam.

Larsson, A. (1996), Introduction. Employment Observatory Conference, Vienna, 24 October 1996 (speech: hand-out).

Ministerie van Sociale Zaken en Werkgelegenheid (1996), Sociale Nota 1997, Sdu Uitgeverij Plantijnstraat, Den Haag.

Nicoll, W., T.C. Salmon (1994), Understanding the new European Community, Harvester Wheatsheaf, Hertfordshire.

Phelps, E.S. (1985), Political Economy, W.W. Norton & Company, Inc., New York.

Sociaal-Economische Raad (1992), Convergentie en overlegeconomie, Sociaal-Economische Raad, Den Haag.

Volkskrant, 13 November 1996: 'Europees Hof maant Londen werktijden snel aan te passen', and 'Major dreigt vanwege 48-urige werkweek Maastricht II te vetoën'.

Waart, P. de (1996), Minimum Labour Standards in International Trade from a Legal Perspective, in: P. van Dijck, G. Faber (eds.), Challenges to the New World Trade Organization, Kluwer Law International, The Hague, ch. 12.

About the Authors

Tineke Bahlmann studied Business Economics at the Erasmus University in Rotterdam. In 1988 she received her doctorate for an intensive research about strategic reorientations during a crisis in six Dutch companies. She is part-time professor in business economics with the Economic Institute/Centre for Interdisciplinary Research on Labour Market and Distribution Issues (CIAV), Utrecht University and director of the Centre for Organizational Learning and Change at Nijenrode University. She advises organizations about organizational change processes and organizational learning, which are also her research topics.

Inge van Berkel studied human geography in Utrecht. After she completed her studies in 1990, she worked for the municipality of Utrecht in the field of urban renewal and was involved in research projects on various subjects (urban planning, health care, education, social housing). From 1993 to 1997 she was a researcher at the Economic Institute/CIAV, Utrecht University.

Hetty van Emmerik studied Industrial and Organzational Psychology at the Free University of Amsterdam. Her PhD project at the Faculty of Economics and Econometrics, Department of Business Adminstration, focused on the careers of men and women in a service-oriented business firm. Currently she is an associate professor at Utrecht University, Department of Sociology. Her current research concentrates on careers of women and human resource management for target groups.

Gerrit Faber is associate professor of international economics at the Economic Institute/CIAV, Utrecht University. His main research interests are trade policy issues related to European integration and development cooperation. He has published widely on these subjects.

Jeroen van Gerven studied personnel sciences at the Catholic University of Brabant in Tilburg. He did a thesis on Industrial Relations in Europe and graduated in 1994. Currently he works at the Hugo Sinzheimer Insitute at the Faculty of Law of the University of Amsterdam. He is writing a PhD thesis about Coordination of Employment Service and Social Security in historical perspective.

Bart Hessel read law at Utrecht University and wrote a thesis on The Constitutional State and Economic Politics (1987). Since January 1986 he has worked as an associate professor of public economic law at the Law Faculty, Utrecht University and is now Professor of European Law and Decentralized Administrations. He is co-leader of the research programme 'Coherence of the social and economic dimensions' of the research school AWSB. He is furthermore a deputy-judge with the Regulatory Industrial Organisation Appeals Court in The Hague.

Saskia Klosse obtained her degree in law at Utrecht University, where she also wrote and defended her PhD thesis *Menselijke schade: vergoeden of herstellen?* (1991), a study into rules and regulations concerning disability in the Netherlands and the Federal Republic of Germany. From 1985 to 1995 she worked as an assistent professor with the section of Labour and Social Security Law of the department ISEP of the Faculty of Law of Utrecht University. Since 1996 she is an associate professor with the same section. Besides, she is a deputy-judge with the sector of administrative law of the district court of The Hague and lectures on the theory of human damage at the medical faculty of the Catholic University of Leuven.

Robert Knegt read law and studied sociology at the University of Amsterdam. He received his doctorate at this university in 1986. His research is primarily concerned with the implementation of legal programmes, in particular those concerning social security. He is executive director of the Hugo Sinzheimer Institute for research on labour law of the University of Amsterdam.

Yvonne Konijn studied law at the University of Amsterdam. She worked successively at the University of Amsterdam, the University of Leiden and Utrecht University, department of labour law and social security. She published several studies about labour law and flexible work and is now finishing her PhD thesis on the influence of civil law on the labour contract.

Maaike Lycklama à Nijeholt studied Business Economics at the Free University of Amsterdam. During her study she was undergraduate assistent. After her graduation in 1994 she worked as a lecturer at the Free University of Amsterdam and as a research assistant at the merchant bank MeesPierson. Since 1995 she is assistent professor business cconomics at Utrecht University. Her research is primarily concerned with the motives for and the consequences of acquisitions.

Joop Schippers is an associate professor of economics at the Economic Institute/CIAV, Utrecht University. His main field of research is labour economics, especially issues concerning labour market inequality between men and women. The latter theme was also the subject of his PhD thesis (1987), a study on wage differentials between men and women. He was also a member of the Netherlands National Council on Equal Opportunity (Emancipatieraad; now disbanded).

Jacques Siegers studied economics at the University of Amsterdam. He received his doctorate at Groningen University in 1985. He is Professor of Economics at the Economic Institute/CIAV, Utrecht University; co-leader of the research programme 'Coherence of the social and economic dimensions' of the research school AWSB; associate with the Interuniversity Center for Social Science Theory and Methodology (ICS).

Rudi Turksema studied sociology at Groningen University and is presently a PhD student at the Interuniversity Centre for Social Science Theory and Methodology (ICS), Utrecht University. His current research is into changes and differences in the supply of day care in the Netherlands.

Stella den Uijl studied Business Economics at the Free University of Amsterdam. After her graduation in 1993, she started doing research for a PhD thesis 'Rehabilitation of partially disabled workers in the work force in various European countries; decisive factors seen from an international perspective'. She is assistent professor at the Economic Institute, Utrecht University.

Bart Verkade studied Business Administration (BBA 1992) at Nijenrode University. During his study he did several projects on Management Development at the Management Development Centre of Nijenrode. His PhD thesis was about the development of the sales force of Nedlloyd Districenters Nederland B.V.
At present he is assistent professor with the Economic Institute/CIAV, Utrecht University. He lectures Business economics, Marketing and Organizational Behavior. His research topic is Business Ethics, with focus on ethics and values as driving forces in organizations. He is also freelance Dilemma trainer at the European Institute for Business Ethics at Nijenrode.

Mies Westerveld obtained a degree in law at the Erasmus University Rotterdam in 1971. Subsequently she has been practicing law for about ten years and she is currently employed as a senior researcher at the Netherlands School for Economic and Social Policy Research, Utrecht University. Her main field of research is social security law, with an emphasis on issues such as solidarity, family related benefits versus individualism and the position of women in present and future schemes. The latter topic formed an important part of her PhD thesis ('Yesterday's choices, tomorrow's blueprint?', 1994), a study on social insurance pension schemes in Germany, Great Britain and the Netherlands.

The Netherlands School for Social and Economic Policy Research (AWSB)

AWSB as an interuniversity, interdisciplinary and thematically oriented initiative
The Netherlands School for Social and Economic Policy Research (AWSB) is an interuniversity and interdisciplinary research school, officially recognized by the Royal Netherlands Acadamy of Arts and Sciences (KNAW). AWSB has a guaranteed staff of 29 fulltime senior researchers, 6 post-doctoral positions, 4 international fellows and over 60 PhD-students (so-called AIOs). Within the Research School the faculties of Law and Social Sciences of Utrecht University, the faculty of Social Sciences of the Erasmus University Rotterdam, the Catholic University Brabant (Tilburg) and the Law Faculty of the University of Amsterdam jointly organize a post-graduate teaching programme. The institutes also collaborate in carrying out research on the changes affecting the Dutch 'welfare state'. Topics under investigation include the underlying legal, economic and moral principles and these principles' manifestations in relation to policy and practice within the labour market, and in terms of social provision.

The AWSB member institutes are the following:
- Utrecht/Law, Utrecht University Institute for Legal Studies (AWSB/SERB)
- Utrecht/Social Sciences, the Interdisciplinary Research Institute for Social Sciences, University of Utrecht (AWSB/Isor)
- Tilburg/Social Sciences, the Work and Organization Research Centre (AWSB/Worc)
- Rotterdam/Social Sciences, the Rotterdam Institute for Sociotific Policy Research (AWSB/Risbo)
- Amsterdam/Law, the Hugo Sinzheimer Institute (AWSB/Hsi)

The purpose of AWSB
The central aim of the AWSB-programme is to chart the forms and the causes of the contemporary transformation of the Dutch welfare state in a European comparative perspective. What are its characteristics and how do socio-economic, legal, administrative and socio-cultural aspects interrelate? What social problems, what new identities and what problems of distribution will result? How do citizens, administrators, policy-makers and public and private organisations anticipate and react? The programme's guidelines represent its greatest challenge, namely to integrate the relevant social, behavioural and legal disciplinary expertise available in the

Netherlands into a multi-disciplinary perspective on the interconnected contemporary developments within the welfare state regime.

The research programme
The actual research within the School is done under the auspices of 12 research groups. Some of them already existed before AWSB was established, others have been newly set up, and bring together expertise from the various research centres. Nearly all groups are interdisciplinary and all groups participate in the AWSB-teaching programme.

A post-graduate teaching programme
The Research School offers PhD-students a curriculum of theory, methods and skills required for effective participation in the field of social and economic policy research. An individual practical component, the PhD-research project, is complemented by modular class teaching. This includes both general and specialized compulsory courses and a variety of optional elements. The teaching programme offers far more than the basic requirements for the succesful completion of particular PhD-projects. Its aim is to prepare the participants for all positions requiring advanced skills in carrying out, managing and evaluating social and economic policy research, be it in the public or the private sector.

Recent developments
The Ministries of Social Affairs and Employment (SZW) and of Public Health, Welfare and Sports (VWS) have showed considerable interest in the AWBS-initiative right from the outset in 1989. Within both departments the need existed for the identification and analysis of a number of long-term developments. SZW, VWS and AWSB reached an agreement on long-term cooperation in 1991.

The board of AWSB aims to stimulate closer coherence between the school's various research programmes. The accumulation of knowledge has also been a major incentive for the Government in terms of support for research schools. Research schools are expected to develop into expert centres in the field of their own research in the Netherlands and thus be able to compete at European level.

To achieve these aims AWSB has been experimenting with various modes of research programming in the past years. The departmental funds played an instrumental role in these experiments. Research which is financed by the two ministries must meet stricter criteria with regard to subject and coherence than research financed by the research centres themselves out of their own budgets. From

1995 onwards the strategy has been to formulate research themes which encompass roughly half of the schools' AIO-projects starting in a particular year. These projects are then matched by departmental grants which are made available for that theme. 1995 saw the start of the programme 'Minimum Protection in the Light of the European Integration', 1996 heralded the programme 'Employment and Social Participation', and in 1997 two programmes started, 'Government and the Market Place' and 'The Future of Social Security'. These programmes will continue in the years thereafter. In 1998 the last two mentioned programmes will be complemented by two more core programmes, 'Citizenship' and 'Pluralism and Equality'.

The cooperation between SZW, VWS and AWSB was externally evaluated in 1995 and all partners agreed to renew their agreement for another four year period. Obviously the financial benefits of this extension are considerable: each department will make available up to f 500,000 per year. More important though is the continuation of the strategic research alliance between the three partners. This has proven to be of considerable benefit to both the academic community and the policy makers.